Turia Pitt has a double degree neering and Science. She spends endeavours, and through her co tional speaking is helping thousands or people mindset, overcome challenges and achieve their wildest goals. She is a well-recognised humanitarian, dedicating her time to causes she is passionate about. Turia was named the NSW Premier's Woman of the Year in 2014 and was a finalist in 2017 for Australian of the Year. She is a judge for the Australian Woman of the Future Fund, as well as being an ambassador for the charity Interplast. Visit her at www.turiapitt.com or on

 : facebook.com/turia.pitt

 : @turiapitt

 : @turiapitt

Bryce Corbett is a journalist and author. He has worked for newspapers and magazines – both in Australia and in the UK – for almost twenty-five years. He co-wrote 2015 Australian of the Year Rosie Batty's best-selling *A Mother's Story* and co-authored with his wife, Shay Stafford, *Memoirs of a Showgirl*, based on her twelve years dancing at the Moulin Rouge. Born and bred in Sydney, Bryce lived and worked in Paris for a decade, where he wrote his first book, *A Town Like Paris*. He currently works as a producer at *60 Minutes*, and – when he is not trekking Kokoda with Turia – lives in Brisbane with Shay and their two children, Flynn and Rose. Visit his website www.brycecorbett.com or follow him on 🐦 @brycecorbett.

Also by Turia Pitt

Everything to Live For
(with Libby Harkness)

Unmasked

TURIA PITT

AND BRYCE CORBETT

EBURY
PRESS

An Ebury Press book
Published by Penguin Random House Australia Pty Ltd
Level 3, 100 Pacific Highway, North Sydney NSW 2060
penguin.com.au

Penguin
Random House
Australia

First published by Ebury Press in 2017
This edition published in 2018

Addresses for the Penguin Random House group of companies can be found at
global.penguinrandomhouse.com/offices.

A catalogue record for this
book is available from the
National Library of Australia

Cover design by Christabella Designs
Cover photography by Elizabeth Allnutt
Internal design by Midland Typesetters, Australia
Typeset in 12.5/17.5 Minion by Midland Typesetters, Australia
Printed in Australia by Griffin Press, an accredited ISO AS/NZS 14001:2004
Environmental Management System printer

Penguin Random House Australia uses papers that are natural, renewable
and recyclable products and made from wood grown in sustainable forests.
The logging and manufacturing processes are expected to conform to the
environmental regulations of the country of origin.

CONTENTS

'In the midst of winter, I found there was, within me,
an invincible summer'

Albert Camus

To the nurses at Concord Hospital – thank you

FOREWORD

As I wheel Turia out of her room in the burns unit at Concord Hospital, my mind wanders. Three months earlier she could run for hours upon end. Now she can't even walk. It's hard not to rail at how unfair it seems, how I don't want our lives to be this.

We pass a tightly sealed window and glimpse the outside world – a concrete jungle of houses, at that moment being covered with misty rain. Then out of nowhere a bright red-bellied king parrot appears, its olive-green wings spread. Turia, her mother and I watch as it lands on the railing in front of us. 'Look at the pretty parrot,' Turia says softly. It checks us out. 'Everything's going to be all right, everything's going to be all right'. Turia is trying her hardest to sing Bob Marley's lyrics.

I am overwhelmed with emotion. This moment will be with me for the rest of my life because it was then I knew that my girl was going to draw on every ounce of strength she had and charge on into her recovery; and I would be right by her side every step of the way.

As Turia slowly clawed her way back from death, her plastic surgeon told me, 'You have a mountain to climb, mate.' Five years on, we have finally reached the peak. As you will discover in this book, Turia is pushing the boundaries of life, absorbing every precious second she has on earth. Most of all, she is happy to be living her life 'like a boss', as she likes to say.

It's been both humbling and fascinating to have witnessed the resilience of the human body, her transformation from near-death to profound strength. Yeah, it's been hard. Hard for me. Harder for Turia. Testing on our relationship? Of course. But I'm super-proud of the woman who is by my side. I'm continually floored by her strength and tenacity, and by her will to live life to the extreme. She embodies the indomitable spirit of humanity, which we all have somewhere inside of us.

Enjoy her book!

Michael Hoskin
Ulladulla, January 2017

PROLOGUE:
FIRE

Sydney, spring 2015: I'm dancing with five thousand strangers and feeling like an idiot. The music is pumping over loudspeakers, the auditorium is in darkness, lights flash as if we're in a nightclub. Except that it's eleven in the morning.

Not for the first time today, I wonder if this was such a good idea. My dad has always been a big fan of Tony Robbins, so when he heard the great man himself was coming to Sydney, he bought me tickets to see him. And certainly, reading the brochure, it seemed the day could be an interesting experience.

Entering the Sydney Entertainment Centre an hour ago and being ushered into a VIP section – I had a regular ticket, but the organisers offered to upgrade me – was confronting enough. The two hundred or so people here have paid a premium for a chance to sit up the front of the auditorium and enjoy a meet-and-greet with the man himself. I know people know who I am. Turia Pitt: the burns survivor. I've never quite got used to walking into a room and have people I don't know recognise me.

Now, in a stadium filled with madly gyrating Tony-enthusiasts, I feel like a dick. If he comes on stage and, as I have heard, tells us to hug the person next to us, I might just have to leave. I throw a look of mortification at Jess – the girl from Adelaide I have befriended. She seems to be treating all of this with the same mixture of cynicism and apprehension. She shakes her head – laughing – trying, like me, to look like dancing in the middle of the morning in the company of complete strangers is the most normal thing in the world.

The music increases in volume, the lights flash more intensely, and with a burst of game-show-host energy and baring a set of impossibly white teeth, the man mountain that is Tony Robbins bounds onto the stage. The crowd goes wild. I'm more shocked than impressed, but I figure I might as well scream along. If you can't beat 'em ...

'You are here to transform your life!' Tony shouts at us, to thunderous applause. He doesn't so much talk as boom. Energy seems to radiate off him; he looks as though he's in some sort of trance.

'Today we are going to dig deep. Look deep inside ourselves and identify what is holding us back.' More cheers. 'We're going to learn how to put ourselves in a peak state to overcome any fears we might have and push our lives forward. Are you with me? Can I get an aye?'

An 'aye' rumbles forth from the crowd – starting at the back of the auditorium and crashing over me like a wave. 'We're going to face off whatever issues you have, confront them, crush them and at the end of the day, we're going to do the fire walk.'

The *what*? I'm suddenly seized by panic. On the huge screen behind Tony footage flashes of uniformed men raking red hot coals in the car park outside. The crowd goes wild – chanting, 'Tony! Tony! Tony!'

And then I hear it: the noise of the coals crackling in the heat; a sound that is amplified over huge speakers and reverberates around the auditorium. It takes me back to the Kimberley, back to a gorge in the outback. Back to the race. I feel sick and instinctively look around me for somewhere to throw up. I cast a nervous glance across at Jess. This isn't funny anymore.

'You don't have to do the fire walk!' Tony shouts in his hoarse, breathless delivery, pausing for dramatic effect. 'But just think about how you will feel tomorrow if you don't.'

It hangs in the air as a challenge. I am completely positive I will feel absolutely fine tomorrow if I don't do the fire walk. My mind starts to race. Is this some kind of sick game? I'm gripped by an irrational fear that this whole charade has been concocted as a test for me: a poor-taste punk for the cameras, in which five thousand people are complicit.

There's no way I'm walking across those coals. No way, no how.

1

THE FIRE

My life will be forever divided into two parts: before the fire and after the fire.

As much as I refuse to be defined by a few seconds, I can't escape the fact that what happened to me one September afternoon in 2011 will give shape to the rest of my story. I'm determined it won't be the most important event in my life, but it will always be a significant one.

The day started with so much promise. We had all risen early, and in the bus transporting competitors to the ultramarathon start line, I remember chatting animatedly, proudly showing off the Kimberley. It had been over six months since I had arrived in the region to start work as a mining engineer at the Argyle diamond mine. I struck up a conversation with three men at the back of the bus: fellow engineers, as it happened, from the nearby Newcrest mine. We spoke excitedly about the day ahead. As the bus rumbled through the early morning stillness of the outback, I remember seeing the sun peek over the horizon and set the countryside alight. If there is a more visually stunning part of Australia, I have yet to see it. The colours are so vivid, the landscape so varied. My boyfriend Michael and I had fallen effortlessly in love with the area, and in the short time we'd lived there we'd begun to build a life there and get to know the place. I'd been doing some volunteering for the ambulance service, which is run out of Kununurra, and we'd gone on lots of camping trips and walks on the weekends, swimming and fishing in waterholes and visiting the local towns.

I had registered for the race six months before. A lover of all things extreme, to me the thought of running 100 kilometres in a single day through the Australian desert was oddly appealing, and I was fairly sure I was fit enough: I'd been doing runs between the mine and the mine camp, had won a half-marathon recently, and was certainly acclimatised to running in the heat of this part of Australia. And I wasn't bothered about how long the race took me – I just wanted to push myself and finish.

As the date got closer, however, I changed my mind. The $1500 entry fee was too steep, I finally decided, when Michael and I were saving up for a holiday to Tahiti. So I pulled out.

As it happened, the organisers wanted some locals in the race, so they contacted me and offered to waive the fee. I agreed. It was one of those sliding-doors moments.

At the starter's gun, I set off amid the forty or so other competitors. I knew the race was going to be about endurance rather than speed, but after about 10 kilometres I pulled away from the three guys I had been running alongside and set out at my own pace. As per my custom, I had my earphones in as I ran, my iPod rolling through the hip-hop tunes on my running playlist.

At the 19-kilometre mark, I stopped at the second checkpoint to have some water and catch my breath. The day was getting warmer as the sun rose in the sky. The landscape around was scrubby, rocky and dramatic: red earth against a clear blue sky. Leaving the checkpoint and running towards Tier Gorge, I passed a pair of fellow competitors sitting by the track and having a quick bite to eat. A father and son duo, I would later discover. I took my earphones out briefly to say hello, and heard a roaring noise in the distance. I figured it must be a road train rumbling along the nearby Great Northern Highway. I put my earphones back in, put my head down, and headed into the gorge. It was just after 1 pm.

The terrain was uneven, so my focus was on where I put my feet. Behind me, two other competitors, Hal Benson and Kate Sanderson, had also entered the gorge, emerging from its narrow, high-walled entrance and onto its floor – a space about 800 metres wide. The course, marked by fluorescent pink flags, wove its way through the valley and out the other side. A shoulder-high wall of brittle desert grass spread out on either side of the track to the rocky escarpments that formed a sort of natural amphitheatre.

Kate and Hal say they stopped in their tracks, taking in a smouldering grass fire to their right. The roaring noise I had heard minutes earlier had started to build to a thunder. They saw me running just ahead of them, directly into the path of the fire – but with my earphones in and head down I hadn't registered the danger. Behind them, three more runners were making their way into the gorge – unaware of the fire trap into which they were stumbling.

By the time Michael Hull and father-and-son pair Martin and Shaun Van der Merwe had caught up with Kate and Hal, I had seen the fire and was sprinting back to join them. I was terrified. Where seemingly there had been no fire moments before, there was now a wall of flames advancing towards the five of us. The grass crackled noisily as the radiant heat from the blaze swept across the valley floor. Smoke engulfed us, restricting our vision. Embers flew wildly around us. Everything seemed to move in fast-forward.

We hurriedly considered our options. Going forwards was out of the question: it would have meant walking directly into the furnace and certain death. Going backwards seemed fraught with danger: the narrow, rocky gorge entrance had been near impossible to navigate in the full light of day. Now shrouded in smoke and beginning to funnel the heat of the fast-moving blaze, it was quickly deemed by the group to be not an option.

'I'm scared,' I said to no one in particular, and started to cry. I felt a hand rest gently on my arm and give me a reassuring squeeze.

'It's going to be fine,' said the stranger. 'We'll be all right if we all stick together.'

I wasn't sure I believed him, but I appreciated the gesture.

There was barely time to think as the wall of fire screamed towards us. The roar of the blaze was so loud now, I could barely hear the person shouting next to me.

I looked around for somewhere to hide: a crevasse, a rock, a creek bed – anything that might provide a fire break. But there was nothing. Halfway up the side of the valley, to our right, I could just make out a rocky outcrop. It appeared not to have too much vegetation on it: perhaps the fire would jump over it? As the heat started hitting us in ever increasing waves, Kate made the call to run for it. With no other option, and terrified at being left alone, I followed.

In the back of my mind, I knew that fire moved faster uphill, that trying to outrun a fire was pointless. But when faced with the choice of standing still and being engulfed by flames or running for your life, there's little time for reason.

As we ran up the hill, I could feel the flames getting closer and closer. The roar was deafening – an apocalyptic, otherworldly rumble that seemed to pass right through me. The heat grew more intense, it felt like it was melting my clothes into my skin and setting the ends of my hair alight. I was crying as I clambered up the rocky slope, losing my footing, slipping, falling and dragging myself upwards, adrenaline coursing through my veins. I couldn't see the others – we'd all scattered as we tried to flee. I scrambled onto the outcrop – the ledge looking far smaller and more exposed than it had appeared from below. With flames licking at my feet and the crackling sound of burning spinifex in my ears, I looked desperately around me for a depression in the rocks in which to hide. The time for running was over; I thought my only hope was to find some sort of barrier, squeeze myself into it and hope the fire might pass over me. But I couldn't see shelter anywhere.

I dragged a long-sleeved shirt out of my backpack and draped it over my legs, curling myself instinctively into a ball. The heat was unbearable, so hot I couldn't breathe. Each breath I took felt like I was inhaling flames.

Finally, I couldn't stand the heat anymore. I stood up and started to run further up the hill, and as I did I fell. That's when the fire caught me. I remember looking down at my hands and arms and they were both on fire. I was screaming. The pain was indescribable.

The only person I could think of was Michael. *This is it*, I thought. *I am never going to see Michael again. This is how I die.*

And then, just as quickly as it was upon me, the fire passed. The roar stopped and there was silence. An eerie silence. Everything around me was black and smouldering. Smoke rose in wisps off the charred remains of tree stumps. I stood there flailing – a mixture of panic, confusion and extreme pain. The flames on me had gone out, somehow. I couldn't see anyone else. All I could hear, distant at first, then getting louder, was a wild, animal-like hysterical scream. Then I realised it was me.

'Wake up!' I remember telling myself. 'Wake up, Turia! This is a dream – it's all just a bad dream. You need to wake up.'

It's from about this point that my memory gets a bit hazy. The shock began to set in, and the next few hours passed in a blur.

I vaguely recall Martin stumbling towards me in the first few minutes after the fire. His legs were burned to the thighs and he had burns to his right hand. We may have exchanged words, I don't remember. All I remember is him moving me gently to try to make me more comfortable. He reached into what was left of his backpack, brought out two Panadol and gave them to me with the remains of his water bottle.

'How badly burned am I?' I asked.

He looked at me, uncertain how to reply, before answering: 'You're okay. And you'll heal well.'

I recall seeing Kate, huddled not far from where I was. The back of her shirt had melted and the skin on her back was burned. The blackened landscape around me started to come alive with fellow competitors. Fellow survivors of the fire storm. It was like a war zone – bloodied, bruised and variously burned bodies limping towards one another to take stock.

It's hard to describe what I felt. I was in shock. Everything seemed to unfold around me in a slow-motion fog.

I remember the three mining engineers from Newcrest appearing after a while. As it happened, they had arrived at the top of the gorge just as the fire was advancing on us down below. They had watched in horror as the flames overtook me and Kate, and heard our screams echo across the valley.

They were uninjured and busied themselves with first-aid duties: dousing with water a few crepe bandages and applying them to the worst of the burns, then pulling space blankets and silk sleeping-bag liners from their packs and fashioning a pair of temporary shelters above Kate and me.

I had come across the Newcrest three, including one who had introduced himself as Trent, at the second checkpoint and briefly considered hanging back to run with them. Again, sliding doors.

One of them made a manifest of names and set off back along the track to raise the alarm. The sun beat down and the wind blew hot on my wounds, the full extent of which I had no concept. At a certain moment, I am told, my voice broke the silence.

'Excuse me, please,' I apparently said. 'Can someone please get the ants off me?'

I had been sitting on an ants' nest for over an hour and only just realised. It was decided to move me into the shade next to Kate. As Shaun and Trent took hold of my arms to help me to stand, my skin peeled off at their touch.

I don't specifically recall the first helicopter arriving. I do recall how elated I felt that help was at hand. It landed in the valley below, some 300 metres away, there being nowhere for a chopper to land on the side of the canyon. The pilot ran towards us, only to discover that there was no way either Kate or I could be moved. In a bind, he took off again to collect the race-appointed medic and to radio for back-up. Returning some time later with the event's doctor, Dr Julie Brahm, he managed to hover the chopper close enough to a nearby escarpment that Dr Brahm was able to leap down and tend to us.

She took stock of the medical emergency before her, recognised that Kate and I both needed emergency intravenous hydration and set about trying to insert an IV drip into my arm. I was so swollen from my burns, however, that she couldn't find a vein. It was the first hint I had that my injuries were perhaps more serious than I had believed, or than anyone had let on. I didn't know it at the time, but the burns were so deep that my nerve endings had been destroyed: pain had become the least of my problems. Without medical attention, Kate's body and mine were on the verge of shutting down.

In between the first helicopter departing and the second arriving, an ambulance crew had located the gorge and driven in. I looked up to see the familiar face of Bonny, an ambulance officer I had got to know while doing my volunteer work with the ambos.

'Hi, Bonny,' I said, in a moment of lucidity. She looked at me quizzically.

'It's me. Turia.'

It took her a moment to register, and when she did her eyes widened in shock and she began to cry.

Up until that point, part of me thought I would be back at work at the mine on Monday with an awesome story to tell at the weekly safety briefing. It was when I saw Bonny's confusion, the fact she didn't recognise me at first, and her expression of undisguised horror, that I wondered if perhaps, after all, my life was never going to be the same again.

When the pilot of the second helicopter, Paul Cripps, arrived, he hovered uncertainly above the scene, assessing the danger of performing a risky one-skid landing in order to medivac Kate and me out of there.

Because we were so high on the canyon wall, and because it had been deemed too dangerous to try to move us, Paul had to manoeuvre his helicopter to a rocky outcrop just below where I was stranded, then gingerly place one of the chopper's skids on the narrow rock platform and hold it there while Kate and I were lifted inside.

And because, with each transfer, an attending medical officer had to be loaded aboard too, Paul's only option was to perform the feat twice, dropping the first of his two precious cargoes on the valley floor before returning to fetch the second.

My fellow racers, all of whom had remained, began to hurriedly push down the small trees that surrounded me and remove loose rocks in preparation for the chopper. Flying blind as he came towards me, Paul had to rely on his co-pilot who had moved to the back of the chopper and was leaning out the door to verbally guide him in.

Kate went first, clambering awkwardly into the helicopter, with lots of support. When the chopper returned a few minutes later to collect me, it seemed to hover for an eternity above the outcrop, its right skid searching for the certainty of the ledge.

Once it had finally landed and I'd been helped up to the door – I couldn't stand without support, much less walk – I reached out my arms for the co-pilot to pull me into the cabin. I detected a moment's hesitation in him, as if he didn't know where to touch me.

Thirty minutes later Paul brought the helicopter down in an emergency landing on a patch of grass opposite Kununurra Hospital. As he helped me down from the helicopter cabin, I could make out a team of doctors and nurses in surgical gowns running towards me, pushing a couple of gurneys.

'Please!' I heard myself say as they rushed me towards the operating theatre. 'Can somebody call my boyfriend.'

2

ON A KNIFE EDGE

In the early morning of Sunday 4 September, barely two days after I had set off from the start line of the ultramarathon, I was admitted to the intensive care unit at Sydney's Concord Hospital.

In an induced coma, my body reeling from the emergency procedures that successive medical teams had undertaken at Kununurra and Darwin hospitals, I had no idea where I was or what was going on. My body was working overtime to keep up with my injuries: I'd been burned on my legs, arms, hands, face, neck and some of my torso. The resting heart rate of a normal person is 60–80 beats per minute. Even though I was lying completely still, my heart was racing at between 120 and 150 beats per minute as my body battled to fight infection.

The escharotomy that had been performed by the doctors at Kununurra had already saved my life. In crude terms, it's a slicing open of burned flesh down to the level of body fat to relieve pressure as the body throws everything it has at the rehydration of affected organs. And the debridement doctors had performed in Darwin had played its part in ensuring I was still alive. Debridement is the surgical process of removing dead skin – to allow for the regeneration of new skin. In my case, however, the burns were so deep and so severe, the debridement process had stripped me back to bare muscle and exposed nerve endings.

The immediate task for the intensive care team was to keep me alive. While my relative youth and fitness level meant my heart was strong and immune system efficient, because of my low body fat I had less insulation when the fire hit, so the burns had gone deeper into my tissue.

Without bandages, I would have been a confronting sight. Fluid retention had swollen my head to the size of a basketball; my arms and legs had been sliced down the middle. I would have looked for all the world as if I had been skinned and flayed.

I didn't know it at the time, but my friends Briggsy and Nicola were the first people to see me in ICU at Concord Hospital, and even to this day Briggsy finds it hard to talk about what she saw.

Dad, Mum, my brother Genji and his wife Angela arrived not long after. I can't imagine how hard it must have been for them to walk into my room; for my mum to see her child in such a state. A mix of horror and helplessness, I suppose. A wish you could swap places, then and there, and take on all the pain so your baby doesn't have to endure it.

Michael and his dad arrived not long after, and had to take in the full realisation not only of the extent of my injuries, but also that if I pulled through (which at that point was a big if), there would be a long and painful road to recovery in front of us.

I might have kicked off solo in the red dust of the Kimberley two days previously, but now I was caught in a life-and-death struggle in which many others had a stake.

Early the next morning, I was rolled into theatre for my first encounter with two men to whom I will be forever indebted: Professors Peter Maitz and Peter Haertsch. I didn't know it at the time – because I didn't know anything, such was the level of my sedation – but this was to be a fateful meeting that would change the course of my life.

Over the next four hours, the two men worked on me, debriding dead and damaged skin, one attending to my face while the other worked on my hands. My nose had been burned off, my ears were barely there. Because there is so little flesh on the fingers, the prospect of me keeping them was never great from the outset. But the two doctors worked assiduously to see what tissue could be salvaged, what was healthy enough for grafting, and what required an immediate layer of artificial skin. Neck, arms, legs, feet, torso. By the time they had finished, they had removed 60 per cent of my body surface and applied a temporary artificial skin.

Any healthy skin they were able to locate was removed and taken directly to a lab, where it underwent a process to stretch it to four times its original size in preparation for skin grafts. (Something I've learned from this experience, from a medical point of view, is how remarkable, durable and elastic human skin is.)

Three days later I was back in the operating theatre. Sections of the artificial skin that had been applied to my legs, arms and face had become infected, requiring the doctors to debride once again, scraping back this skin and starting over. Test results indicated I had picked up an infection – most likely during the wait on the side of the canyon before being airlifted to hospital. Thanks to this infection, my face became irreparable as they lay me once again on the operating table and started scraping back the infected tissue.

So extensive were my injuries, the sites on my body from which they could harvest healthy skin for grafting were severely limited. And with the artificial skin causing me so many problems, it was decided I needed donor skin. Australia's low rate of organ and tissue donation meant supplies of suitable skin at local skin banks were low to non-existent. I learned later that what little there was available had already been requisitioned by Rugby World Cup authorities in New Zealand, who had stockpiled it in the event of a terrorist attack during the World Cup.

Professor Haertsch located donor skin at a bank in the States and immediately arranged to have it cryo-packed and sent to Sydney. Upon arrival at Sydney Airport – and with my life hanging in the balance some 20 kilometres away in Concord – the skin was held up by customs officials concerned that the importation contravened the Human Tissues Act, which prevents the sale of human tissue products.

Thankfully for me, Professor Haertsch is not a man to be messed with. A message to customs officials from his registrar read: 'If we don't get it this afternoon, this patient will die.' The skin was released on the spot.

The operation that took place a day later saved my life. Again. Without the donated skin, without it being let through customs, without the expert surgical work of Professors Maitz and Haertsch, I wouldn't be here today. Professor Haertsch applied the skin to no less than 40 per cent of my body. It was to be a critical turning point in my recovery.

This was point zero. The slide had been arrested, but the hard work was only just beginning.

There were many points during my recovery when I felt like I didn't have the strength to keep living, and easily one of the worst was waking up to discover that all the digits on my right hand and two fingers on my left hand had been amputated. It's impossible to describe the feeling of desolation.

Hands, fingers and thumbs are bodily assets that you don't appreciate until you lose them. Think about the number and variety of things you do each day that require the dexterity of your hands and each of your digits, not least your thumbs. Opening a door, doing up a zip, fastening a button, holding a toothbrush, gripping a knife or fork, opening a jar, reaching into a purse and pulling out coins.

And after twenty-four years of being used to fully function- ing hands, it was incredibly hard to teach my body to have to get by with only three fingers. I know the doctors had no choice but to take them. I know it was an agonising decision for Michael to have to make while I was in a coma, but their loss was devastating.

At the time, though, I had plenty of other reasons to cry.

Each morning of my five-month stay in Concord Hospital – and each morning for a good six months after my release – my dressings had to be changed. And each morning for the first three of those months was a horrible lesson in what I would call 'anticipatory pain'.

I was one of many people in the burns unit at Concord during my time there and each one of us had to endure a morning dressing change. The nurses would work in teams, making their way from one ward to the next. I could always tell how far away they were by how loud the screams were coming from fellow patients. The louder the screams, the closer they were getting, the sooner it would be me.

I would work myself into a state of high agitation. Each time a bandage was removed it was like tearing off a top layer of my skin; like taking a block of sandpaper to a set of exposed nerve endings and grinding away at them. It was a process, in my case, that could last up to four hours. Every morning the nurses would come in and ask me which area I wanted them to start in. I would burst into tears. I couldn't move, and even if I could, there was nowhere to run. They would begin their grim work and try and remove the bandages as delicately and efficiently as they could. I would scream and writhe in agony, calling out for Mum or Michael to intervene.

'Make them stop! Please, Michael! Make it stop!'

More often than not Michael and Mum had to remove themselves from the room. There was nothing they could do to help.

As the months progressed, it got easier. Or maybe it didn't get easier, I just became more used to it. Accepting that there was no way of avoiding the daily torture, I started volunteering to go first. At least that way I didn't lie in wait for up to an hour listening to the screams of fellow patients. I also got Michael to help psyche me up each morning – filling my room with loud gangsta rap. Tupac was my constant companion during these sessions: his angry rants against the system played at top volume before the nurses arrived to flay me anew were the perfect way to prepare me for the pain that was to come.

'I'm going to nail this today,' I would tell myself, before instructing the nurses to do the most painful bits first. At the same time, they were trying to wean me off my pain meds, making for a perfect storm of doctor-ordained torture.

At the end of each session, I was spent: both from screaming or sobbing in agony, and also from the adrenaline rush and fear that preceded it.

During the months I spent at Concord Hospital, every day I was completely focused on my recovery. In there, to me it was as if time had stopped, although really I had gone back in time and was having to re-learn all of the things that most of us take for granted.

My body had to re-learn how to perform the most basic motor functions. I couldn't walk. In the intensive care unit I'd had to have a tracheotomy, so I could barely talk. Later, because I couldn't bend my elbows, and even if I could, I had only limited use of my hands, I wasn't able to even feed myself. So I became utterly dependent on Michael, who, since the very first day of my admittance to hospital, had been by my bedside almost constantly from 7 am to 7 pm – he was there every single day for six months.

Mum split her time between Ulladulla, our home town, and Sydney, doing a week in each. At home, she would get my younger brothers organised, make sure they were doing their school work, keep the household running. In Sydney, she was 100 per cent dedicated to me.

Both Mum and Michael had moved into my brother Genji's spare room in the apartment he shared with his wife, Angela, in North Sydney – a good forty-minute drive east of the hospital.

Every morning she was with me, Mum would spoon into my mouth the food she had painstakingly prepared the night before. There was hospital food I could have eaten, but Mum was determined to take personal charge of fattening me up. She also helped me to use the bathroom, wiped my bum, cleaned my teeth. If I had an itch that needed scratching (literally), I called on Mum or Michael to scratch it.

And while you might think this slavish dedication on the part of people who quite clearly love me would produce a surge of gratitude in return, sometimes I was just so angry at the world I'd end up shouting at them, lashing out at them for want of anyone else to lash out at.

I remember one time with my physios – the first time they got me out of bed to try to walk. One of the guiding principles of physio in situations like mine is to get the patient mobile as soon after the accident as possible. The sooner you move, the less likely your skin is to begin to stiffen, which would of course affect your range of movements. Unfortunately, the sooner you move, the more painful it is.

Standing upright for the first time, I was in excruciating pain. Supported on all sides by nurses and physios, I cried. Standing barely a metre away, and fighting back tears of his own, was Michael.

As I took one or two faltering steps, looking more like a hundred-year-old invalid than a twenty-four-year-old woman used to running long distances, Michael did his best to encourage me.

'All right, Turia! Way to go,' he said. 'Turia, champion of the world!'

In a flash of anger I spat back at him, 'Get lost, Michael! I am *not* a champion. I'm a fucking cripple. Your girlfriend is a cripple! It's nothing to celebrate!'

The nurses and physios supporting me went quiet. Michael turned a shade of red, gathered himself, and walked silently out the door.

I felt like such a bitch. Here was this guy who had shown nothing but compassion and support since my accident, who was giving up his life to be there for me in my time of most extreme need, and I was telling him to get stuffed.

Is it something I am proud of? Of course not. Was it inevitable? Probably.

This was the weird world I inhabited. On the one hand, my injuries were so severe and my disability so complete, I invited the cooing encouragement that parents utter only when their baby performs the most basic task. There were days, after enduring a dressing change and rounds of exhausting, painful physio, when I would want nothing more than to be treated like a baby.

But there were other times when I would push back. Moments when the well-meaning attempts to mollycoddle me only served to get on my nerves. I was an adult, a twenty-four-year-old woman, a mining engineer with a double degree. The fact I could put one foot in front of another or hold a spoon was not a reason to celebrate; it was pathetic.

To this day, that remains one of the harder things for me to cope with: the complete plummet in people's expectations of what I am capable of doing. When I'm at the gym and people come over and congratulate me for still doing my workouts, it almost kills me. I think to myself, *I could outrun you any day.* And I know I shouldn't be ungrateful and I know they only mean to be kind, but I hate being underestimated. In my case, it only makes me more determined to show people what I can do. To do something extraordinary – something that even able-bodied people struggle to do.

The flip side, of course, is that for every person who thinks it's amazing that I can walk up a flight of stairs, there are those who think I could walk to the moon if I put my mind to it, now they've seen my recovery.

Time passed so slowly in the burns unit. I used to watch other patients being discharged and seethe inside that it wasn't me. All I wanted to do was be home again: running, swimming, surfing. Instead, I had to be content with mastering the most basic of motor skills: closing my lips together; coordinating sufficiently to get my special, long-handled spoon to my mouth; lifting my arm above 90 degrees; and trying to sit on the toilet seat. It was impossible not to sometimes ask myself, *Why has this happened to me?* But then I'd get angry and think, *It happened; deal with it, mate; harden up, focus on your recovery.* I saw a psychologist a couple of times, but I didn't really gel with him. And most days I'd be so busy I didn't much think about the details of what *had* happened.

An important part of my physical rehabilitation was climbing steps. If you've been doing it all your life, climbing a step or two is not so much of a big deal. But when you are learning to walk again as an adult, a flight of steps is your Everest.

The first time I attacked the portable staircase in the physio ward, I managed only one. One step, that is. I was a curious mixture of elation and deflation. Elated that I had walked up my first step. Deflated that it was apparently a cause for celebration.

Within a week, that one step had turned to two steps. Progress, I was starting to understand, was measured in millimetres when you are recovering from burns such as mine – not leaps and bounds.

When finally I managed an entire flight of stairs, I could have punched the air I was so ecstatic. Except that I didn't have full movement in either of my arms, so air-punching was out of the question.

I couldn't wait to tell my surgeon. His reaction, however, could not have been more underwhelming.

'One flight only?' he asked, with an air of studied indifference. 'You know there are nine of them out there in the hospital?'

If I'd had opposable thumbs, I would have strangled him.

But he knew, and I was far too lacking in self-awareness to understand, that the best way to get me to do something was to tell me I couldn't do it.

Nine flights of stairs. Two hundred and thirty-four individual stairs. From the very bottom of Concord Hospital to the top. I was determined to climb then, so I'd take myself, Mum and Michael off each morning, and eventually one day I walked every one of them. It took me three hours, I was in enormous pain for four days afterwards – but it was worth it.

When I told my surgeon he just smirked.

Leaving Concord Hospital and returning to Michael's parents' home in Narrawallee, near Ulladulla, was a watershed moment. In some respects, I couldn't get out of the hospital fast enough. In other respects, the idea of leaving the burns unit, clinically sealed as it was from the rest of the world, made me anxious. I felt like a bird leaving the security of its nest for the first time. Excited but scared.

My doctors had initially booked me into a rehab facility in Sydney, where they wanted me to spend a few months.

Michael had done a recce and told me I would hate the place. Mum, being the optimist she is, tried to focus on the positives. 'There are some lovely frangipani trees outside,' she said. Having a mum who is a writer has its benefits, but a grounding in reality is not one of them.

The place was a dump. The facilities looked rundown and felt dirty. I hated it from the minute I walked in there, and felt for all those who were stuck there. Surrounded as I was by elderly people who had suffered strokes, and others who had been in car accidents, it gave me an insight into how poorly equipped our health system is for young people who find themselves in care. There are thousands of care facilities set up to cater for our elderly, but where are young people supposed to go when they suffer an accident like I did?

The nursing staff stuffed up my meds, I started to feel sick, the physio was cursory. On my second week there I went back to Genji and Angela's. I lay next to Michael and I cried – I was so incredibly grateful to have him in my life, and I thought about all the times I'd slept next to him and never appreciated it.

We began to campaign for me to return home. Michael convinced the doctors he was more than capable of undertaking the daily dressing change, and moreover, he argued, the healing qualities of being at home would only fast-track my rehabilitation.

The whole episode underscored the lesson I was beginning to appreciate was vital to my recovery: I had to listen to my heart, I had to trust my intuition. And while a doctor's advice would always be paramount when it came to my recovery, Michael and I also knew what was best for me.

The decision to live with Gary and Julie (Michael's parents) for the remainder of my convalescence was made because they had recently become empty-nesters and were knocking around inside a four-bedroom home by themselves. Their house was larger than Mum's apartment (the only other viable alternative) and, thanks to a large backyard ringed by a high fence and a line of trees, it was a purpose-built haven in which I could lick my wounds (and do my daily exercises) in private.

By the time I left the hospital, I had progressed to wearing a full-body compression suit of extra-tight, thick Lycra. Its purpose was to smooth down my scars as they healed. I also had a mask. Because a girl has to accessorise. Once on, the only parts of my face that were visible were my eyes, mouth and what was left of my nose.

Being back in Narrawallee, and driving the streets of Mollymook, Milton and Ulladulla (neighbouring towns that all form one very special area), was a tonic all its own. The countryside I knew so well seemed to welcome me back, take me to its bosom and assure me that everything was going to be okay. The sight of the ocean had a healing effect as well. The water was my second home and I wanted so much to be back in the sea, to allow myself to be rocked gently back to health. But even dipping a toe in it was painful. Forced to swim in my compression suit, the entire experience was deeply unpleasant. I was so weak and so cold, at first I would last all of twenty seconds before I had to get out again. But I knew that a future that didn't involve the ocean was out of the question, so I persisted.

Michael would take me to the sea pool at midday – when the sun was at its strongest. At first I just walked up and down the pool, to get used to being back in the water. Then I progressed to doing a lap across the width of the pool – maybe 12 metres. Then I did a lap lengthways. Then two laps.

With my mask on, my goggles couldn't sit flush to my face, meaning they were basically useless. So I would close my eyes and Michael would swim alongside me to keep me going in a straight line. I also couldn't breathe through my nose anymore, which didn't make being in the water any easier.

When eventually I plucked up the courage to swim at the beach and take on the waves, it was a whole new disaster. I was so weak I didn't have the strength to keep my footing and the waves would knock me down. As Michael raced towards me I would flounder in the whitewash, my compression suit full of sand, seething with anger, embarrassment and frustration.

Setting a long-term goal became a really important part of my recovery. Back in the early days in the burns unit, even before I had learned to properly walk again, Mum had urged me to get up each morning and make my own bed. 'You're not going to have nurses around to do it for you when you get home,' she would say.

Every day physiotherapists and other kinds of therapists had tended to me. The physios attended to my range of movement; occupational therapists helped me to work on my independent functioning. I also saw a speech therapist, who taught me to swallow, and speak, again. But I was only making the most gradual of progress, so I knew I needed to set myself a goal that was well and truly out of the ball park. I settled on Ironman – arguably the toughest test of physical and mental endurance on the world's sporting calendar. Each year, only a handful of the world's fittest people are selected to take part in the official Ironman championship at Kona in Hawaii, and a slightly larger group of ridiculously fit Australians participate in local, satellite Ironman events.

It wasn't something I'd ever considered doing before the fire, but the idea was sown in the first month of my hospitalisation. Some of my doctors gravely informed me that I would need constant care for the rest of my life. I should have felt deflated when I heard the experts tell me stuff like this, but one of the nurses in the hospital, Penny, was brilliant. I came to think of her as my angel. She always made me feel good about myself, and whenever I was given hard news, she'd quietly remind me later, 'Only you know what you're capable of, Turia.' That really resonated with me. I resolved to prove those doctors wrong.

'I'm going to do an Ironman,' I would tell my physios as they tried to restore even partial movement in my knee and elbow joints.

'Of course you are, darling,' they'd reply, humouring me. But inside, the seed was germinating – the resolve was starting to harden.

3

BACK WHERE IT ALL BEGAN

Dusk is falling on Ulladulla. As daylight fades and the afternoon slips into night, a brother and his sister are sprinting up a beach. Their tiny hands are clenched into fists. As they run, a trail of sand spills from their hands. It's 800 metres from the beach to where their father is waiting. He stands out the back of their house – a modest suburban home. Nearby is a shallow trench he has dug. As the children reach the backyard, panting, they throw what small amount of sand they have managed to transport from beach to backyard. The brown earth of the trench bottom has only the lightest dusting of sand on it.

It's a scene I remember well. Etched into my memory. The two children are my older brother, Genji, and me. Running back and forth to the beach to collect handfuls of sand to fill the hole my father has just dug in the backyard.

'And you're not coming inside until the trench is filled,' I remember my father saying.

To say that my dad was a tough bugger would be a major

understatement. He took discipline very seriously, and treated the raising of his children as a project.

Born in Werris Creek, a small country town near Tamworth in country New South Wales, Michael Pitt's own childhood was tough. His dad was a bank manager and the family moved around western New South Wales. When Dad turned fifteen, they moved to the beachside in Maroubra in Sydney, where Dad promptly became a surfer.

He was pretty blessed in the looks department. A mop of blond hair, olive skin and piercing blue eyes, he fitted in immediately with the working-class surf culture of Sydney's southern beaches. He fell into modelling and briefly in the early 1980s his face – and other bits of his body – were featured on magazine covers and advertising campaigns. He even used to model underwear for Calvin Klein. He was signed to the prestigious Chadwick Models in Sydney. He was tall, he had swagger. He appeared once or twice in *Vogue* magazine.

Back in those days, male modelling wasn't the thing it is today, but the money was good. All my dad really wanted to do was surf and travel, and this was an easy way to earn the money to do both. He even appeared on the cover of the *Australian Women's Weekly*, modelling one of the magazine's knitted jumpers. It was an 'Advance Australia' jumper on a 1981 issue of the *Weekly*. He could never have imagined that a daughter he didn't yet know he'd have would also appear on the *Women's Weekly* cover thirty years later – for completely different reasons.

Dad was sent to Tahiti for a photo shoot in the mid-80s when he was in his early twenties and he fell in love with the place. I guess he figured he'd found his spiritual home: a chain of volcanic islands where the surf-break was sweet, the beaches were all but deserted and the people were the living definition of laidback.

When the photo shoot crew packed up and came home, Dad opted to stay put. He was going to become a surfboard shaper, he decided, and settled on the little town of Taravao, a beachside hamlet on the opposite side of the island of Tahiti from its capital, Papeete.

Taravao juts out into the turquoise waters of the Pacific, surrounded on both sides by expanses of sea. A coral reef lies just off-shore and a lagoon sweeps in a lazy arc around the township's southern border. It's about idyllic a spot as any to fall in love.

It was in Taravao that he met Mum.

She was all of fifteen years old and working at 'Le Snack' – the mobile food van parked down at the beach. I've seen photos of Mum at the time: she was a knockout. A stunningly beautiful island girl: long dark hair, deep-brown eyes, skin like velvet and smart as a whippet. Dad was a goner.

Being a bright cookie, Mum had won a scholarship to the best school in Tahiti. She loved reading. Nothing gave her greater pleasure than losing herself in the world of books. To this day, she's exactly the same. Her apartment in Mollymook is stuffed with books. Back in Tahiti, growing up in French Polynesia, and with the canon of French literature at her fingertips, she would often be found under a tree in the town square, head buried in a book, oblivious to the world bustling around her, lost in myriad other worlds. Her favourite author, bar none, was Guy de Maupassant.

During my recovery in hospital, I did much the same thing. In the rare moments I was left alone, I would treasure being able to pick up a book and lose myself in its pages.

Dad says he still remembers the first time he clapped eyes on Mum. She was a demure (yet if I know Mum), slightly coquettish young girl. Dad's attempt to crack on to her at their first meeting was roundly rebuffed. She thought he was too cocky. And besides, she was a good Catholic girl. She might have been innocent in the ways of the world, but she knew enough about these surfer dudes who would blow in from across the oceans to give them a wide berth.

For a whole year Dad persisted. He spent a lot of time trying to woo Mum. I can't say with any authority if she was the only local lass he was courting at the time, but for the sake of this love story, let's assume she was.

I suspect it was partly her reluctance to yield to his considerable Aussie charm that kept him coming back for more. Dad wasn't used to being rejected by members of the fairer sex. As Mum slowly warmed to the idea of this larrikin from a far-flung land, Dad found himself falling further and further under Mum's spell.

After flirting with one another for a year at Le Snack, Mum and Dad met at a party one night and finally got together. I don't know the exact details – because, well, I'm their daughter and there are some things you don't need to drill down on. But I do know that they were inseparable after that. Mum was sixteen. Dad was twenty-two.

In Tahiti, it's common for people to get together when they are young and have children before they turn twenty. As a society, the Polynesians are a lot more relaxed about that sort of stuff.

After a while, they became engaged and Dad packed up his exotic French-speaking fiancée, brought her back to Australia and married her in Bowral, in the New South Wales Southern Highlands.

They returned to Tahiti as man and wife. Upon arriving home, Mum got straight into her school uniform and trotted off to school. She had just turned seventeen.

Not long afterwards, she fell pregnant with Genji. She managed to finish school, was awarded her baccalaureat (the French high school finishing certificate) and not long after gave birth to my brother. Soon after she fell pregnant with me.

Mum and Dad's house in Tahiti was about as basic as they got. It didn't have electricity or running water. It was essentially a little wooden shack. But they were loved up and living in paradise with two beautiful bambinos – if I say so myself.

Not long after I was born, Mum went to work as a primary teacher. She loved teaching – she was in her element. Surrounded by children, doling out books, daily exalting the virtues of education and learning, she couldn't have been happier.

When I was two years old and Genji was three, Dad packed us all up and moved us to Australia. It was the middle of July when we touched down in Sydney and moved into a little terrace house in Chippendale, in inner Sydney. We had come from tropical Tahiti to the dead of a Sydney winter. Mum unpacked her suitcase and looked uncertainly at her collection of sarongs. Although, knowing her, she was determined to make the best of the move, she must have realised at that point that it was going to be a lot tougher than she'd anticipated.

I often think about what coming here must have been like for her. She was all of twenty years old, with two children under the age of three, in a city where she didn't know a soul, only vaguely spoke the language and had barely any money.

At least Dad got a job almost immediately – as a graphic designer. He had no qualifications apart from a flair for drawing, so I guess his great eye coupled with a can-do attitude got him the role.

While the job meant they had a regular income, it also meant long days for Mum with two small kids in a rundown terrace at Chippendale as she tried to get her head around this strange new city. She had spent her entire life living in an island paradise. Now the only jungle she could access was a concrete one.

But my mother is made of stern stuff. She had, to all intents and purposes, spent a lifetime looking after herself. Now she had children who were also depending on her. So instead of allowing herself to be overwhelmed by these new circum-stances, she did what many thousands of migrants before her had done. She knuckled down and applied herself to the task of assimilating.

For Mum, that meant reading every women's magazine she could get her hands on until such time as her English was good enough that she could apply for a job. And apply for a job she did, becoming before too long a customer service manager at a bank not far from our home.

She was helped enormously by Dad's parents, my grand-mother and grandfather, both of whom could see she needed support. They took her shopping, bought her and us kids the clothes we were going to need to get by, and in all ways set themselves to the task of welcoming us into the Pitt family.

After a year or so, we moved to Daceyville, near Maroubra, to be closer to them, and to be closer to the beach so Dad could surf more regularly.

I cried on my first day at school. Not for any particular reason other than it was my first day at school. Daceyville was full of new Australians – it was a real working-class pocket, and our little school was a melting pot of different cultures and backgrounds.

Dad used to make Genji and me ride our bikes to school even when we were in kindy. I'd get a smack on the bum if I put my foot down on the ground while trying to learn, or for not riding my bike properly. Dad was determined we would learn to do things properly from the outset. There were no shortcuts. There was no mollycoddling because we were kids. Every time we stopped for a traffic light, we'd have to get the bike moving again and hurl our leg over the saddle to make our wobbly way across the road. I was all of five years old.

As much as he was a task master, Dad was also a big kid at heart. I remember him letting us run through a sprinkler on a hot day – even if we were on the way to school he didn't mind, as long as we knew we had to take the consequences of arriving with wet clothes. But we certainly didn't have a television – Dad thought TV ruined children's brains. At night, Genji and I used to sneak out of our bedroom window and climb up onto the neighbour's roof to watch TV through their skylight.

*

I don't have especially vivid memories from that time, but I recall there was a lot of fighting between Mum and Dad. Probably because on a fundamental level they were not well-suited. They'd had kids really soon after they'd got together, they never had a lot of money, and Mum was living on the other side of the earth to her friends, family and everything she knew.

Dad was young when he had us – only twenty-six. To his way of thinking, it was part of his job as a father to ensure we didn't make the mistakes he believed he had made in life (I think he felt one was having kids too young). He wanted to make us strong and prepare us for the big bad world. Even when we were young, he'd make us do push-ups, and sit with our legs straight and elevated for as long as we were able to hold them up. He would time us, and yell at us if we dropped our legs. He treated Genji and me like his little soldiers. He had two rules. Rule number one was 'no whingeing'. Rule number two was: 'no bloody whingeing'.

He thinks now he was probably a bit too much. Maybe he was. But I don't resent it for a second. In fact, looking back I appreciate it. I hate how some parents wrap their kids in cottonwool these days. And as I have got older I can see there was method to his madness. Just as I'm grateful to the fire for all the things it taught me, I'm indebted to my dad for everything he taught me in life: and especially the resilience he worked so hard to instil in me. I love him dearly, and wouldn't have him any other way. To this day, he is one of my best mates and greatest supporters. Yes, he could be tough, but then the world is tough. And though he was always fast to discipline, we were never in any doubt that he loved us. He sometimes just had a funny way of showing it.

I suppose on reflection Dad's intense parenting style could all have so easily backfired. I could have turned out to be insecure and unsure of everything I did. Instead, and even without my knowing it, he was slowly but surely crafting a little human with enormous reserves of fortitude.

4

SOUTH COAST DREAMING

I was eight years old when we moved to Ulladulla. It was a place I vaguely knew – we'd spent a few holidays down there. Lazy, salt-crusted summer days swimming and surfing. Dad had fallen in love with the surf there, so we moved out of the city and down the coast.

Back in the 1980s, Ulladulla was a sleepy little seaside town. Its main industry was the fleet of fishing vessels that chuntered out of the port before dawn and returned each day with a noisy crowd of seagulls crisscrossing the sky in their wake. A three-hour drive south of Sydney, and smack bang in the middle of the stunning Shoalhaven district, it's a physically stunning pocket of the world. Lush, rolling green hills tumble down to the coastline, herds of plump dairy cattle graze the days away. Long stretches of yellow-sanded beach, verdant patches of sub-tropical rainforest and the odd, square-topped peak of Pigeon House Mountain rising up above it all.

It was kid heaven. And with its ready access to any number of sick surf-breaks, it was Dad heaven too. He got work as a graphic designer and we settled in.

I think Mum felt instantly more at home with the gentler pace of South Coast life. It was small-town living – not even the physical isolation from anything you would otherwise call civilisation could take away from the sensation of staring out across the glassy waters of the Pacific Ocean on a clear day.

Our lives became all about the outdoors. We seemed to exist in a state of perpetual motion. Most mornings – summer, winter, rain, hail or shine – Dad would wake up Genji and me and take us down to the beach for a run. If I lagged behind at any point, he would come up behind me and smack my bum to speed me up.

After school we would come home, grab our surfboards and find the best break on any of the numerous beaches within a five-minute drive of our home. Dad had taught me to surf in Sydney when I was only six years old. It won't come as a massive surprise to learn he wasn't the most patient of teachers, so it fell to Genji to educate me on the finer points of catching and riding a wave. He had a softer touch and was a better surfer than Dad anyway.

Dad was stoked when we got waves, but he always had corrections for us at the end of every ride: how we could have ridden the wave better, how we needed to improve our paddling technique. I'm sure it's clear by now that he was the disciplinarian in the family. Mum, on the other hand, is the complete opposite. When she used to try and smack us we would just laugh at her. And now, no matter what I, or any of her four kids, do – she thinks it's amazing. On the speaking circuit, every time I get up on stage and utter more than two syllables, if Mum is with me she's in raptures. Dad, on the other hand, will listen to me do a speech and be proud of me for having done it – but he'll always suggest ways on how it could be improved. Mum shows her love so easily – I sometimes take it for granted. But with Dad you feel you have to earn it.

Genji and I went to Ulladulla High School for a couple of years, before moving to St John's Catholic School. Ulladulla High was a perfectly fine school and we had lots of friends there, but I think Mum and Dad wanted us to be a little more stretched academically. I had begun to show signs of being gifted when it came to school work, but I was also inclined to be a bit lazy if I wasn't pushed.

I loved St John's. The school was just the right mix of discipline and freedom, academia and sports to keep me satisfied. Before long I had a great group of new friends.

St John's was located in Nowra, a forty-minute bus ride up the coast. The road was a two-lane affair and wound its way through thick bushland. Most days I would pass the time staring out the window as we rolled past forests of tall gum. My bestie in those days was Genevieve. She and I were inseparable, both on the bus ride to and from school and in the playground.

One afternoon during the ride home I was sitting next to Genevieve as usual when I saw a car swerve on the road in front of us and clip the bus. The bus driver yanked on the steering wheel, hoping to avoid a collision, only to tip the bus onto its side and send it skidding along the road. The seconds between us being upright and sliding out of control along the bitumen seemed to pass in slow motion. There was a screech of brakes, a moment when we seemed suspended in thin air, and then a final gut-churning lurch as the bus lost balance and tipped onto its side at speed. I was on the upside and fell with a thud, crashing down on top of other kids and the hard metal of unforgiving bench seats. After what seemed an eternity, the bus skidded to a halt. And for a moment, there was silence.

I remember Genji grabbing me and pulling me towards the back window, where we followed the stream of dazed and confused students who were clambering out. I turned to grab hold of Genevieve and pull her out behind me, but she stayed crouched inside the bus, bent over her brother, Kristian. In the crash, his arm had got caught between the bus and the bitumen. He was in a bad way.

We stood on the side of the road in a state of shock. If I close my eyes now, I can still see the image of a bus on its side, dust settling around it and Kristian trapped inside. The road was covered in his blood.

We were twenty minutes from Nowra, on a road in the middle of bushland. It seemed to take forever for an ambulance to arrive. Kristian died at the scene from blood loss. He was fifteen.

By some miracle, and despite being thrown about the bus like a rag doll, I hadn't suffered any physical injuries. I was, however, in a state of shock for the next few weeks. Being a kid, I couldn't really process what had happened. Looking back, I seemed to sleepwalk through the immediate aftermath. None of it felt real.

We all went to Kristian's funeral and afterwards Genji and I went home and played video games – something our dad had rarely let us do before.

Not long after the accident, Mum and Dad pulled Genji and me out of St John's and enrolled us at Shoalhaven Anglican School, no longer prepared to let us travel that road twice every day. I remember Genevieve coming over to visit one day because she wanted to get out of her house. We went for a walk and I held her hand, but I didn't know what to say to her. I felt uncomfortable and I stopped making an effort to see her so we gradually lost contact. When I look back on it, I know I was a bad friend. I was just too self-involved. That was my first encounter with death. And now, after my own experience with the fire and my long recovery, it throws my guilt into ever-sharper relief.

I still have old friends and acquaintances make contact with me to apologise for not reaching out or being there for me in the days, weeks and months after the fire. 'I wanted to text or call, but I didn't know what to say,' they say. And it's a cop-out. You just need to show up. Just show up. Even if you stand there and say, 'I don't know what to say, but I wanted you to know I am thinking about you.' That's all it takes.

I wasn't happy at Shoalhaven. In retrospect, I think my anger was a deep-seated reaction to the bus accident – feelings I took out on my parents, accusing them of ruining my life by moving me to a new school. I only lasted two terms before I was asked to leave. I was a shit to all my teachers: swearing in class, defying any attempts at discipline, generally being a teenage pain in the arse. One afternoon, I wagged school with a girlfriend; we ended up having a fight, during which I pushed her to the ground and she broke her arm.

I went back to school the following Monday and everyone hated me. As I say, I'm sure this sudden lurch into delinquency was my way of processing the bus crash. As far I know, none of us received counselling – I certainly didn't. It would never have occurred to anyone in my family that I might have needed professional help to deal with what had happened.

Being thrown out of Shoalhaven and forced to return to Ulladulla High School was the perfect outcome as far as I was concerned. I was in Year 10, I had inherited a fair smattering of my parents' good looks and I was suddenly very interested in boys. I fell in immediately with what you might call the 'popular kids'. I was also smart, which could have proved to be social death, but because I was considered to be pretty and could hold my own with the 'cool kids', I never suffered the stigma of being a nerd.

Teenagers are so shallow. I know because I was once a very shallow teenager. The extent of my interests in those days didn't stretch far beyond surfing, who was going out with whom, and which guys were 'hot'. Nevertheless, I did well in my studies. In my final year, I won the school medal for maths and physics. I was also really good at chemistry. And while I do have a science-oriented brain, the fact I chose those subjects at the time in fact had more to do with a teacher telling me I was rubbish at them than any particular passion for them. One of my teachers laughed at me when I told him I was planning to take advanced maths, physics and chemistry for my HSC. 'You're not smart enough to do those subjects,' he chuckled.

As my surgeon at Concord Hospital realised years later, if there is a surefire way to motivate me, it's to appear to under-estimate me – or otherwise seek to put limitations on what I can and cannot do. It was always like that when I was at school and it remains that way to this day.

The fact that this teacher didn't think I could handle those subjects spurred me on. I studied like a maniac – burning the midnight oil and setting my alarm to get up early and squeeze in extra study hours before school.

I came first in all my subjects for the HSC, got a TER score in the high 90s and graduated with flying colours.

It was around this time that Mum started to achieve her own professional success. Her love of reading had always manifested itself in a passion for writing. Encouraged by my father, she sat down to write a novel – the result was a book called *Breadfruit*. It told the tale of Materena Mahi, 'the best listener in Tahiti' according to the book's blurb. 'A warm and generous woman, a natural problem solver, versed in the folk wisdom of her native island home.' In the book, Materena juggles her relatives, her new baby boy, church on Sunday, cleaning her boss's house, her fiancé and an upcoming wedding.

The fact that Mum had applied herself to the writing of this book at all was, in retrospect, an amazing achievement. Not only that, but after the usual round of disheartening rejection letters, she finally received news that her book was going to be published – the realisation of her every professional dream. But I was a self-obsessed teenager so the significance of what Mum had achieved was lost on me at the time.

Even if Mum had been inclined to celebrate her achievement, she would have had precious little time to do it. Two more siblings, my brothers Toriki and Heimanu, had arrived on the scene, the first when I was nine and the second a year later. And *Breadfruit* failed to find the audience its publishers hoped it might. So, with what I can only imagine was a heavy heart, Mum went out to find a job. She took a position with the Mission Australia charity, working in job placement. She had four kids, was working full-time and running a household. But she'd had a taste of writing. She had come to learn what it was to sit at a keyboard, tell stories and lose herself in an imaginary world. She was hooked.

Determined to have another crack at this whole author caper, she decided to write a second book. Her office was next to my bedroom, and I used to fall asleep to the sound of her tapping away at the keyboard. This was an important lesson for me. It emphasised the importance of hard work and discipline, and made me realise that with a 'never give up' attitude, anything is possible.

Her second book, *Frangipani*, was a massive success. It was immediately embraced here at home, was translated into ten different languages and published all over the world. Mum travelled to America, China, Canada and all over Europe to promote the book.

To become an internationally successful author in a language that was not her maternal tongue was an amazing feat. Certainly now I realise we didn't give her the credit she deserved.

It would have been hard for Dad – he would have been proud of her, but their relationship was starting to show signs of strain.

When I was in Year 11, Mum and Dad divorced. It was sad, as marriage break-ups always are, but for the most part it was a relief for the entire family. Towards the end of their marriage, all Mum and Dad ever seemed to do was argue. It was tough on my little brothers, for sure, but they were both so young when Mum and Dad split that in lots of ways them living apart has been their normal. Then again, they've had to deal with adjusting to different social situations in a way that I never had to. Unsurprisingly, the two homes in which they now split their time were poles apart. Mum's place was a riot of colour: Tahitian sarongs and sea shells everywhere you look. Dad's place was spartan.

Mum and Dad might have been fractious at times, but they were a constant, as a unit, for most of my childhood. And even now, though they are not together, they remain my staunchest supporters and biggest fans.

With high school done and dusted, I decided to take a gap year before starting university. And what better place to while away a year as an almost-eighteen-year-old than the ski fields of Queenstown in New Zealand? I saw a job ad online for a ski-lift attendant and fired off an application. They wrote back telling me I was hired, and I couldn't get there fast enough. Ulladulla felt like it was getting smaller by the day; I was ready to spread my wings and fly the South Coast nest. I remember my uncle gave me $500 before I left, which I thought was a fortune. I promptly arrived in Queenstown and spent it all in a week. It was my first lesson: I had to learn to budget.

I lived in staff quarters for the first month or two before moving into a share house with a couple of newly minted mates. We would work all morning, snowboard all afternoon and party all night. I was there for a year and can safely say I made the most of every second.

For my eighteenth birthday, my best friends Kristen (or Briggsy as she's known) and Nicola surprised me by coming to see me on a lightning visit. Soon enough, however, real life reared its head – as it has a habit of doing. A new year was upon me and with it the prospect of starting my uni degree. I packed up my snowboard, bade farewell to my friends and came home.

5

MEETING MICHAEL

The University of New South Wales (UNSW) in Kensington, in Sydney's east, sits on a sprawling campus. It teaches all the usual subjects that seats of learning of its stature offer. Aspiring lawyers mingle with aspiring linguists, the scientists and doctors of tomorrow rub shoulders with the business people and economists of the future. But far and away the students on the UNSW campus who make their presence most clearly felt are the engineers. Loud, brash, poorly dressed and extremely fond of beer – it was into this hot-bed of academia that I was thrust upon arriving at university.

Having decided to pour myself – and my hard-earned high-90s HSC mark – into a double mining engineering and environmental science degree, I took a room in Baxter College on the UNSW main campus and happily let the debauchery of uni life wash over me.

How did I come to choose a double degree in mining engineering and environmental science? Because I had watched mine bomb blasts on YouTube and I thought they looked awesome. I cared about the environment. I had also returned from New Zealand with a hefty credit card debt, and had heard mining grads sometimes landed first jobs with pay packets in the vicinity of $130,000. Hey, I never claimed to be one of the world's deepest thinkers, all right?

I threw myself into campus life with so much gusto that I failed my first year. No matter. In a class of sixty students, I was one of only three girls. Problem was, it didn't take me too long to work out that while they were fine to share a beer or ten with, engineers were not high on my list of potential boyfriends.

Med students, however, were. Which is how I came to be involved with Tyson – my first serious boyfriend. Like me, Tyson hailed from the south coast of New South Wales. He was an extroverted, smart medical student from Batemans Bay. We met in Orientation Week and soon after became insep-arable – even going to the lengths of meeting one another's parents. But we were young, and university seemed to stretch on in front of us for years. Though passionate, ours was a love affair that was destined not to last; essentially, life had differ-ent plans for us both.

While at uni, and as if to prove that beyond the hard-partying exterior there did in fact beat the heart of someone who took an interest in her fellow humans, I travelled to Mongolia to join a Habitat for Humanity house-building team. I flew to Ulaanbaatar in Mongolia, and then on to Erdenet – a god-forsaken, windswept place situated for no reason that I could discern smack bang in the middle of absolutely nowhere. The famed steppes of Mongolia were just featureless and flat. All of the families we had been sent to help lived in gers – the traditional tent their forebears had inhabited for centuries.

They weren't much interested, as it turned out, in having a bunch of privileged, upstart uni students from the other side of the earth coming over and telling them they needed to move house. These people were nomads. They had livestock that – for their livelihood – they needed to constantly move. And here we were providing them with a solution for a problem they didn't know they even had.

We set about making them a collection of poorly constructed concrete bunkers, and we couldn't work out why they were getting really annoyed with us. Given we were a bunch of uni students with a collective house-building experience of next to nothing, the houses we built were truly awful. They had neither sanitation nor electricity.

For the most part the locals stood by and watched with bemusement – or ever-increasing levels of frustration. We would put a bit of cement on a wall and they would come over and scrape it off. All they wanted was a new ger. And quite probably they wanted the $3000 in cash that each of us had spent flying over there to make ourselves feel like we were doing something for the world. Three thousand dollars, after all, was the average annual salary in Mongolia at the time.

It taught me to ask questions of the charities with which I became involved in later years. To make sure I aligned myself with charities that directly serviced a particular need. Charities such as Interplast, which, though I had never heard of it at the time, was to become a cause close to my heart.

Undeterred by our Mongolian experience, and still determined to foist our help on an unsuspecting third world, Briggsy and I headed off to Cambodia the following year. We spent a year fundraising, including staging a huge event in Ulladulla that was kindly patronised by everyone we knew – to raise money for a school in Cambodia. We then took the money over and were able to see first-hand what a difference it was going to make in the lives of those children. Then we rode our bikes 400 kilometres around Cambodia to raise more money. The whole exercise reinforced how lucky we are in the developed world, how much we take for granted and how easy it is to give back. It was formative in that respect.

During this time, I would visit Ulladulla to spend time with Mum, Dad and my little brothers. At the occasional party or in the street, or sometimes even at home with Mum, I would cross paths with Michael Hoskin – or 'Hosko' as he was known to his mates. He and Genji had been best friends since high school. They worked together at the local Tuckerbag super-market, stacking shelves after school. But mostly they surfed together – and no doubt cut a swathe through the local female population.

Michael was cute – the home-town, surfer-boy kind. I had fancied him for years in that way that younger sisters have crushes on their older brothers' friends. Not only was he was incredibly good-looking but also he seemed like a genuinely nice guy. Uncomplicated, wholesome, with just the right amount of glint in his eye.

Of course, through Genji we had met many times in our school days in and around Ulladulla. There had been a few near misses where we almost got together at various parties, but it never seemed to quite happen.

Michael had recently graduated from the Police Academy in Goulburn and taken up a posting in Maroubra, of all places.

We had never run into each other in Sydney, but we were often back in Ulladulla on the same weekends. And I distinctly remember one evening being at home and getting ready to go to a party, knowing it was likely that Michael would be there. It was a summer's evening in early December, and there was that wonderful, pre-Christmas festive mood in the air. Whether I had consciously or subconsciously made an extra bit of effort with my appearance, or whether my mum simply employed that intuition with which all mothers (especially superstitious Tahitian ones) are equipped, she remarked on how attractive I was looking as I headed out the door.

'Woo hoo! You look hot tonight,' she cooed. 'Are you going to kiss anyone?'

I smiled and shot back. 'Only if Michael Hoskin is there.'

And he was. So I did. It was 11 December 2009 – an unforgettable day in my life, as it turned out.

A happy year began in the blush of an exciting new relationship. We were both living in Sydney – Michael working and me studying – but almost every weekend we would jump in the car and drive south to Ulladulla for an uninterrupted forty-eight hours of surfing, swimming, diving and running. If physical attraction to one another was the initial spark that got us together, a mutual love of all things outdoors – and a deep-seated respect for the genuine goodness of one another – kept us together. I felt completely at ease in Michael's company. He was warm, loving, funny and utterly generous of nature. Michael was the guy who was friends with everyone. He never had a bad word to say about anyone, and only ever saw the best in everyone he met. He was the gentle, quiet yin to my brash, extroverted yang. More than anything else, he was good of heart, with a moral compass that was unshakeable. We were still young, and we had so much more life ahead of us to live, but in our quieter moments, whether on the deck of his boat, bobbing on the ocean, basking in the sun after a morning spent diving for lobster, or curled up in bed next to him, my head on his chest, I imagined this was a man with whom I just might be able to build a life.

6

THE RIPPLE EFFECT

Have you ever seen one of those movies where there are multiple stories branching out from one single incident? An exploration of how several lives can be affected in different ways by a single event in one person's life? The ripple effect.

Much has been written and said about how that day in September 2011 irrevocably altered my life. But comparatively little has been committed to paper about how that brush fire in the Kimberley all those years ago marked a turning point in the lives of so many others, too.

It's a source of constant wonder to me when I stop and think about the love that was poured into me by my loved ones, and the patience and devotion they showed on a daily basis during my recovery. It makes me emotional every time I think – or talk – about it.

If I lived a hundred lifetimes I could still never repay so many people for everything they have done for me or properly express how grateful I am. But I hope that by giving them an opportunity to tell their story, to share their own personal experience of the fire and its aftermath, I might in some way be able to honour them.

So scattered throughout the following chapters are first-person testimonials from those who are closest to me, as well as those who, because of their role in my life at the time, have a unique perspective to offer on the how and why of my recovery. Because someone can tell what you are like (or what they think you are like), but it's only when you speak to those who know you best that the portrait becomes fully dimensional.

And where better to start than with Michael? The man who knows me better than anyone. This is his story, in his own words.

Michael

I was born on Christmas Day 1984 in Narrandera, a little country town near the border of New South Wales and Victoria. Mum says I was her special Christmas present from Santa.

I am the eldest of three siblings. There's me, my sister Shae and my brother Aaron – all born within a few years of each other. We lived on about five acres, with a big swimming pool that the neighbours used to come and swim in. Dad would often take me out shooting rabbits – any we shot we would take back to my nan and she would make a stew out of them.

Our weekends were spent mostly riding motorbikes about the property or down at the creek catching crayfish; we'd put a kangaroo leg in the trap, drop it down to the bottom of the creek and wait for the crays to come. I remember lots of nights spent camping down by the creek or alongside the Murrumbidgee River, sitting around a campfire and eating freshly caught cray. It was a pretty good life.

When I turned nine, Mum and Dad decided to swap country life for coastal life, so we moved to Narrawallee, a little collection of houses just north of Ulladulla. That was the start of my love affair with the ocean. I was in or on or next to the sea for pretty much the next ten years of my life. To this day I still get antsy if I'm away from the coast for too long. Although you have to have a heathy respect for the ocean, I still regard it as my happy place.

Dad bought a boat when we moved to Narrawallee and straightaway we started fishing. We had no idea what we were doing at first – pulling up and scaling and eating all sorts of weird fish, stuff we would throw back if we pulled it up today. But it was all new to us back then.

Weekends were the typical blur of little athletics and cricket. As he got older, Aaron was pretty handy with the cricket bat, and he started playing rep, which meant travelling all over the place for his games. Mum was a teacher at my primary school. I never had her as my teacher, but she was always around when I needed a lift home or pocket money at recess.

I met Turia's brother Genji at Ulladulla High School in about Year 8. We both started working around the same time at the Tuckerbag supermarket in Ulladulla, packing shelves after school. We became good friends – spent a lot of time surfing together and just hanging out as you do when you're fourteen and fifteen.

The first time I saw Turia was one afternoon when she came into Tuckerbag to see Genji. She was at a different school to us, and she was wearing her uniform. What do I remember from that first encounter? I don't know. I think I was just curious that Genji had a sister. He'd never mentioned it before.

I stayed at school through Year 12 and got my HSC. I wasn't sure what I wanted to do afterwards, so I joined a mate and headed overseas. We went to London, where I worked for a year as a builder's labourer. I was nineteen, there was a lot of partying and it was a lot of fun, but after a while I'd had enough. The weather was rubbish, I was getting paler and fatter by the day. What do they call it? The Heathrow injection.

I had a return ticket, so I left my mate and came home.

Back in Ulladulla I worked around town for a bit – in a bottle shop, that sort of thing. Otherwise I just surfed and hung out, got myself back into shape. I applied for and was accepted into the Police Academy in Goulburn. I had done work experience at the cop shop in Ulladulla in Year 10. Most of the time I'd just sat in the back of the patrol car while the coppers drove around checking the surf and handing out subpoenas – I remember thinking it looked like a pretty cruisey way to make a living.

The reality was of course a bit different.

After ten months of training at the academy, I was stationed in Maroubra. It's a bit of a mixed bag, Maroubra: next to some awesome beaches with great surf, there are million-dollar properties alongside acres and acres of housing commission. In the immediate vicinity, you have Long Bay Jail, the hospitals in Randwick, the Coogee pubs. What I initially thought was going to be an easy, beachside posting turned out to be anything but. Maroubra Police Station, I would later learn, is one of the busiest in the Sydney metropolitan area.

It's fair to say the experience opened my eyes. More than anything else, it made me appreciate how well I had been brought up. I visited a lot of homes where the kids weren't as lucky as I had been. You could see their potential, but they were struggling through life and mainly that was down to peers who were a bad influence, and alcohol and drugs, which were even worse ones.

I attended a lot of domestics – going into homes where husbands had bashed the crap out of their wives. I saw more than a few dead bodies – car crashes, suicides, even one particularly gruesome murder. For the most part, I managed to compartmentalise what I was seeing. You learn pretty early on how important it is to separate the emotion in any given situation from whatever action needs to be taken. You're either the kind of person who takes all of the shit on board, or you work out how to let it slide off you. Some of my colleagues needed counselling. I had my own form of therapy: I would go into the ocean, to surf or fish.

I remember seeing Turia at a mate's barbecue, back in Ulladulla, during a visit home. We'd bumped into each other on and off throughout the years, but at this barbie I remember thinking how beautiful she looked. I had always been attracted to her, I suppose. But I thought she was out of my league. Bubbly, tall, pretty and strong-minded. She was always active and out there and doing things for charities. I honestly didn't think I had a chance with her.

So, at this party, I was being silly. I'd had a few beers and she'd had a few beers and – I don't normally do this – but we were having a chat and in the middle of talking to her I just blurted out, 'So, are we going to kiss?' and she replied, 'I've been waiting for you to ask.'

I somehow managed to talk her into staying at my place that night. And she agreed, but only on the proviso I didn't try any funny business. I thought she was kidding. Turns out she wasn't.

We were pretty much inseparable after that night. She was just so charismatic and magnetic – I couldn't help but be drawn to her. She has this fantastic energy that makes me want to be near her.

When she graduated from uni with two degrees I was so proud, and amazed that anyone could have the capacity to study for and be awarded an engineering degree and an environmental science degree. Towards the end of her degree she'd got a job in the mines up north. A little place called Kununurra in the middle of nowhere at the top of Western Australia, in the Kimberley, about 800 kilometres from Darwin.

I was pretty much done with the police force by then. I couldn't get excited by work, it was starting to get me down, and the prospect of a change really appealed. So, I resigned, packed my bags and went with Turia up there.

It was 2011 and we were about to have nine of the best months of our lives. I got work at the mines, Turia was busy with her job – an internship with Rio Tinto in their Argyle diamond mine – and every chance we had we would take off with a tent and explore the Kimberley. It's some of the most beautiful country you will find anywhere in the world. We spent our weekends hiking and camping and swimming in gorges.

The mines were booming at the time. Our plan was to work as much as we could and save our money to put down a deposit on a house. Even back then we were talking about a future together. I think we both knew we wanted to be with one another.

We used to run a lot together up in the Kimberley. Keeping fit was definitely one of the things we had in common. I'm not competitive with Turia – she's the competitive one – but I do love exercising with her. I try to push her further until she's completely busted.

When Turia first told me she wanted to sign up for the ultra-marathon, I had my doubts. A hundred kilometres in the desert in one day – I knew she was super-fit, but I worried she wouldn't be up to that distance. She'd only got the call-up for it two weeks before the race and hadn't had time to do any special training for it. But she's determined when she wants to be. And when the organisers offered to waive the entry fee, I knew there was nothing I could say that was going to stop her.

In the week before the race, we went down to Sydney for her graduation ceremony. I sat in the auditorium with her mum and Genji and cheered when she stood up to receive her degrees. I remember thinking how remarkable Turia was; how she had the world at her feet; how we were about to embark on this exciting new chapter in our lives. It felt like the world was our oyster and anything was possible.

We went back to Ulladulla for a few days. Turia was going to return to Kununurra alone, to prepare for the race, while I stayed back to go to a friend's party. I dropped her at the train station at Bomaderry so she could get back up to Sydney and fly north. It was all a bit of a rush – we were probably running late for the train or something – and as she jumped out of the car, I kissed her and wished her luck. I told her I'd see her in a couple of days and we would celebrate her killing the ultramarathon. She smiled as she turned and got out of the car. I didn't know it at the time, but that was the last time I saw the old Turia.

On the day of the race, I flew back from Sydney to Darwin. It's a four-and-a-half-hour flight and I didn't arrive until late in the afternoon. I had to overnight in Darwin. I checked in to the airport motel and had a swim in the pool before a beer and dinner. I knew Turia would still be running, and that there was no reception on the course, so I didn't bother trying to call her.

It was about 11 pm, when I was asleep in bed, that I got a phone call from the race organisers.

'There's been a fire. Turia has burns to more than sixty per cent of her body,' I was told. 'She's currently intubated in Kununurra Hospital.'

It took a moment or two to register. I thought it had to be a bad dream, or a joke. I went numb. My head started spinning. I felt sick. I hung up and immediately called my dad.

'You have to come, Dad,' I said. 'It's serious.'

He started booking flights straightaway.

The organisers had told me Turia was being transferred directly from Kununurra to the burns unit at the Royal Perth Hospital, so I raced directly to the airport and tried to get on a plane to Perth. The next available flight wasn't until the following day, but the attendant told me it would be faster if I flew to Sydney and took an early morning flight from there to Perth. So I bought the tickets.

On the plane to Sydney, I kept hanging on to the snippet the organiser had told me: that Turia had walked from the helicopter into Kununurra Hospital. Surely that was a good sign.

I arrived in Sydney the next morning and met Dad, Turia's mum, Celestine, Genji and his wife Angela. Just as we were about to make our way together to Perth, I received a text message informing me that Turia had been transferred to Darwin. Her injuries were so severe, the burns so deep, they didn't think she would survive the flight to Perth. I was horrified; I can't even describe how I felt. Physically sick. And I didn't know what to tell Celestine, who was already a mess.

We all changed our flights to travel to Darwin, but then in the departure lounge I received another message: Turia was going to be transferred to the burns unit at Concord Hospital in Sydney. However, first she would undergo surgery in Darwin – a process called 'debridement' where doctors surgically remove the worst of the burned skin. We all boarded the flight to Darwin, as everything started to happen in fast-forward. Even if we were only going to be by Turia's side there for a minute, we were determined to be there.

As it happened, I didn't see Turia until she was in intensive care at Concord Hospital. I could have gone in and seen her at Darwin Hospital – after the operation she had stabilised. But the doctors were pessimistic. I remember specifically one German doctor coming out of theatre and telling us bluntly that Turia might not live. That hit me hard.

Dad went in to see her. He came out and told me it wasn't pretty, and it was then I decided that if she was going to die, I wanted my last memory of her to be a happy one. At this stage she was in an induced coma, so I knew she wouldn't be wondering where I was. I went outside the hospital and found a place by myself and had a massive cry. It was real. I might lose this girl I had fallen in love with.

I have always dealt with my emotions in my own way. I didn't want comfort from anyone. I just wanted to have a cry and then get back in there, roll up my sleeves and deal with it.

Walking into the burns unit at Concord Hospital a day or so later, I could barely believe what I was seeing. It was one thing seeing stuff during my years with the police force, but this was so far removed from any of that. It had happened to the girl I loved.

Turia was on a hospital bed, wrapped in tin foil to keep her body temperature stable. Underneath all the bandages, I could just make out her eyes. They were closed. She was heavily sedated, in an induced coma. Her arms, legs, torso and head, apart from her eyes, were all wrapped in bandages, like a mummy. There were doctors and nurses everywhere, buzzing about Turia, checking monitors, connecting her to machines. It felt like panic stations. I wanted to be sick; I don't have the words to describe it.

The doctors took Celestine and me into a room and sat us down. They started explaining the burns treatment process and kept emphasising how serious it was, how we had a long way to go before we were out of the woods, but that with perseverance, a bit of luck and a whole lot of hard work, there was still a good chance that Turia could lead a relatively normal life.

The first weeks at Concord were dark times. Days and weeks of not knowing whether she would pull through. Turia's doctor, Professor Haertsch, took me aside one day and told me frankly that it could go either way. He told me I needed to think about her survival as being like a ladder. 'Our aim at the moment is to get her to the top of that ladder,' he said. 'Right now, she's about one-third of the way up. But you have to be prepared that for every step we go up, there could be three steps back down again.'

I went home every night and spent hours researching burns on the internet. I read everything I could get my hands on, to understand the nature of burns recovery. It didn't give me a whole lot of comfort, but at least I felt a little better informed when talking to doctors.

Throughout it all, remarkably enough, her organs were functioning normally. She was never on life support per se. Her body could have given up at any time, but it never did. Her heart was pumping as if she were running a marathon – working hard to repair her damaged body. But, thanks no doubt to her high level of fitness before the fire, all her vital organs kept working as normal.

One day, my parents were visiting the hospital. We'd all spent time next to Turia, quietly talking to her, never knowing if she could hear us (we found out later she couldn't – she had no idea we were there), and chatting to one another in hushed tones. I stepped outside the room for a moment and asked Dad to follow me. I handed him a small box. He knew straightaway what it was.

Before the fire, Turia and I had sometimes talked about getting married. We had even shopped for rings on a recent visit to Perth, but it hadn't gone further. When we were living together in Kununurra, I had seen a ring I liked in a jewellery store that was linked to the diamond mine where Turia had been working. It was a beautiful ring, and I liked the symbolism of it too. After Turia was first admitted to Concord Hospital, I had called the lady in the store and arranged to buy it and have it sent to Sydney.

'If she gets through this, I am going to marry her, Dad,' I said, passing him the ring box. 'I want you to take this and put it in the safe. But don't tell anyone. In case she doesn't pull through.'

Dad took the ring, hugged me and said, 'Good on you, mate.'

It was a father–son secret we kept for four years.

I remember the day in the intensive care unit when Turia regained consciousness. The doctors told me they had decided to pull her out of the medically induced coma, but that I shouldn't expect much – she was going to be very, very drowsy.

It seemed to take forever before she came around. Slowly, I started to see movement and after a while her big eyes rolled open. I sat there anxiously. We made eye contact, but I couldn't be sure if she recognised me. I started talking to her – telling her to wriggle her big toe if she could hear me. It was the only part of her body that wasn't wrapped in bandages.

She seemed to pause, as if the message was getting to her brain through a fog. And then she wiggled her toe. It was the best day I had had in a very long while.

Every day that Turia was in the Concord burns unit I would wake up at 6 am and drive with Celestine from Genji's apartment across Sydney to the hospital. We would give Turia her breakfast at 7 am, then her physios would come and work with her. Her days were busy: she'd have an early physio session followed by bandage changes, and then speech and occupational therapy, as well as visits from doctors.

The days took on a routine as Celestine and I worked as a kind of tag team. She brought the mother-nature, touchy-feely side of things to the table and I was more useful on the practical aspects. Celestine was a bundle of positive energy – lots of colour and movement. In the morning on the drive to hospital, she liked to talk. It was a forty-minute drive and she would pretty much talk the whole way, about anything and everything. I would usually just sit there quietly and nod.

I remember when Turia spoke her first words. It was about two months into her stay at Concord. Up until that point because of her tracheotomy we had only been able to communicate with her via a board – she would point to the letters and I'd spell out the words, and she would nod or shake her head. Later, we had whiteboard on to which she could write messages using a pen taped to her hand. And this is a girl who can talk the leg off a chair. It must have been so frustrating for her.

I had left my job by this stage, because this had become my job. I was all of twenty-six years old at the time. I didn't make a conscious decision to be by her side every step of the way, I just took every day as it came. But I guess I knew I was going to be there for her. That was what I needed to do now: help Turia get better. So I completely shut off the outside world and focused all my energies on her.

There was no moment when I thought I needed a break. The nurses kept urging me to take some time for me, but I never felt like I needed it. I did go away one weekend, to a friend's wedding, but I spent the whole time wanting to be back in the hospital. No one at the wedding really asked me about Turia, and I wasn't in the mood to talk about it. Friends knew that she had been burned and was in hospital, but no one beyond her closest friends knew the extent of what had happened. We had kept it all strictly in the family; not for any particular reason other than closing ranks and concentrating on Turia and her recovery.

While there were never moments when I felt like giving up, going away or just leaving, Turia would occasionally do her best to drive me away. There were times when she was really unreasonable. Times when the frustration and anger would build up to the point where she couldn't hold it in anymore, and she would lash out at whoever was closest at the time. And that was usually me. I'd just let her get it off her chest, then put myself in her shoes and soldier on.

Besides, I knew she didn't mean half of the things she said. There was one time when she had had a particularly bad couple of days and was just losing patience. We all were. Everything about her recovery seemed to be going so slowly. And she'd had enough this one day and lashed out and told me she didn't want to see me anymore. That she wanted me to leave her – to get out of the bloody hospital, find someone who wasn't a cripple and get on with my life. That was hard to hear. But I knew deep down she didn't mean it. I figured it was a test.

I used to think it was weak when people would say to me, 'Why don't you just leave? You have your whole life ahead of you.' I only ever thought in terms of us. The fire wasn't something that had happened just to Turia, it had happened to the both of us. It was a problem for us both to solve together.

I suppose I am a pretty placid person with lots of patience, and I guess that helped. But the bottom line is if I didn't love her as much as I did, I wouldn't have done what I did. If it was some girl I had just met a few weeks before the fire, no way would I have lasted. But she was my girl.

Which is not to say it was all plain sailing. There were plenty of times when it all became too much. I cried one night at Genji's. Again, I was really upset at how slow everything was moving. Everyone else I knew was out having such a good time. We were supposed to be at the peak of our lives, but we were stuck in a hospital. At the end of each day, I might see Turia progress with something – whether it was taking a step or having a bit more food – and I would cling to that as if it was some sort of major development. But then there would be a setback – some reason why she would slide back down the ladder a rung, and it would break my spirit completely. It was hard not to think negative thoughts. I did talk to the doctors, though, and I took real solace in their professional advice. Turia and I are both very practical and logical people. So if the doctors told us to try something, we'd always give it a go, and that kind of positive action helped us a lot.

The first time she walked was a milestone. It was also the hardest thing I think I have ever had to watch. Two nurses and two physios got her out of bed and managed to get her upright. She was howling in pain, with people on either side of her, holding her up, ignoring her pleas to be put back into bed. She was hunched over like an eighty-year-old woman, and begging for it to stop. She looked at me and screamed at me to make them stop. I couldn't watch. It was too traumatic. I had to leave the room. I knew that pain was going to be a necessary part of her recovery, but seeing someone you love in agony, and knowing this was only the beginning – it almost broke me. I went around the corner where she couldn't see me and had a cry.

When it was finally time to leave hospital, the decision to move in with Mum and Dad was a no-brainer. Their house was private, it had space, a big backyard where she could do her exercises. It wasn't really a conversation, I more or less just called Mum and Dad and told them Turia and I were coming home to live with them. They never hesitated for even a second. She was like a daughter to them anyway at that point – they had a really strong bond with her.

So I became her full-time carer. I had learned from the nurses at Concord how to change her dressings, how to help her with her physio exercises, what to do in the case of an emergency. I just figured that if she was going to recover, she was going to do it more quickly if she was out of a hospital environment and being cared for by me, rather than someone who came in once a day and didn't really know her.

Life at home settled into a kind of rhythm. I would change Turia's dressings every morning, a process that would usually take a couple of hours and still caused her a lot of pain. Then there were her appointments for physio and massage and with her exercise physiologist. And after a while, I could start to see the results of our efforts. I could see the healing process take place – even if it was still terribly slow.

She was in the house for a couple of months before she felt strong enough to go out in public. We found the walking trails around the headlands or alongside the beach and they became a part of our daily routine. The soft sand at the beach was good for her to run in, though it wasn't so much a run as it was a slow kind of shuffle at first. Still, some of the doctors had said she'd never get near to running again, so even this was a good start.

I treated every outing as part of her rehab, part of her training. Right back at the start when she was in hospital, she had said she was determined to do the Ironman. So, every time I got her up and moving, I would tell her we were training for the Ironman. Whether it was her climbing three stairs or taking her first swim in the ocean, I would time her and get her into the mindset of competing – if only with herself.

The local community was fantastic. Turia was a South Coast girl – she was one of theirs, and they were determined to protect her and help her get back on her feet. Which is not to say she wasn't self-conscious about going outside. It took a good two months of being back home before she mustered the courage to venture out in public. At this stage she was wearing her compression suit and black compression mask, to help the scars heal smoothly. She stood out like a sore thumb wherever we went, and it made me super-protective. I found myself walking down the street, always on edge, always on the lookout and ready to run interference if I thought there was going to be someone staring or, worse, coming up and saying something stupid. If anyone stared, I would look them straight in the eye and they would look away, embarrassed.

When I look at Turia now, I barely recognise her from the girl in the hospital bed. She's so full of life and love and enthusiasm. She's back to the old Turia. But it's funny. People ask me what I see when I look at Turia now, and the answer is: I see Turia.

I've forgotten how she looked before the fire. I don't look at old photos – because I'm not interested. I look to the future rather than the past. I see the girl I fell in love with and am going to spend the rest of my life with. And I feel proud of the job I did in helping to get her better.

I always knew she would do well in life, but I think out of all of this, Turia has realised how much potential she has inside her. She would always have been successful at anything she had done, but she's been tested in a way that few of us will ever be tested. And she has come out on top. I think she is doing amazing things for the world. And in the end, when all is said and done, she won't be defined by having survived a bushfire, but rather by the difference I know she is going to make in the world.

7

LAMALOU-LES-BAINS

In the south of France, not far from the Spanish border and close to the Mediterranean, is a small village called Lamalou-les-Bains. Set in picturesque hills above the city of Montpellier, it's one of a chain of little villages in that part of the world renowned for its thermal spas.

In Roman times, the villages thrived: playing host to well-to-do members of the sprawling Empire as a place of relaxation and rejuvenation. The mineral-rich waters emanating from nearby mountain springs were thought to have healing qualities, and to this day millions of French people flock to this corner of Languedoc to undergo what the French reverently refer to as *thalasso therapie* – or water therapy.

When Michael and I arrived in Lamalou-les-Bains in May 2013, in place of the Romans was a quaint little town whose tourist numbers were swelled in summer with French and international visitors descending for stints in the many day spas, or to wander the region sampling its world-famous wines.

In the year since I had left hospital and returned home to Ulladulla, I'd been busy on the internet, researching burns and burns victims and the best-practice rehab options around the world. Dad and Genji had taken the lead, tracking down and passing along anything online that bore any relation to my circumstance.

In their research, they stumbled upon the story of Katie Piper. Katie was a vivacious Londoner, a pretty and popular early-twenty-something leading a full life in one of the world's most exciting capitals. Then one day, the boyfriend she had recently broken up with talked one of his friends into throwing sulphuric acid at her face while she was walking to a Tube station. Witnesses described Katie's screams of pain. Others watched as she ran to the nearest public toilet and stuck her head in the bowl, desperate to splash water on her face.

Katie sustained horrific burns to her face and upper body. Her oesophagus was burned through from the acid she ingested. Both her ex-boyfriend and his accomplice were jailed for life.

As part of her recovery, Katie spent time in Lamalou-les-Bains, at a clinic purpose-built for the rehabilitation of burns victims. I bought and read her book. I looked up every photograph online that I could find. It had been eight years since the acid attack and she had not only got back her life, but built a new one – emerging as a national figure of inspiration in her British homeland. I was sold.

The Centre Rééducation et Réadaptation sits right in the middle of Lamalou-les-Bains. Housed in a hotchpotch collection of old and modern buildings, the centre is very much the lifeblood of the town. At any given time, the village's permanent population of some two thousand is bolstered by a couple of hundred visitors, many of them in-patients at the clinic. They come from all over the world – an international parade of tragedy. The severity of our injuries, and the misadventures that led to them, may have varied, but at a basic level we were each of us fundamentally broken and in need of repair.

Researching the place on the internet back home in Ulla-dulla required a whole lot of translation help from Mum. The website was entirely in French, as was the application process. I'm sure it gave Mum a little thrill to be able to put her maternal tongue to such good use.

Boarding the flight with Michael some months later, I practically tingled with nervous anticipation. Driving the 70-odd kilometres in the car from Montpellier to Lamalou-les-Bains, I just felt plain scared. For the first time in almost two years, I was going to be alone. Not alone, exactly, because I would still have nurses and doctors and therapists tending to my every need, but Michael would not be with me each day as only in-patients could stay at the clinic. Up until that point there hadn't been a day of my recovery for which Michael wasn't present. His had been the first face I had seen every morning, the face I instinctively turned to whenever I needed anything during the day, and the last face I saw at night.

I was about to lose my security blanket – to finally have to stand on my own two, still-very-wobbly feet. I knew it would be good for us both, that I had become way too dependent on him, but it scared me. In fact, as we pulled into the car park and carried my suitcase to reception, I wanted to turn and run. Michael dropped me off and was hovering (like a parent does sometimes) in the reception, reluctant to leave me there. Eventually I told him he could go. I needed to make some friends!

*

The therapy at Lamalou-les-Bains is considered world class. After a couple of days there, I could see why. I would never say a bad word about the quality of medical care we have in Australia, it really is second-to-none – I've lost track of the number of times I have counted my blessings that I lived and was caught in a bushfire in a developed country such as Australia – but even so, the French have taken *le traitement des grands brûlés* – the treatment of severe burns – and elevated it to a whole new level.

My days were structured around exercises to redevelop the muscles and dexterity in my hands, to sessions in the spa where I was put under high-pressure water jets, or laid out on a bed where automatic rollers pinched, pressed, massaged and stretched my skin. The basic idea was that constant stimulation of the skin would improve blood flow and promote the creation of new collagen.

I would sit in group occupational therapy sessions where we all had to play board games, to improve our hand coordination. The entire thing took place in French. At first I didn't understand a word that was being said, but eventually, the snippets of French I had gleaned from Mum through the years started to resurface and serve me well in most situations.

Almost everyone in my classes was a burns victim. The only other English-speaking patient was a young Irish guy, but he was so depressed about his condition and so determined to be constantly negative about it, I finally decided it was better to give him a wide berth.

Besides, as bad as his and my burns were, you only had to look around the room to see someone who was in a worse situation. One of the people in our class was an eighteen-year-old guy who had had both his eyes burned. Another had been burned in a gas explosion; another still had fallen asleep in bed while smoking. I can see this now, though at the time I was still too self-absorbed to properly muster a whole lot of empathy. You become incredibly selfish when you are on a recovery trajectory like I was on. It's almost necessary. In order to get better, to get back to point zero and return to anything even resembling a normal life, you have to focus all your energies on yourself. Empathising with others' misfortune would have to wait. My journey was only just beginning.

I stayed in the clinic for six weeks. So full-on was my schedule, I didn't really have time to get lonely. There were always people around, prodding or pulling at me or dragging me off to another therapy session. I would normally get to the end of the day, eat my dinner at the nanna-hour of 5.30 pm and collapse into bed exhausted.

Michael could only visit on weekends, so he spent the weekdays travelling the region by himself. When we were reunited on Saturday mornings we would gleefully jump in the car and explore the nearby towns. Carcassonne, the stunning walled city; Nîmes, the glorious former Roman outpost with its beautifully preserved coliseum; Montpellier, the stylish student town, bustling with activity. The weekends were our escape: we would find a little hotel in a tiny town, seek out a restaurant and gorge ourselves on amazing French wine and food. I got the sense that Michael was a little lonely travelling mid-week on his own – not speaking the language, having no one to share his day with – but he never said as much and was always really positive about the wonderful sights he was seeing. And the time we spent in the Languedoc together more than made up for it.

My maternal grandfather lives in France and he made noises to my mum about wanting to come down to see me, but I just didn't have the energy for it. I hadn't known him at all growing up, he was virtually a stranger to me, and while I appreciated his offer, I wasn't in the frame of mind to have to reconnect with someone I barely knew – much less someone to whom I was supposed to feel some kind of bond. So I put him off. It had become standard practice during my recovery to only do what I absolutely wanted to do at any given time. Catastrophic injuries like mine can allow you to dispense with the social niceties that make up our normal lives. I was lucky, too, that my family were supportive of my choices: they agreed, if I didn't want to see someone, I didn't see them. If I didn't want to go somewhere, I didn't go. Not only did no one ever begrudge me my selfishness, they encouraged it for that first year or two of my recovery.

Ultimately, that meant that there were regrets along the way. For instance, Michael and I missed his brother Aaron's wedding in Vanuatu. It took place not long after I had returned to Ulladulla from hospital, so it was probably a moot point anyway whether I could have sat in a plane for an extended period of time. But Michael could have gone – except leaving my side for more than an hour was out of the question for him in those first six months we were home. We were a two-person, self-sufficient little unit dedicated solely to my recovery. Nothing else registered, nothing else mattered.

While that was fine for the first year or so, we were slowly becoming so anti-social that it threatened to jeopardise my rehabilitation. Exposing myself to other people, learning again to interact with a relative or complete stranger without feeling so self-conscious I wanted to crawl into a hole and hide myself from the world, was crucial.

As important as the re-learning of everything from brushing my teeth to dressing myself unaided was, it began to dawn on me that there were other things I needed to re-learn: things like being a friend again, taking an interest in the lives of your nearest and dearest and not being dismissive when someone says they have had a hard day – as if *they* would know what a bad day was.

There's no doubt being in France at the clinic was important to my physical rehabilitation, but it was vital also to my mental recovery. I learned how to live day-to-day independent of Michael. For so long he had been my protector, always there to run interference, to anticipate problems before they happened and step in to solve them. At the clinic, if I didn't like something, I had to speak up.

But probably the biggest advance I made in France was getting used to being without my mask. Pretty much constantly since I had left hospital over a year previously, I had worn one of the three black compression balaclavas that the burns unit had issued me upon my release. As much as wearing the balaclava served a medical purpose – helping to compress and smooth out the scar tissue as it formed – it was also a convenient mask behind which I could hide. A protective barrier between me and the world.

The mask had become so much a part of my identity, locals in Ulladulla and Mollymook barely flinched when they saw me in the street. The photos on both my driver's licence and passport were of me wearing the mask. Looking back now, I looked like a bank robber.

While it was my security blanket in so many respects, I was also conscious of how much it made me stand out. The townsfolk of my home town might have got used to it, but it was a magnet for stares wherever else I was in public.

In the clinic in Lamalou-les-Bains, a large part of my treatment required me to take off my mask and get used to being in mixed company without it. The prospect filled me with both excitement and fear, so at first I would gingerly remove it and take a brisk walk down the corridor, before scurrying back to the safety and privacy of my room. Not long after, I was able to sit in group therapy sessions without my mask. After all, if ever I was going to feel inconspicuous in a group, these were my people.

Increasingly, the therapies I underwent required me to take off not only my mask, but my entire full-body compression suit. More than feeling naked, I felt utterly conspicuous walking to the treatment rooms in only a flimsy cotton gown. I was sure people would stare at me, but of course they didn't.

Eventually, I was coaxed to take my mask off and go outside. I wasn't sure I could do it at first: it seemed like such a big step. Was I ready to be that exposed in public – even if it was on the grounds of a private clinic in a town where I didn't know a soul in a country where I was unknown?

I took off the mask and stepped outside. For the first time in almost two years, I felt the breeze on my face. The feeling was one of indescribable joy.

8

CONFIDENCE

If I were asked to draw a graph on confidence, with the x axis listing all the facets that comprise confidence, they would include (but not be limited to): believing in yourself, backing yourself, having a high level of self-esteem, being comfortable in your skin and embracing your uniqueness. Physical appearance would only be one of those facets.

To my way of thinking, a beautiful person is a confident person. Confident in who they are and what they are capable of doing. Not cocky, just self-contained. Someone can be physically perfect but have zero confidence. And that's not attractive.

There are a lot of things that make us feel confident. Our appearance is one, but more important is a sense of self-belief, a faith that you can achieve amazing things. It's accepting compliments from people with grace and having the presence of mind to understand that our physical appearance is just an outer shell and that ultimately we are each of us so much more.

And it's not even physical appearance per se – it's how you present yourself to the world. Do you respect yourself? Because, as trite as it sounds, people are much less likely to respect you if they can see you have no respect for yourself.

I'm not saying every day I feel attractive – everyone feels off from time to time. But everyone's appearance changes over the years – from a kid to a teenager to an adult. The difference with me is that my appearance changed really quickly. It's like the frog in a pot theory – if change happens gradually, you don't notice as much, or it's less jarring. With me, it happened in a few seconds.

Talking about beauty – body image – is missing the point. That's not what my story is about, that's not my journey.

Since the fire, I've been really careful with the words that I use to describe myself: I could describe myself as skinny or slender. Disfigured or different. Burns victim or burns survivor. The words we use to describe our experiences influence our experience of the world.

I wore my compression mask for two whole years. In the end, I hated wearing that mask. It was uncomfortable, it drew attention to me whenever I was out, and worst of all it affected my ability to communicate easily with people. No one could read my facial expressions. It's not until you lose the ability to use the cock of an eyebrow to express a reaction that you realise how many cues are passed between humans without the use of words.

But the more time I spent in that mask, the more I came to realise that we all wear masks. It's like I was let in on some great big human secret. I began to wonder: why are we all so afraid to show people who we really are? So even though I've always been pretty true to who I am, I resolved while inside that mask that I wouldn't waste a second of the rest of my life pretending to be anyone other than myself.

Living through an experience like mine forces you to come face to face with yourself. When you are stripped back to nothing – literally and metaphorically – when you have all the time in the world to sit and think and stew and worry and ponder, you do a lot of soul-searching.

You learn very quickly not to sweat the small stuff. You become expert at separating the things that matter in life and the things that don't. You also learn a lot about the values and opinions and behaviours that gave shape to the person you once were, and you work out very quickly how many of them you will incorporate into You 2.0.

We're all used to looking in the mirror and seeing a face we recognise staring back at us. Every line, every imperfection, every wrinkle, dimple and blemish is familiar to us: and it makes up an important part of who we think we are and the sort of image we project to the world each time we step out the door.

Towards the end of my stay in the clinic in France, it was announced that a local beautician would come in for a make-up session with anyone who was interested. I couldn't sign up fast enough. A professional make-up artist! I was convinced she would come in and, with one magic wave of her make-up wand, transform my face.

When she held up the mirror after our session, I started to cry. Of course, I knew that no amount of mascara was going to miraculously change anything, yet I had hoped, while she tended to me, that the expert application of foundation would make my skin look less red.

If there is one saying that I have grown to hate more than others it is 'beauty is on the inside'. I've lost track of the number of times someone has said that to me and I have had to resist the urge to thwack them. I understand the sentiment, and it is only ever meant as a sort of a compliment, but it still grates.

A watershed moment for me came when I was featured on the cover of the *Australian Women's Weekly* magazine. It was July 2014 and it happened almost by accident. I'd been asked by the magazine's editor, Helen McCabe, to be a judge in the *AWW* scholarship program 'Women of the Future'. It meant going through an impressive list of young Australian female entrepreneurs and philanthropists and choosing the ones whose ideas, projects or work within the community were most worthy.

As a judge, I had to take part in a photo shoot along with my fellow judges. By then I'd done enough magazine shoots to have a fair idea of what to expect, but nothing could have prepared me for the scale of the *Women's Weekly* shoot. Multiple hair stylists, make-up artists and fashion consultants buzzed around for a good three or four hours, fixing my hair, painting my face and slipping me in and out of outfits.

When the time came for the photos to be taken, I took part in a group shot – each fellow judge was either a woman of substance or celebrity or both – then I posed for a portrait. The portrait probably took all of five minutes to capture: a simple shot of me standing with my arms folded, looking directly down the lens of the camera, a wind machine on my hair to complete the look.

After the photo shoot I promptly forgot all about it. When I got a phone call about three weeks later from Helen to tell me they had decided to put me on the cover, I was surprised. Flattered and excited, certainly. Yes, it's the biggest-selling magazine in the country; yes, it's a big deal for a so-called 'ordinary' person to be on the cover instead of a celebrity; and, yes, I look different to most of the women who normally grace the cover of magazines. None of that was lost on me. I knew what an honour it was to be on the *Weekly* cover, I understood that it ranked up there in terms of 'media achievements'. But in the grand scheme of things it is just a magazine, and I was about to submit myself to another surgery on my hand. So I thanked Helen, gave her a few words about what an honour it was, and went about my week.

The day the magazine hit newsstands, the world went into some sort of psycho meltdown. Okay, maybe not the entire world. And maybe we are not quite talking a Kardashian-style internet breakage, but things definitely went a bit nuts. My email inbox started filling at a crazy rate, my social-media accounts could barely keep up with demand and messages were left on my mobile from CNN, BBC, *People* magazine and the *New York Times*. I received calls from journalists as far afield as Singapore, India, Indonesia, Mexico, Israel and Canada, all desperate to write the story of what this 'bold move' by an Australian magazine editor meant for 'the industry's perceptions of beauty'.

I did a handful of the interviews and I read a few of the stories. Some of the journalists were so excited by the *Weekly* cover that they wrote things like 'what we consider to be beautiful may never be the same again'. And while I couldn't imagine one magazine cover single-handedly undoing centuries upon centuries of human conditioning about beauty, I could still see it for the significant gesture it was.

Then again, to be honest, the whole thing mystified me. As I told one interviewer from the BBC, 'I just don't understand what all the fuss is about.' And as I said to Helen McCabe the next time I saw her, 'Am I the only one who feels like maybe people are reading too much into it?' She just laughed.

During one radio interview with a BBC presenter, who had called me from London and was broadcasting live to his millions of listeners, I took issue with his line of questioning. 'Turia,' he said. 'We can't ignore the fact that your face is disfigured. Can we say that this is a major step forward for magazines and the notions of beauty that they peddle?'

I arced up immediately, taking issue with the use of the word 'disfigured'. It's a word that has such negative connotations. Would you ever call a Picasso painting disfigured?

I prefer to think of my face as being different, that's all.

As I told the journalist who had interviewed me for the original *Women's Weekly* article, putting me on the cover was 'humbling' and rather than sending the message that 'beauty is on the inside', it sent the message 'that confidence equals beauty. There are a lot of women out there who are so beautiful but don't have the confidence, and at the end of the day, that's what gets you over the line.'

That issue of the *Weekly* was its second-bestselling of the year, outselling even the souvenir royal edition that recorded the visit to Australia a couple of months earlier by Prince William, the Duchess of Cambridge and baby Prince George.

Before the fire, my sense of who I was and what I had to offer the world was never defined by my looks. For me, it had always been about how far I could run, how good I was at surfing, how much I could do in any given day. It was measured by the relationships I had with friends and family, the enrichment I got from those around me, my ability despite myriad distractions in an increasingly fast-paced and shallow world to prioritise the things that matter: family, friends, kindness and health.

Did I take pride in my appearance? Absolutely. I got my hair cut and wore make-up and dressed fashionably as much as the next person. Just as I still do to this day. I don't think there is anything wrong with wanting to present the best version of yourself. If you want to dye your hair, pierce or tattoo yourself to oblivion or get plastic surgery – all power to you. It's everyone's right to do what they want with their body. And if it makes you feel better or more confident, knock yourself out.

The fact of the matter is that before my accident, I really liked how I looked. And since my accident, I have grown to really like how I look. At first it was confronting to see how much my face had changed. All those contours that I knew so well were no longer there. The eyebrows, the nose, the lips, the chin. All of it has changed and it's taken some getting used to, but I genuinely do look in the mirror and like what I see.

I constantly have people come up to me and ask how it is that I am able to be so confident. As I've said, confidence comes from within – it's got nothing to do with your shell. How do you talk to yourself? What words do you use to describe yourself (do they have positive connotations, or negative connotations)? Are you grateful for your life? Do you surround yourself with positive people? Are you aware of your strengths, and of your value? Do you look after your body in terms of eating well and exercising? All of this stuff adds up to make you a more confident person.

The truth is there are no shortcuts. Obviously, if we could take a pill and miraculously all our problems would go away, we'd all want it. But unfortunately, life doesn't work like that. Nothing worth having is going to be easy. It takes work. You want results, you have to be willing to put in the work.

It has taken me four years of almost constant surgeries to get to how I look now. People cannot understand why, if I have been through so much and undergone so many procedures, I continue to go under the knife. And the answer is: because I am determined to constantly improve myself. If there's a new technology that might give me even a tiny bit more movement in my fingers, I will try it. Just as if there's an operation that will slowly rebuild my nose or otherwise improve my face, I will do it. It's all about being the best version of myself possible. That said, there's a balancing act between enjoying my life and doing cool things, and progressing with my operations. I try to have four a year – enough to see progress, but not so many that I'm constantly in hospital and recovering.

If I could have anything back from my pre-fire life, it would not be my face. It would be my fingers. Until you lose the use of them, you don't realise how vital your hands are to your everyday life. It's got easier as the years have gone by. People are generally great, and now if they ask me if I 'need a hand', I'll reply, 'Actually, two would be great.'

Doing up buttons on my jeans, putting dishes away, push-ups, baiting a fishing line, playing guitar or typing: these are things I cannot do as easily as I used to.

At the airport, there's a series of things you need to do: get your laptop out of your bag. Lift your suitcase onto the conveyor. Then on the plane, put your suitcase in the overhead compartment. Sometimes I do need help. So I normalise it. Most blokes would help a girl get her suitcase from the overhead compartment if she needed it. I've helped people get their bags down from the overhead compartment (one of the advantages of being relatively tall). I think that's beautiful, strangers helping each other.

People often ask, 'So what do you want me to do in that situation? Do you want me to ignore you fumbling with your zippers? Or do you want me to offer to help?' What I want is to be treated like you would treat anyone. If you see a woman struggling with her suitcase, and you would typically offer to help, then offer to help me.

I have a contraption at home that helps me open jars one-handed. I wedge it between my thigh and a countertop, place the jar in the contraption and twist it. Before I got it, it was not uncommon for Michael to return home to find the remnants of some foodstuff or another smashed against the kitchen wall – hurled by me in a fit of frustration.

Do I notice people staring at me when I walk down the street? The truth is, I notice it less and less. And I guess that's because I look for it less and less. I used to be so self-conscious, acutely aware of the reaction of everyone I passed or came in contact with. Now, as I have got more and more used to Turia 2.0, I'm back to how I used to be: comfortable enough in my skin to not think much about the image I project to the rest of the world.

If I have learned anything, it's that whatever you look for in the world, you'll find. If you go through every day looking for the worst in people, you'll find it. If, on the other hand, you assume the best of everyone and believe people are essentially well-meaning and good-intentioned, then that will be your experience. If I go out every day looking for people staring at me: guaranteed I will find them.

The way I see it, we all of us have a self-esteem bank. Being kind to yourself, being able to look at yourself in the mirror and give yourself a compliment, accepting other people's compliments graciously – all of these things put a 'deposit' in your emotional bank account. The same goes for positive interactions with people – each one makes you feel good about yourself, and leaves a net deposit in your account. Negative interactions are withdrawals from your account. Someone saying to you: do you really need that second piece of cake? People staring at you enough to make you self-conscious. That could be another withdrawal.

There will always be people who – either inadvertently or on purpose – will make a withdrawal from your self-esteem account when you deal with them. The important thing is to be aware of it, and to make sure you make enough deposits to create a cushion so it doesn't bother you.

So, does beauty matter to me? Only as much as it matters to the next person. I understand that well-meaning people want me to be the poster-girl for beauty being 'on the inside', but that's not what I am about. Body image, beauty myth: it's not my thing. I am about the power of the mind. If anything, I want to be a shining example that anyone can do anything if they have the mental fortitude.

I've thought about this a lot, and at the end of the day, it's like this: I honestly don't waste time or energy thinking about how I look. Do I look different to how I looked before? Yes. But then we all change over time. The way I see it, now I am unique. And that's the most beautiful thing of all.

9

MUM

If you were to meet my mum, the first thing you would notice is how warm and soft she is. Big brown eyes; wide, open smile. She has one of those faces that tells you immediately you have met one of the world's gentle people. And it's a pretty good indicator of how she really is. Tahitian to her core, Mum is a living, breathing embodiment of her Polynesian heritage. It's not for nothing, after all, that after visiting Tonga, Captain Cook dubbed the place the 'friendly islands'.

But as cuddly as she seems on the outside, Mum is made of as stern stuff as any woman I know. You can't watch your daughter go through what I have been through and not have an inner reserve of steel.

Read any one of my mum's books and you'll see they're about the inner strength of women. Her heroines might get a raw deal from the men in their life; they might – by an accident of birth – find themselves dealing with a set of social and cultural circumstances that leave them at a distinct disadvantage;

but in the end, they are lifted to greatness by the sisterhood. Even if only in their own little world.

I love my mum. Which is not to say we always get along. I am more like my dad than my mum in many ways. She's all creative and arty and right-brain; I'm all scientific and spreadsheets and left-brain. In many respects, you couldn't meet two more different people. And that means we don't always see eye to eye. We most certainly had some almighty clashes when I was growing up. (Then again, find me a daughter who doesn't have almighty clashes with her mother on occasion.) Even now, after everything we have been through together, we still have our fallings-out. She can still annoy me more than anyone else in the world and I can still annoy her. Knowing where each other's buttons are and pressing them as often as we can is a mother–daughter thing. But I can honestly say, for all that we can get on each other's nerves, we are incredibly close. There's not a woman in the world I admire more than my mum. She had two kids when she was still a teenager. She moved to another country where she didn't know a soul. She raised me and my three brothers while holding down a job by day and writing best-selling books by night. And then, when one of her children needed her most, she dropped everything and dedicated herself to my recovery.

Growing up, I used to listen to Mum singing Tahitian songs, 'summoning the ancestors' as she would call it, and I would dismiss it as islander myth, just another example of her crazy eccentricities. But now I look at her in a different light. Now I see that she comes from a long line of proud warrior women. Women whose strength, patience and love have borne and nurtured generation after generation.

If there is a greater healing power in the world than a mother's love, then I don't know what it might be.

This, in her own words, is my mother's story ...

Celestine

It's a strange thing when you're a mum and your baby is in pain and there's nothing you can do to alleviate it. If you could swap places, you would do it in a heartbeat. If you could take their place in that hospital bed and experience all the pain for them – absorb it all so that they didn't have to – you would do it without thinking twice. But you can't. So you feel helpless.

Turia was in such a bad way at the start, I used to go out of my mind at not being able to do anything to help her. And because I'm her mum, and because I had to do something, I started to cook. Food is love, I firmly believe that. If you want to show someone you love them, you cook for them.

I would prep everything the night before, then wake up every morning at 5.30, sneak into Genji's kitchen and start cooking. I had been to St Vinnie's and picked up a superfoods cookbook. One of the recipes was for a juice with twenty separate fruits and vegetables in it. It used to be my morning ritual. I would make the juice, being sure not to leave out a single fruit or vegetable, then I would make pancakes – because Turia loved pancakes – then I would make something like a stir-fry, packing it with fresh vegetables and herbs because taste is so important. When you are in hospital and your days are stretched out before you like one great stretch of beige, you need little explosions of taste and colour to get you through.

Each morning, I would pack my little esky and drive with Michael over to the hospital. We would cross the Gladesville Bridge and we could glimpse the hospital in the distance.

I would call out, 'I'm coming, darling!' God only knows what the hospital made of this Tahitian woman with an esky bustling into the hospital each day. By the end of Turia's stay there, Michael and I were regular fixtures.

When she first told me she was running an ultramarathon in the Kimberley, of course I was worried – just as any mother would be. I never doubted her ability to run the race, but I was scared something could happen, like a branch falling on her head as she ran through the bush. It never occurred to me might be caught in a bushfire.

The afternoon of the fire, I was at home in Ulladulla. Turia had graduated from uni two weeks previously and I had asked my husband, John, to collect her degrees from Ulladulla Picture Framing. I felt a surge of maternal pride as he walked back in the door with them. My baby girl – my clever, accomplished baby girl. All I could think was that the world was at her feet.

Coming in from the backyard later that afternoon, I remember being struck by how the light from the afternoon sun was filtering through the door and catching Turia's graduation portrait. Turia laughs at me when I tell her this story now. Just another one of Mum's crazy islander superstitions. Mum's writer brain working overtime. But it has always stuck in my mind.

I was working late that night and turned in to go to bed around midnight. Not long after, the phone rang. I used to hate it when the phone rang after midnight. Nothing good is ever on the other end of a phone line after midnight.

It was Genji. He was calling to say there had been an accident; that Turia had been caught in a bushfire and was hurt. He didn't know anything other than she was being flown to Darwin.

My whole body was trembling as I hung up the phone. I felt like a cigarette, but my hands were shaking too much to roll it.

It was the cruellest of news: I knew my baby was hurt, but I didn't know how badly. I knew she had been in a fire, but I didn't know the extent of her injuries. I knew I had to be by her side – I knew that more certainly than I had known anything in my life – but it was going to take me hours and hours before I would be. And in the meantime – in the horrible meantime – I would be consumed with the terror of half-knowledge. In the absence of any real information, my imagination would be left to entertain only the worst-case scenarios. It was a kind of hell.

I went to the shower as John packed me a bag. I stood for a moment under the water and cried silently.

The flight to Darwin was excruciating. I couldn't think straight, I couldn't get comfortable. Surely, I told myself over and over, if she was well enough to walk to the helicopter, she couldn't have been injured too badly. I clung to that snippet of information more out of hope than anything else.

When we finally landed, we rushed to the hospital. Eventually, a doctor came out to speak to us. She wasted no time getting straight to the point. 'I'm afraid she may not live. I'm afraid she might not survive.'

It was too much. Before I even knew what I was doing, I began wailing. The anticipation, the travel, the exhaustion had all built to this point. It was the guttural cry of a mother mortally wounded. How could this be? How could this be happening?

The doctor asked if I wanted to go in to see Turia. But I couldn't. If she was going to die – if my only daughter and baby girl was about to die – I didn't want that to be the last memory I had of her.

Arrangements were being made to airlift her to Sydney. To have a chance of surviving, she needed to be transferred as soon as possible to a hospital with a specialist burns unit. So for us it was back to the airport and back on another plane.

The first time I laid eyes on Turia after the fire was in the burns unit at Concord Hospital. It seems funny now to think the place seemed like a labyrinth to me at the time. I could draw you a map of the burns unit now, I know it so well. Every corridor, every door, every nurse station, every corner around which I would sometimes scamper mid-visit to have a quiet cry.

Walking into Turia's room there for the first time was one of the hardest things I have ever had to do. Every cell in my body was aching to be somewhere else. Anywhere but here, about to be confronted with the unimaginable reality. I stood beside her bed, trying to detect some sense of Turia – trying to discern how or if under all those bandages there was any essence of my second-born – with tears rolling down my face.

'She's not supposed to be here,' I kept repeating over and over. 'She's just graduated, her life is supposed to just be beginning.'

All I could make out of my daughter beneath the tubes and dressings was her teeth. Her eyes were covered, her head was swathed in bandages, her arms, legs and torso were tightly wrapped. The only indication she was alive was the steady beep of the heart monitor.

'She might be able to hear you,' one of the doctors said in a hushed tone, breaking the silence.

Beside me was Turia's dad, whom I hadn't seen for months. He looked in shock. Before I knew what I was doing, I began to sing.

E te varua maitai e aroha ma. 'Dear Lord, have pity on us.'

I had no words, so I resorted to music – the words, the melody, they all just came tumbling out, channelling the islands, calling on the gods.

So began a pattern. Each day I would go to see her and each day I would sit by her bedside and sing. I never knew if she could hear me, but at some level, I reasoned, the sounds must be registering and – wherever it was that she was, in whatever realm she was hovering – reaching her and giving her some comfort.

Then one day when I showed up at the hospital with Genji, they had taken off some of the bandages and her eyes were visible. Genji had been in before me and came out warning me not to go in there and cry.

'I'm not a coconut head, Genji,' I told him. 'I'm a warrior woman.'

It did shock me to see parts of her unbandaged for the first time. But there were her eyes – closed peacefully for the moment. It seemed like such a good sign.

Again I started singing, and as I sang Turia's hand started waving. My heart leapt. It was the smallest thing but just the greatest feeling. Then she opened her eyes and I saw those gorgeous green eyes that I knew so well.

'You are not alone, my darling. We are here for you!' I said, staring hopefully into her eyes. 'It's okay, darling. Mum is here.'

From that moment, I treated her recovery as a project. There were other burns patients in the hospital, and their loved ones seemed not to know what else to do but sit around and cry. I was determined not to be like that. If Turia was going to get better, she needed her team around her to be strong and decisive. So Michael and I became a two-person team, and Turia became our project.

Before Turia was able to communicate, nurses would come in and speak to her like she was a baby. This was my clever daughter with a double degree. I called John and had him send up Turia's university degrees, and promptly had them hung up on the wall beside her bed. My daughter was a mining engineer – an accomplished, educated young woman.

Then, after a few days of listening to Michael and her father and Genji repeat the same encouraging platitudes to Turia – 'You can do this!' 'We're going to beat this together!' – I thought, *Enough!* She's a smart girl. She will be bored out of her brain hearing the same things over and over and over, no matter how well-meaning they might be. So I instructed everyone to read to her. Michael was told to read her poetry; her father was told to read from newspapers or scientific magazines, which I knew would pique our girl's interest; and I pulled together a collection of her favourite novels and spent my days slowly reading them out loud to my immobile daughter.

As her recovery progressed and she was able to move a little more, I asked the doctors whether it was mandatory for her to wear the nondescript hospital gown. This wasn't my daughter. This outfit gave nothing away about her personality or interests. So, with the doctor's blessing, I had Michael bring in a whole wardrobe of Turia's clothes. Then we made getting dressed part of her daily ritual. Wake up, eat breakfast, get out of bed, choose an outfit. I had brought in the singlets she liked to wear when she exercised, all emblazoned with the sorts of motivational messages that used to be her mantra: 'Nothing

Worth Having Comes Easy', 'Laugh, Dream, Believe' and 'Be Strong, Be Brave'.

It was a small thing, but it made a big difference. After she was moved from intensive care, I brought in Tahitian sarongs from home and hung them about her ward, to add a splash of colour to her surroundings and provide her with a little more privacy between the nurses' station and her bed.

The cleaners, who monitored her progress on a day-to-day basis at least as carefully as any nurse or doctor, used to smile and laugh at the funny lady with her esky and eccentric ways. One of them, Ron, who took a special interest in Turia, gave me a wink, as if to say he understood. It was a mother's way of trying to make sense of the unfathomable. It was my own possibly silly way of trying to restore some kind of order to a world that had been turned upside down.

By now I had taught myself massage – a technique called effleurage – so I went in most days and sat for an hour massaging Turia's head.

'Do you like that, darling?' I would ask. She would nod in reply.

Some days, right back at the beginning, a simple nod would have me walking on cloud nine. She could communicate! She could hear and understand and respond. When you are told that your child is going to die, the smallest achievements are the biggest things.

When they first took her out of intensive care, all she could do was scream. If they managed to get her upright in bed, she would sit there propped, unable to move, and cry quietly like a voiceless animal. As she became more mobile, humour was our ally. If we didn't have a day with at least one outbreak of giggles, it was a day wasted, to my mind. There was a balcony at the end of the corridor. We used to go out there and jam the door open with a towel. Turia would stand on the balcony and pretend to be a queen speaking to her subjects. It was silly, but it never failed to raise a smile.

With each day that passed, she became better and better. As if the spirit of the old Turia was reinhabiting this strange body she now found herself in.

I would massage creams and oils into the exposed parts of her burned skin. Touch is such an important sense. And when you are in bed for months on end, and when finally after weeks of recovery, your skin can be touched without it hurting, you crave human touch.

Towards the end of her hospital stay, when she was having a good day, I would catch her looking at Michael as he sat by her bedside reading.

'Take your shirt off,' I heard her say to him one day. And he blushed, and threw her a look and replied, 'Darl, not here.' But I pulled the curtains across and stood at the door and left them together for a moment's privacy. Massage, kiss, caress, touch: they were all such an important part of her recovery.

As indeed was Michael. There's no way Turia would have recovered as quickly as she did if it wasn't for Michael's love and unwavering support. He is such a beautiful human being and I marvel at how blessed we are to have him in our lives.

His life had been cruisey up to this point. It was surfing and diving and taking his boat out for a fish. Then without warning his world was turned on its head. And he stepped up. Not for a moment did he hesitate or falter. To sit and watch it happen, it was almost as if he had been preparing for this all his adult life.

Nothing would faze him. Nothing would make him angry or upset. Turia would rail against the unfairness of it all. She would lash out at him in her lowest moments, take out all her pain and frustration on him. And no matter how much she threw at him, he would just smile and nod and wait for it to pass.

I remember back in the early days of their courtship, back when they first got together. He was so happy. He had been wanting to be with Turia for such a long time. And he waited patiently as she flitted off to uni and travelled the world, knowing that she would be back.

He was Genji's friend before he and Turia got together. I've known him since he was fifteen. He used to drop by my place and give me seafood he had caught or abalone he had plucked from the bottom of the sea. He always made out he was dropping by to see Genji, but I always knew he had an ulterior motive. My mother used to say, 'Turia should marry that one. She will never go hungry.'

And though we knew each other, we didn't know each other especially well before Turia's accident. He's a man of few words, after all. But living together at Genji's apartment, and spending every day together in the hospital, I came to understand him better. The three of us were like a triangle of healing, with Turia at the point. And it worked because we were all striving towards the same outcome. I would come up with ideas to improve her day or lift her spirits – 'Michael, we need to brighten up this ward. Michael, I think toe rings would look good on her feet' – and he would go out and make them happen. Nothing was ever too much trouble. Turia's journey would have been so different if it had been any other boyfriend. Michael has got what I call the humble gene. He doesn't need to be the loudest or most important person in the room. Of course, we had our moments. I can be a bit over-bearing and emotional at times, but when I got too excited, Michael would gently take me by the arm, calm me down.

It was as if he could read Turia. When she couldn't communicate, he would communicate for her. Yes, she was my daughter, but he had such a calming influence on everyone, including Turia, that I knew it was always better to defer to him.

He was also strong. Right back at the start, before even Turia had properly regained consciousness, doctors were making life-and-death decisions that were going to have an enormous impact on the rest of her life. Within the first weeks of Turia arriving at Concord Hospital, we were faced with the dilemma of what to do about her fingers. They had been so badly burned in the fire, infection had taken hold so compre-hensively, that there was a danger without amputation that the infection could spread. Michael and I were presented with the heartbreaking dilemma of making the call on whether or not to amputate.

Can you imagine a mother having to make that decision? I wasn't strong enough to do it, so I deferred to Michael. He agonised over it, carrying the responsibility like a millstone. He knew Turia – his Turia – was such an active, independent girl. Yet he made the call. Because at the end of the day, her living was more important than anything else. Disability they would deal with down the track. The important thing at that point was to keep her alive.

They monitored the progress of the infection for about a week, and every day they put off amputation there was hope.

But finally they decided they had no choice. I was very sad that day – probably the lowest I had been. The nurse gave me a hug.

'Go home and have some whisky,' she said as she pulled me into her. I started crying.

I went home that night with Genji, and he insisted we go to the pub – not to drown our sorrows, as he put it, but rather to celebrate the beginning of Turia's recovery.

'This is the end of the paring back,' he said. 'From this point on, everything they do is to rebuild our Turia – everything that happens from here is to make her better and give her back to us.'

It was a Friday night. I saw all these young people Turia's age, having fun, out socialising with their friends. I wanted to get into the spirit of it, but it was too hard.

When Turia came to after the operation and learned her fingers had been amputated, she was devastated. She howled. For a mother to see her child in that much pain is really the worst experience. You want to comfort them, you want to take away the hurt, but there is nothing you can do. Nothing at all. It was just so frustrating. Your one job as a mother is to protect your children, to keep them out of harm's way. But I couldn't break down in front of Turia. I felt like I needed to be strong for her. And so I would hold back the tears until I got home at night. I also had a special bench at the hospital, tucked away out of sight. It was my bench. And when it was all too much, I would sometimes go there and sob quietly to myself. And in the first weeks, every day was touch and go. There wasn't a morning we didn't come into the hospital terrified at what we would find, scared to turn the corner of Turia's ward and discover she'd deteriorated through the night. Every slight improvement in her condition was jumped on and clung to, and every setback sent a dagger to our hearts.

Did I ever think Michael would leave, just decide one morning that it was all too hard and he didn't need this in his life? You know, strangely, I didn't. So complete was his dedication to her recovery, it never occurred to me that here was a boy who had his whole life in front of him, who was eligible enough to wander out the hospital door and find a new girlfriend, and get on with living a normal life.

Michael and I talked a lot in those months. We were pretty much inseparable for the whole time. And I saw a boy turning into a man before my very eyes. Being the crafty old islander woman I am, I managed to sow a few seeds into that young mind, but honestly – and this is largely due to the excellent job his parents had done – there wasn't much refining needed. He was that rarest of creatures: a young Australian man with a kind heart, a gentle nature, a strong backbone and a really strong sense of right and wrong.

He taught me the power of silence, the importance sometimes of being still. I taught him that it is okay to express your feelings, that it is important to be open. We had such different energies, and in many respects, it was the fact that we were so different that made us work so well as a team. I'm sure the hospital staff used to look at us and laugh. We really were the odd couple. But he couldn't have done what I did, and I wouldn't have been able to do what he did. I couldn't brush her teeth, for example, because I was too indelicate. He was better than me at changing the sheets on the bed, and more delicate when it came to the removal of scar tissue. Every night he would sit with Turia and coax her into doing the leg exercises on the machine that she was required to do as part of her rehab. But he would never have known how to make a soup with twenty-seven ingredients.

'She's your little baby,' he would say to me as I tended to her. And he was right. She was.

Not that Turia always took well to being overprotected. She would swing from wanting me to baby her, to wanting me to treat her like an adult. It was a fine line. You lose so much in the way of dignity and independence in a situation like that. For example, she wasn't able to wipe her own bottom, so I had to do it for her. She was being infantalised, and of course I didn't mind resuming the role of mother-and-helpless-baby, and if she was feeling weak or small or tired, she would let me mother her. Even if along the way I would remind her 'You are a very intelligent person, Turia, you will have to work this out yourself, find a way.'

Then there would be the days when she would push back and lash out. 'I'm not a baby!' she would yell at me. Only half-jokingly, she came to refer to me as 'the pest'.

It really was like having a baby, though. There were so many milestones we had to build up with her: the first time she walked, the first time she climbed a flight of stairs, the first time we left the burns unit, the first time she saw her reflection. All of these firsts were hard-fought. And while Turia's strength throughout all of them was phenomenal, it wasn't without a lot of coaxing – from me, from Michael and from the amazing medical professionals who tended to her each day.

I remember the first time she walked. It was agonising to watch. Michael had borne witness to her taking her first steps the day before and had come home in a state. It had deeply affected him. The following day, I went in to cheer her along and it almost broke my heart. Here was this daughter of mine, who had run marathons and won school medals and graduated with a double degree, and she looked like an old woman. Five or six people were around her, helping her stand, willing her to take a single step, and she could barely do it. Her bottom lip had fallen down – I could hardly watch. Michael had turned away, overcome. So I mustered all the enthusiasm I could and from nowhere I pulled out a Martin Luther King quote. 'Take the first step,' I piped up. 'You don't need to see the whole staircase, just take the first step.'

Turia shot me a look of contempt, and out of the corner of her mouth muttered, 'Shut up, Mum.'

The next day she walked up three steps.

Leaving the burns unit for the first time was a big milestone too. The hospital had fashioned her a compression mask, and Turia was excited about getting the mask and leaving the unit. For months she had been in the same small corner of the hospital. Out her window she could glimpse the sea. I used to see her looking longingly towards it.

But for some reason on the day the mask was supposed to come, it didn't. Or maybe it did come and it didn't fit or didn't work; I don't remember exactly. But I do remember that it set Turia off. She had built herself up to this moment – finally leaving. Her walking had progressed to the point where she could almost do it unassisted. I was so proud of her. But she has this meltdown and started crying.

'Darling,' I told her. 'It doesn't matter.'

'It does matter, Mum!' she shot back at me. And Michael said, 'Okay, you want to go out? Let's go out. But be prepared. Because you look different and people are going to stare.'

So, we got out of the unit and we walked into the general area of the hospital. And this stupid woman bowled up and asked, as if Turia wasn't even there, 'What happened to the boy?'

But we forged on, because Turia wanted to be out. And then another man came up. He had no teeth, he looked rough. And he came up to us and said something like, 'Oh no – she's been burned.' To which Turia, quick as a flash, replied, 'At least I have my teeth.'

We came back laughing. As I said, it was so important to find at least one moment to laugh every day.

It took a long while before Turia saw her own reflection. Understandably, there are no mirrors in the burns unit. There are posters and photos and pamphlets scattered around the place, with messages of hope and motivation and contact numbers for support groups; some of them were illustrated with photos of burns victims, so Turia had an idea of how her face might look. But she hadn't seen her reflection for a couple of months, and I think in her mind's eye she was still presenting to the world the same face she wore before the fire. I worried about this. Turia isn't stupid; she knew her face had been burned. She could tell by the way people looked at her that the burns were significant. But until she saw the extent of the damage with her own eyes, she couldn't possibly imagine it, much less process it.

I think the first time she glimpsed her reflection was in the blank, black screen of an iPad. It was purely by accident and she wasn't prepared for it. But with each shock, she had to summon the will to regather, to recompose herself and forge on. You hear people talk a lot about the strength and resilience of the human spirit, but to see it manifested daily in my daughter was something I will never forget. It was humbling.

I went with her recently to hear her give one of her speeches, and I almost exploded with pride. We were in Mount Isa, and it could have been a tough crowd, but they hung off her every word. I watched as she held this entire auditorium in the palm of her hand, raising them up with her words, and it reminded me of when we were first approached by *60 Minutes*. Turia and Michael debated the merits of doing that sort of publicity, inviting that sort of attention and scrutiny, because it's a lot to take on. But I knew that she could do some good, that we could turn this suffering into empowerment – to make sense of it somehow. If she had gone into hiding after the fire and become a hermit and refused to even leave the house, it would have killed me.

If I were to stand in front of a crowd and say, 'You can do anything you put your mind to' and 'Life is a gift' it would have no impact. But when she says it, it sets the room alight.

And she's been able to use the public profile as a tool, so that when people see her in the street, they know her story, and they are inspired by her without even having met her. 'I know you,' they say. 'And I think you are amazing.' And each time it happens, it helps her to heal just that little bit more.

The week before the fire it was my birthday, and I had asked the kids to pick up a paintbrush and paint a canvas that I would hang on my wall. The boys painted Tahitian motifs and designs, dolphins and whale symbols and frangipanis – all the stuff they know I love. Michael contributed by painting a fish – because I call him *moana tane* – which means 'ocean man'. And, perhaps just to humour or tease me, Turia and Michael had been talking in the car on the way to her graduation weeks before about having a baby and calling it Moana. I remember being excited and enthusing about what a beautiful name it was. So Turia's contribution to the painting was to paint the name 'Moana' in a corner of the canvas.

I was born into the Catholic faith, but in Polynesian culture the ancestors are also hugely important. I draw strength from them every day. In Tahitian, we call it the *mana* or 'energy' – it comes from all different places. So there were nights I would come home from the hospital and stand in the shower crying, calling out to the ancestors, 'Moana must be born! Moana must be born!'

And maybe he will be. Maybe he will.

10

DAD

You know how they say people take after one or the other of their parents? As I've said, on paper I definitely take after my dad.

Though we had a pretty strict upbringing with Dad, we were never in any doubt about how much he loved us. And I think since the fire, he has become a lot softer with me. I'm kind of annoyed by that – after all, he raised me to be tough, to always strive for a higher standard, to never be satisfied with 'good enough'. I've called him out on it a few times, and he reckons it's not because of my accident but because he's getting too old to fight.

I'm blessed to have such loving and supportive parents. And I'm acutely conscious of all the sacrifices that both of them have made for me and my brothers. Dad and I don't talk about the fire and its aftermath, but I know, like Mum, he was profoundly affected by it. This is his story.

Michael Pitt

As a parent, one of the great things you can hope for in your children is that they have an enthusiasm for life. You want them to have a bit of spunk, a bit of zest. And from the day she was born, Turia had those in spades.

I remember holding her as a newborn. She was so beautiful, but even then you could sense that she was bursting to get on with life. And it didn't take long for her headstrong, stubborn side to come out. Even as a three-year-old, she and I had some whopper arguments. Celestine was working at a bank in Maroubra, Genji was at kindy and I was working from home. So that meant it was just the two of us through the day. I was never in any doubt about what Turia wanted at any given moment of the day. It was pretty clear from a young age that she was both smart and very, very determined.

I mean, she did a double degree at uni because it wasn't enough to do just one. Plus she figured she might as well get two knocked over at the same time. That's Turia: she is driven.

As sister and brother, Turia and Genji were always competing with one another. They still are to this day. When they see each other, they'll always compare abs and biceps. She was keen on surfing as a young kid and a really good runner. As daughters go, I knew I was really lucky to have one as accomplished as Turia.

The day of her accident? I remember it like it was yesterday. It's not an experience I would want any parent to have to go through.

I had just returned home from a holiday sailing in Greece. I was staying in Sydney and had switched my phone off overnight. When I turned it on in the morning there were loads of voicemail notifications, and a text from Genji. 'Turia has been in a terrible accident,' it read. 'Burns to 60 per cent of her body. May not live. Call me.'

I remember sitting there looking at those words. And even as I read them – 'May not live' – I remember thinking it must be some kind of sick joke. I called Genji straightaway and said, 'Is this for real?'

I went to the airport and jumped straight on a plane for Darwin.

That flight was the longest and most painful few hours of my life. I just sat there staring out the window, thinking about Turia: playing over and over in my mind all of the happy memories of her growing up; what she looked like, what she smelled like, what she was like running around as a little kid. It was as though I was willing her back to the land of the living by dredging up and cementing in my memory all the happy, significant moments in Turia's life. Because at that point, her life was on a knife edge. So I sat on that plane for what seemed like an eternity wondering if I was going to see my daughter again or if I was going to bring her home in a box.

By the time the plane landed, I was numb. All I wanted to do was speak to the doctors and see whether my little girl was going to live.

I am not one of those get-down-on-my-knees-and-pray type of people. I am an atheist. I didn't see this as God's work or any kind of fate. I just knew it was a random accident: just the chaotic nature of the universe. I didn't feel any anger at all.

Genji and Gary Hoskin met me at the airport and the three of us drove straight to the hospital. Having someone like Gary there in a situation like that was a lifeline – he is such a calm, considered person. He told me later that he was only barely keeping his shit together, but in the moment he was like a rock.

The head surgeon in Darwin was remarkable. She told it to us straight: she'd had to pretty much slice Turia from head to toe. I think they call it an escharotomy – where they cut through your skin to relieve the swelling. I went into the intensive care unit and saw my little girl lying there. She was so still. She was wrapped completely in bandages with only her face exposed. It was so swollen I barely recognised her. All I could think to do was talk to her. She was unconscious, but I was sure she could hear me (turns out I was wrong on that).

'Darling, it's Dad. I am here. Mum is here, Michael is here, Genji and Gary are here. We all love you and are here for you.' I think that became my mantra, repeated to her over and over again for the next few days.

The doctors operated on her there and then, and then the CareFlight people came to pick her up to transfer her to Sydney. They were so professional. Just awesome. Your kid is potentially dying before your eyes and you're standing there feeling helpless and these guys fly in like supermen. Just incredible.

None of us were able to fly with Turia, so we all jumped on whatever flights we could get and followed her down to Sydney. At that point it was all about life and death. There was no discussion about how the recovery was going to go or the scope of what would be in front of her physically and mentally. It was just a question about whether she would live.

At Concord Hospital, over the next few days, her heart stopped a couple of times and she had to be reanimated. Can you imagine that? Your daughter dying on the hospital bed in front of you on three or four occasions and them having to drag her back to life? The doctors become demi-gods. You watch them work and listen to them as they calmly explain everything they are doing, everything they are going to do – and you just come away with the most enormous respect for them. She was being looked after by the two Peters – Peter Haertsch and Peter Maitz. Both of them were so professional. The level of intelligence, skill and education these guys have is just mind-boggling. You put the life of your daughter in their hands and it's a comfort. These are the guys who are going to patch her up and make everything okay. And they never tried to sugar-coat anything. She's going to look different, they told us. She's going to have skin transplants. She could be in hospital for twelve months. And it was information that they drip-fed to us, telling us what we needed to know as we needed to know it.

Once Turia survived the first two weeks, I knew she was going to be okay. I knew she was going to make a miraculous recovery. As I've said, she had always been so determined as a little kid. If she set her mind to doing something, she would sit there and sit there and practise it until she got it right. Emotionally, too, she was tough. I suppose I tried to raise all my kids to be emotionally self-sufficient. And I knew by then that in life you cannot rely on other people, or blame them for things that don't go your way. You are ultimately responsible for your own life.

For the next six months Turia was in hospital. I was working in Ulladulla and had my two youngest sons with me a lot of the time. Celestine had essentially moved up to Sydney to dedicate herself to taking care of Turia. And hats off to her. She is a remarkable woman: so caring, so full of warmth and affection. She poured herself into Turia's recovery, and I can say with certainty that Turia would not have recovered as quickly or as comprehensively as she did if it hadn't been for Celestine.

I would drive back and forth on weekends. At first, it looked as though the recovery was going to be long, slow and painful. But I knew how determined Turia was, and I knew that medical barriers were being broken all the time, and that my daughter would take those boundaries to the limit. She was deeply scarred, but gradually the old her started to shine through.

I had done a lot of online research and discovered burns victims who suffered worse injuries than Turia. People whose limbs had fused, for example. And we chose to focus on the positives. As bad as it was – and it was bad – there were people in worse situations.

I've always been into physical fitness, so whenever I spent time with Turia in hospital, I would try to take her through some stretching, work on the physio aspects of her recovery and rehab. I'm not sure she appreciated it all that much. There were a few choice words that seemed to be used quite a lot whenever we were going through her exercises. But, to her credit, and for all the swearing and cursing – she did them.

Turia and I have always had one of those father–daughter relationships where we talk a lot. Not necessarily about feelings or anything – but always about science and the possibilities of the future. So we spent a lot of time discussing science and technology, boring everyone else to death.

They moved her to a rehab facility but she hated it there and quickly decided to come home. When she finally got back to

Ulladulla, I made it my job to go with her to the gym to do her exercises. I can't speak highly enough about the community in Ulladulla. They really rallied behind her. So many people went out of their way to help. Sometimes you hear people bashing Australia – but I just think it's the greatest country on earth. We are so incredibly lucky to be born here – our health system is second to none. And then to have had this amazing community just wrap itself around us.

Moving in with Michael's parents, Gary and Julie, was probably the best thing that could have happened to Turia at that stage. What can you say about people like Gary and Julie? She was their son's girlfriend – not even a member of their immediate family – and she was utterly broken, requiring round-the-clock care. And they just took her in without a second's hesitation. I will be forever indebted to them for that. They are the most humble, kind-hearted people. And their home was exactly the nurturing environment Turia needed at that point. Out the back is this tranquil little garden and, bit by bit, the little circle of what she was able to do got wider and wider.

Then, of course, there is Michael. He has been her rock. He's got very broad and strong shoulders. Which is not to say he hasn't suffered. I have seen the pain in his face. Imagine what he has been through. The love of his life has nearly been torn from him and then he has to nurse an invalid. And he would never claim it – he would never want accolades for what he has done. How important for Turia to wake up from that coma and see her boyfriend by her side, to spend eighteen months learning to walk, eat and speak again – and her boyfriend never left her side. And let's be honest: Turia wasn't always in the best of moods while this was going on. How could she have been? She was angry and frustrated a lot of the time. It's not easy to be bright and chirpy when you struggle to brush your own hair or clean your own teeth. And for all of this to be dumped on them just as their relationship should be blossoming and in its prime. It tells you everything you need to know about Michael.

Honestly, between Michael and Celestine, they took the whole load. The rest of us were there for distraction, entertainment and support. But it was all on them. I'll be forever thankful to both of them for that.

I suppose the thing that people don't often stop to think about is the toll that this has taken on both of them. It has hurt Celestine deeply to have to go through all of that pain. When someone you love and would give your life for has been hurt like that, it marks you. It leaves scars. And she would never make a big deal about that, because that's the kind of woman – the kind of mum – that she is. But I know it's been a tough journey for her.

Michael, too. He doesn't say all that much, and isn't one for big displays of emotion – but I know there have been moments for him when it has all been too much. How many young men, presented with that set of circumstances, would have stepped up in the way that he did? He is remarkable.

Do I look at my daughter now and feel terrible for her? Not at all. If she refused to leave the house and was completely broken, I would feel terrible for Turia. But the fact that I look at her now and see this incredibly strong woman forging this amazing path in the world, it just blows my mind. It's almost as if she went into those bandages and came out a butterfly – completely transformed and ready to fly. She is like one of those Marvel superheroes. They are near death then dropped into some radioactive vat, only to emerge with superpowers. Would this enormous strength of character ever have been realised if this hadn't happened to her? If she had never been caught in that fire?

Obviously, she closes the door from time to time and closes in on herself. But she is out there inspiring people in a really big way. Was there ever a doubt it would all turn out like this? I suppose she had to decide when she was lying in that hospital bed whether she was going to let it defeat her or whether she was going to rise like a phoenix. Was she going to shrink and shrivel or persevere and put herself out there by going on TV in a mask, then take it off, pose for the cover of the *Women's Weekly*, put herself through some extreme training to do things like Ironman?

I would love to say that I always knew she had it in her – but I didn't. I am so glad she did. A mate of mine said to me recently, 'Mick – you know, she is really special. Not just for today. But in this century in Australia today. She is right up there.'

I see her on magazine covers or on the TV, I watch her give her speeches to rooms full of a thousand people and see the effect she has on them, and I just want to shout from the rooftops, *That's my girl!*

Of course, as her dad, I'm quite looking forward to the day she and Michael produce a couple of grandkids. She keeps saying it's her next big project, but then things like Ironman in Hawaii come along. Then she talks about wanting to climb

Everest. And I am always like, 'Do you think that's such a good idea?'

And she'll look at me and say, 'Seriously, Dad. What's the worst that can happen?'

I was twenty-six when she was born. Young. Being a parent is easily the most important work you will do as a human, but you get next to no training for it. I know she will make a great mum – just like her own mum is. She tries to make out that she will be really strict, but I doubt it. If there's a god, she will have a daughter just as headstrong as she is and she'll start to appreciate what her mother and I went through.

It's funny, because people make a big deal about the fact that she was so attractive before the fire and how she had done some work as a model and how that must make it doubly hard for her to accept what has happened. But I think they miss the point completely.

Men wear their scars as badges of honour: it's a sign of a life well lived – noses broken at footy, scars from smashing into a reef while surfing. Women spend so much time and money on their appearance. And Turia does as well. She can spend hours on her hair or applying eyeliner. And she still has bad-hair days.

I guess on some level she has made the decision within herself that she is as beautiful now as she ever was, and while people may not see it at first glance, they won't fail to see it if they spend any kind of time with her. And that's true.

As far as I am concerned, she is at least as beautiful now as she used to be – maybe more so because of the amazing person she has become. Besides, she is looking better with every year that passes, such is the skill of the surgeons who work on her. And when all is said and done, she could so easily have been dead. Because that's the alternative, really. I mean, if it really bothered her – she could take her life at any time. If her life wasn't worth living, she could end it all tomorrow. But as I have said to her on one or two occasions when she's been down: if you were dead, you wouldn't be doing all these remarkable things. You live, and live scarred – but what a remarkable life you have ahead of you.

Is it a happy ending for her? I think it absolutely is. But the story is far from over. I really hope to be talking about her again in ten years' time, looking back on a decade of remarkable achievements, because that's what she has ahead of her.

Not one of us on this earth can turn back time. If I could, I would love to reset the clock. Of course I wish it had never happened. Seeing the physical and mental pain she went through for the amount of time she went through it – I wouldn't wish that journey on anyone. But given this is the hand she has been dealt, and given what she has done with it, it just makes me burst with pride.

She has been fast-tracked to a level of maturity that few of us will ever know. And in the process, she's gained wisdom that few of us will ever have. She's had to draw on resources that not many people know that they have and very few of us will ever have tested. Having said that, in some respects she's still the six-year-old kid I remember. She has that child-like enthusiasm mixed with a profound wisdom.

Would I say she is thriving? Yeah – I think I would. She has embraced the challenge that is life and taken it on head-on. Around this time last year, she was out in big surf at the Bombie, near Mollymook. And it can get pretty rough out there. All the hardened old salts were out on their guns (big wave boards), and Turia was catching waves on her body-board; surfing these huge waves and getting a thrashing. But each time she got slammed, she just paddled back out to the line-up. And you know, every single one of those locals has come up and told me at some point what a legend my daughter is. And she is. She really is.

11

MY OTHER MUM AND DAD

Gary and Julie Hoskin's home in Narrawallee, a pocket of South Coast suburbia just north of Mollymook, is a haven. For eighteen months, in the early stages of my recovery, it was my haven.

Gary is your typical Aussie bloke, a real product of his generation. A former country lad, he has a gruff-looking, weather-beaten, all-Aussie exterior – but you don't need to scratch too far beneath the surface to discover his soft centre. For that matter, you don't even have to scratch beneath the surface. You just have to walk into his backyard.

The block of land on which Gary and Julie's house sits is long and deep. The house, a comfortable, brick, single-storey, 1980s build, sits at the front of the block, and the rest of the yard is given over to Gary's garden – an immaculately kept patch of lawn, agapanthus and native shrubs and trees. But easily the most remarkable thing about the yard are the high-set rows of bird cages that line its perimeter.

Gary is a bird breeder. It's his passion; an occasionally very noisy one at that. Which is funny, because Gary is one of the most softly spoken men I know. To see Gary with his birds is to understand his nature. It's not uncommon for freshly hatched macaws to require hand-rearing, a process that compels Gary and Julie to wrap the chicks in blankets and hand-feed them until they are big enough to fend for themselves. The sight of this burly Aussie bloke cradling a tiny, defenceless macaw and nurturing it to the point it is strong enough to fly on its own is kind of incongruous, but in many ways it sums up Gary better than anything else could.

After leaving hospital, I spent eighteen months living with Gary and Julie Hoskin. Just stop and think about that for a moment. It wasn't as if their son and his girlfriend were moving in for a bit while they saved money to put down a deposit on a home. I was a broken, angry half-person – determined to make a recovery, but in so much pain, so incredibly frustrated, severe burns to 65 per cent of my body and essentially immobile. Michael – their precious son – was my full-time carer. He waited on me hand and foot, rarely leaving my side. Julie, when she wasn't holding down a full-time job as a school teacher, cooked meals, washed sheets, helped bathe me, ran me back and forth between medical appointments and generally bent over backwards to accommodate my every need. Gary juggled his own job, which required him to travel the region as a food inspector, with the onerous task of nurturing back to full health the helpless chick who was a permanent presence in his living room.

Gary and Julie were both on the brink of retirement when my accident happened. After thirty-two years of marriage, they had only recently got the family home back to themselves after the last of their three children moved out. They would have been well within their rights to gently explain to

Michael that – much as they were prepared to step up and help out – the prospect of housing him and his burned girlfriend for an open-ended period of time was just not feasible.

But in Gary and Julie's case, not stepping up was never an option; it was never even a consideration. When Michael called them and said he thought the hospital had done all it could and that all the medical experts agreed the best environment for my recovery now was a home one, they didn't hesitate to throw open their doors.

And it wasn't as if I was a model house guest. Quite apart from taking up the entire living room most days, or having my electric arm-bending machine whirring away incessantly, they had to cope with my mood swings. I'm not proud to admit that I would regularly have a meltdown – overcome with what I thought at the time was the hopelessness of my situation. I could be sitting at the dinner table, over a meal lovingly prepared by Julie and carefully mashed or cut into tiny pieces to accommodate me, and I would lose it completely because I couldn't pick up the cutlery or I'd had a particularly bad day. Never once did they complain. Never once did they push back. Never once did they intimate that I was being an ungrateful cow. Their patience and forbearance in the face of one of the most trying episodes of their lives is something for which I will be forever grateful.

Who can even begin to imagine the mixed emotions they must have felt as they watched their son – their vital, handsome, eligible son – dedicate himself so fully to this invalid in their home. Proud? Yes, undoubtedly they felt proud at the compassionate young man they had raised. Scared? There's no question they felt scared and worried about the return he might get on that investment. What kind of future did he hope to build with me? What kind of a life was he consigning himself to? Wouldn't it simply be better for all concerned if he just cut and run?

I don't know if Gary and Julie ever thought like that. I think I would have if I had been in their position. But knowing the sorts of people they are, it probably never occurred to them.

There are many people to whom I feel enormous gratitude, and Julie and Gary are right up there at the top. They are the most extraordinary ordinary family I know. And isn't that always the way? Take a couple of people leading ordinary lives and thrust them into a situation where they have to step up: and invariably they do.

This is Gary and Julie's story ...

Gary and Julie Hoskin

Gary: I remember the night of the fire. I got the phone call from Michael. It was late, he sounded confused, panicked. He told me about the fire and asked me to come with him to Darwin. Before I even knew what had happened, I was in the car and on my way to the airport. That was a long drive, and the flight felt even longer. In Darwin we went straight to the hospital, where we were met by a nurse who told us it was not looking good. The sense was very much that Turia would probably not make it through the night, that we should prepare ourselves to lose her.

So I stood there with my son and Turia's mother, Celestine. Neither of them could bring themselves to see her, so I went inside the intensive care unit, and I was confronted by this person – not even really a person – or at least not one that I recognised. It was horrible. Turia's head was swollen, there was so much fluid retention. Her hair was all over the pillow.

I came back outside and said to Michael: 'It's not good, mate.' He was in a state. 'I won't go in,' he said. 'If she dies I want to remember her as she was.'

As it happened, he ended up seeing her in so many worse situations. And he never faltered. Not once. He coped so well. He was a copper for five years and he's never really talked about it, but apparently he saw a lot of bad stuff when he was with the police. You know, throughout it all, throughout all the dark times, and there were plenty of them, he always had such a positive outlook. 'She's alive, Dad,' he would say. 'She's alive.'

Julie: I remember the day the doctors called about the decision to amputate her fingers. Michael was at home, and he'd been agonising over it. They knew they were going to have to amputate, the question was how much. Was it just the fingers or was she going to lose the whole hand? And they didn't know for sure until they got her into the operating theatre and it had been Michael's call to have the operation in the first place. And the phone rang and I was as anxious as he was and I was trying not to show it by busying myself getting tea ready, but of course I was listening to every word and watching for Michael's reaction when I heard him say, 'You didn't have to take her hands! She will be so happy!' And my stomach was churning and I was trying not to cry or show too much emotion and I was looking at my boy, how elated he was that his badly burned girlfriend was only going to lose some fingers and not her entire hand, and all I could manage to say was, 'Tea's ready, love.'

At first it was only us and Celestine who were allowed to see her in the hospital. And we would sit in the ward, on the edge of her bed, trying to be positive. 'You'll be fine,' we'd all be saying, without any of us really knowing how or if she would be. But even in those moments, there would be flashes of humour. And this is the remarkable thing about Turia. She never lost her sense of humour or optimism. I remember in the early days, we were all sitting on her bed, speaking to her in encouraging tones. Turia could barely speak – only through the hole in her neck, through the tracheotomy – or barely move, and we sensed her motioning Gary to lean in closer. 'Gary, Gary,' she rasped at us. And so Gary leaned in further and Turia said, 'You're sitting on my hand.'

Gary: We can laugh about it all now, because she is okay – but at the beginning, gee, she was busted up.

Julie: Turia lived with us for a year and a half. The very first night when we knew she was coming home from hospital, I decided to do a big baked dinner. I called Celestine and John and invited them over. I extended the invite to her brothers. I thought it would be a nice surprise for her to come home and have the entire family here. Finally they arrived after the long drive down from Sydney and Turia slowly manoeuvred her way out of the little Getz they'd driven down in, made her way inside and saw this big party of people waiting for her to arrive. And it was too much for her. She was overwhelmed. And I immediately thought, *Oh no, I've done the wrong thing.* It was supposed to be a happy occasion, a reason to celebrate, a nice surprise – but of course for her, it was just a rush of emotion after what must have been a very long, slow and painful car journey. The trip had taken them much longer than normal because they'd had to stop at regular intervals to allow Turia to get out and stretch. The next morning, I went back to the stove-top thinking I could make amends for the night before by making something nice for breakfast. So I whipped up eggs and smoked salmon. Which of course she couldn't eat because it was too rich.

Gary: Michael had to change her bandages every day. The reason they had let her out of hospital and allowed her to come home early was because Michael had learned from the nurses how to change her bandages. And it would be this morning ritual they would go through. It caused her a lot of pain, and we could hear the moaning and the screaming. Michael would come out of the bedroom after having changed the bandages and he'd have tears in his eyes.

Julie: We did worry about him a lot. Because especially in those first months, he was very quiet. For a year and a half, she would sit in that recliner in our living room basically unable to move. If she needed to go to the toilet, she needed help; at meal times, she needed help. The days were monotonous for her – and I suppose for Michael too. Some days, at the beginning, it took an enormous effort just to stand up and take a half a wander about the living room. Yet eventually our days settled into a kind of a rhythm. I'm a teacher and I went to four days a week at school to try to give Michael a hand. On weekends we'd meet at Celestine's place for lunch, then we'd spend an hour or so massaging Turia. It would be the three of us together, and we had some really fun times. Celestine would call it 'girl power'. Afterwards Turia would come home and walk around the backyard dragging weights behind her.

Gary: Because she was so scarred, even I was always on the lookout for different oils and creams that might help speed the skin's recovery. I remember visiting [our daughter] Shae one time, who told me about an oil that was apparently really good for damaged skin. So of course I went and searched about five chemists until I found it. I used to rub the oil on Turia's face. The poor kid; she couldn't turn around without someone wanting to rub a cream or an oil on her.

I remember looking at Michael and thinking what a special kid he was. When you think about it, not too many young blokes would stick by a girl who was damaged as she was. She went from being a model to being burned to a crisp. And it's not even about the looks; it's about whether a person recovers from injuries like that. And what kind of quality of life are they going to have even if they do? At the beginning, none of us knew the answers to any of those questions. And we couldn't afford to think too much about them anyway. Not that we had any time. It was like every bit of our energy – every bit of Michael's energy – was being poured into Turia and her recovery. I think Michael is a legend. He is my best mate. I had people come up to me and say, 'Surely, he's not going to stay with her?' And you know, I never for a moment thought that he wouldn't stay with her. Because he loved her. She was his girl.

Julie: Turia was just so grateful when she lived with us. Always so gracious and polite. And it's something that struck me. Because she had every right to be angry and frustrated with the world and the cards that had been dealt to her, but she never failed to say thank you whenever anything was done for her. She never once took us for granted.

Gary: We would have people come up to us and say how amazed they were that we had taken them in and had them living with us. But it was never a question for us. It was a no-brainer. We had a big, empty house. Michael and Turia lived in one part of it, we lived in the other. They did their own thing and we'd cross paths at meal times. She hired this contraption, a machine that she would put her arm in every day that would bend it for her, to encourage movement and stretch the skin. And she would sit there for hours on the couch, the machine humming away, her arm bending up and down.

Sometimes Michael would meet me at the door when I came home and he would say, 'Dad, today hasn't been a good day.' And we would know to back off and leave them alone.

Julie: We just didn't want to ruffle any feathers or get in their way.

Gary: We racked up the most incredible electricity bills in those eighteen months. The poor kid was either too hot or too cold. She was so skinny and had no body fat; even in the middle of summer we'd have the heating on constantly. Each day Michael would spend half an hour filling the bath for her and she'd be in and out of it in two minutes. Not that we cared. We were all just focused on getting her better. She's such a strong lady. I honestly don't think if it had been anyone else they would have recovered the way she did. And I never once heard her whinge about how unfair it was.

Julie: I suppose it was emotionally hard more than it was physically hard. I mean, I seem to recall doing a lot of washing for those eighteen months. The washing machine was almost constantly running with the sheets and the towels. Michael used to lie her on towels when he changed her dressings, because her skin was still healing and it was still a messy, painful process. We had to throw out the mattress after the kids moved out, it was blood-stained and ruined. But the physical toll it took on us was minimal really. Certainly compared to the toll it took on Michael. And certainly compared to the emotional toll it took on both of us to see the pair of them struggling through this slow recovery process.

Gary: Michael isn't one to show his emotions or complain, but as his parents, we worried about him.

Julie: Every day he had to put a mouthguard in Turia's mouth to make the skin stretch. And it must have been so painful, and she would cry every day. And I would come home from school, where someone had been whingeing about how hard it had been to be on playground duty, to see Turia on the couch with the mouthguard in and the arm-bending machine going, and it would put everything in perspective.

Gary: I remember parents of Michael's friends asking us why he hadn't been in touch with their kids. But the fact was, he just didn't have time.

Julie: In the beginning he refused to leave her side. He would sit in the living room with her, reading a book, keeping her company and making sure she had everything she needed. I used to urge him to take a break, to go for a surf, but he wouldn't budge. Someone had to be here with her. She couldn't bend her elbows, she couldn't get off the couch. She wasn't able to swipe flies off her face, she couldn't turn door handles. She would wear her mask most days, but sometimes not. And we would get so many deliveries and if Michael hadn't put her mask on, she would hear the doorbell ring and panic that someone might see her. 'Don't let them in!' she would cry, and I would assure her no one was going to come in. In those first months, she was very self-conscious.

Gary: But that changed with time. At first, other than going to the physio and to medical appointments and to her mum's place, she would only go out in the backyard, which is tree-lined and private. No one can see in. I think that was important to her.

Julie: Much later in the piece, we took her to Sydney to see *The Phantom of the Opera*. And I remember being in the theatre foyer, and she was in her mask, and this idiot walked past and I overheard them say, 'Oh, look at that one, she's getting into the spirit of it all with her costume.' And I wanted to belt them. You just feel so protective. And I remember on that same trip walking down George Street with her, and she was so skinny, her jeans were falling down, just sliding off her hips, and I ran along behind her hoisting them up.

Gary: She's a brave girl. She learned pretty quickly to not let anything faze her. One morning, she wanted to go and see her mum in Burrill Lake, about fifteen minutes down the highway. So I put her on the back of my Harley. She could barely hang on. But then, that's the thing about Turia – if she's not pushing herself or she's not being challenged she's not interested. That's why she got so well so quickly. If the doctors told her to do ten reps of a particular exercise she would do thirty.

Julie: I was with Michael and Turia when she went for her first swim down at Narrawallee beach. Michael had put a life jacket on her and she wobbled tentatively into the water in her full-body compression suit. The first wave came along and she ducked under and the life jacket pulled her up and she got a mouthful of salt water. She wasn't happy. She just got straight out and started walking out of the water. I thought that was it, but she stopped, composed herself and turned around and went straight back in. She was just so determined. But I worried the whole time about how thin she was. I was constantly trying to fatten her up.

Gary: And that was the thing. From the outset she never accepted the limits other people imposed on her. She just pushed and pushed herself. We were all there to help with her recovery, but mostly it's down to her own inner strength.

Julie: Humour was really important, too. We would always have tea together at night. The four of us would sit around the table and eat together. There would be times Turia would just sit there taking the mickey out of Gary. She loved nothing more than teasing him – and he can be so easy to tease. She has a wicked sense of humour, a real mischievous streak.

Gary: Yeah. She was always having a dig at me.

Julie: So, yes, we did laugh a lot. But I also cried a lot. Never in front of Michael or Turia. I used to go walking with my girlfriends, and they would always be interested to know how Turia was going – and that's when I would cry. That's when I knew it was taking more of an emotional toll than I realised.

With the benefit of hindsight, we felt privileged to have been there for them, but at the same time, my mind was obsessed with worry. To see a beautiful girl sitting there like that and not able to do anything for herself – you just felt, you poor, poor girl. Within ten minutes I could go from being really happy to being really low. There were times when I would have to put her mask on for her. I could never do it as well as Michael, and I always made a mess of it. But you just felt like you were always trying to please her and do things to make her feel even a little bit better.

Gary: I don't think we are that special. We only did what any other parent would do in that situation. I actually loved having them here. At least we knew what headspace Michael was in all the time. If he was upset, we knew it; if he was happy, we knew it – we could monitor his moods. He was close to us, we were on hand if he needed us, and that made us feel better.

Julie: We just wanted to be there for Michael. When they told us they were moving out, I remember feeling really sad. It was just so emotional.

Gary: I think there's a reason Michael coped as well as he did. He's always been really laidback.

Julie: And I think he has become more laidback since Turia's accident. He's had such a dose of perspective. He's learned to work out the things that are important in life and the things that are not.

Gary: Turia, too. She's come such a long way. At first, she didn't want anyone to see her. Then gradually, bit by bit, she ventured out into public. And that must have been hard. I remember taking her to the pictures and being aware of all these people staring at her. But she just handled it so well.

Julie: She has this amazing way of putting people at ease. And it's ironic that she's the one going out of her way to make others feel comfortable. But she does. When people first meet her, they don't know what to say or even whether to touch her. But she throws herself into any social situation, even with complete strangers, and it immediately puts people at ease. She's remarkable. We just look at where they are now, and all the incredible things she has done since her accident, and it makes us so proud.

Gary: You think back to those first few weeks after the fire, and it's hard to believe it's the same girl. I'll never forget in the hospital in Sydney, when it was still very much touch and go as to whether she was even going to survive, and Michael came up to me holding this little box. I knew what it was straightaway. He handed me the box and said, 'Dad, can you look after this for me, please? If Turia pulls through this, I am going to marry her. But don't tell anyone, in case she doesn't make it.' I brought the ring box home and put it in the safe. And then a bit further down the track, when she started losing fingers, I said to Michael, 'Mate, don't worry about the fingers. You can always put it on a chain.' I was just so proud of him. In all that time, he never lost it once. I was the one in the hospital who would occasionally lose it and cry – and he would come up and support me.

I still remember one of the first questions she asked the doctors when she regained consciousness. She couldn't speak. She had a screen put in front of her and she tapped out the question with a kind of pen in her mouth. 'Can I have children?'

Julie: Can you imagine that wedding? It will be a day of really high emotion. Really emotional.

Gary: People say, you must be proud of your boy. And we are. We couldn't be more proud. People say, it must have been hard on you. And it was hard. Probably the hardest thing we have ever had to go through – watching our son and his partner go through such pain. But do we feel lucky to have been a part of this? Has it brought us closer together as a family? Absolutely. And we wouldn't change it for the world.

12

THE DOCTOR

Since the fire, I've had more than two hundred procedures. Some of them minor day procedures; some of them life-saving, marathon stints in the operating theatre. You'd think, given the amount of time I have spent in their company (not to mention the agony many of them have put me through) that I would want as little as possible to do with the doctors and specialists and nurses and physios who have all been so important to my recovery.

But each one of them is special to me in their own way. Even the physio who used to put me through hell in hospital and who has probably heard me swear more than anyone in the world (and that is saying something) has a special little piece of my heart (it's a dark piece, sure, but it's still a piece).

Two men loom large above them all, of course: Professors Maitz and Haertsch. If there are two medical maestros who have played a pivotal part in firstly my survival, and thereafter in my regaining a normal life, it is these two.

Together with Professor Maitz, Professor Haertsch ripped

133

me back from the brink of death when I was first admitted to the burns unit at Concord Hospital. As he will tell anyone who asks, upon first laying eyes on me when I was transferred from Darwin, he thought I was a hopeless case: that my chances of survival were negligible. In fact, as he also likes to tell anyone who asks, he remembers thinking it would probably be better that I did die. To his thinking, back in those early days, even if I was to survive the catastrophic burns I had sustained, I would be so damaged beyond repair that any life I would go on to have would not be worth living.

Did I mention how I love nothing more than confounding people? Especially people who write me off?

To be fair to Professor Haertsch, he was probably better placed than most to write me off. As one of Australia's foremost burns surgeons, with more than forty years' experience, he was awarded the Order of Australia medal back in 2003 for his work treating the Bali bombing victims. There's arguably no one in Australia who knows burns better than Professor Haertsch – and certainly, in my book, there's no one who knows better how to treat them.

If you were to meet Professor Haertsch for the first time, you'd come away thinking he was your stereotypical surgeon: all gruff and impersonal and completely lacking in humour. But spend as much time with him as I have, and you know he is the complete opposite. He's funny, in a dry-wit sort of way. His gruff exterior masks a big heart as exemplified by the charity work he does for the reconstructive and burns surgery charity Interplast. And while he would occasionally get on my nerves with his tendency to dismiss some of my wilder ambitions when I was recovering – he was among the surgeons who raised his eyebrows when I declared I would complete an

Ironman – I came to understand that my recovery would not have been possible without him.

On a practical level, he is the one who rebuilt me. The skin grafts, the reconstruction of my nose, the multiple operations on my hands, the laser treatment to soften and flatten my scar tissue – they are all his handiwork. I'm his creation, in some ways – and, as I write this, it's a journey we have been on together now for almost five years.

But that's enough from me. Let's let Professor Haertsch speak for himself ...

Professor Peter Haertsch

I remember when Turia first came in to the hospital. It stands really clearly in my memory. In fact, I could never forget it for the simple reason that before me was a young girl who had sustained as deep a burn as I had ever seen. At first, I didn't think she could possibly survive.

The only thing she had going for her was her age and athleticism.

On the spot I made a decision that if she looked like bombing out, if at any point it looked like she wouldn't make it, I would put it to her family that we let her die. It seemed to me that even if she did survive – and that seemed unlikely – her life was going to be severely compromised.

As it happened, she didn't bomb out. Though she came very, very close.

Looking back, it is always Michael who stands out. It was he who at all times adopted a 'let's give it a go' attitude. Each time my back was to the wall, when I thought there was no way of bringing her back from the brink, he would always be there, encouraging me to throw everything we had at Turia's survival.

I knew that if she was going to make it, we needed human donor skin, and we needed it fast. Unfortunately, in burns treatment, skin isn't just lying around waiting for me to collect it and apply it to whichever burns patient I am working on. And donor skin is very hard to find. Skin banks usually have only very limited supplies – people burn themselves all the time – so the small amount of skin available at any given time is almost always in high demand. And because the Rugby World Cup was being played in New Zealand at the time, much of the skin that was readily available had already been requisitioned by New Zealand authorities in anticipation of a possible terrorist attack at one of the rugby matches. So I investigated the possibility of bringing in donor skin from the United States. Which meant it had to clear customs and quarantine – a complicated, time-consuming process. And the one thing Turia didn't have on her side was time.

The biggest problem we faced was the extent of gross burn wound contamination. When Turia first arrived from the Northern Territory, we performed a series of grafts, using mainly her own skin, taken from the few parts of her body that had not been burned. You see, with skin grafting, it becomes a mathematical equation. You look at a body surface area and if you have 50 per cent burns, it means you only have 50 per cent from which to take a graft. If you have 65 per cent burns, as we did in Turia's case, you only have 35 per cent of the body from which to take grafts.

Within days of performing the original skin grafts, it became clear the grafts had not taken, because she had picked up an infection. So we pretty much had to start again. That meant scraping back all of the skin we had already applied, clearing up the infection and applying new skin. But because it had to be imported from the United States, and the clock was ticking, the whole exercise came down to the wire. As I recall, the skin we had ordered from America was held up in customs and quarantine. Some well-meaning official, who I suppose was only doing his or her job, refused to give clearance to the skin until it had spent time in quarantine. My colleague had to make several increasingly desperate calls to customs officials, trying to explain the situation. Eventually he managed to convince someone that unless clearance was given for the skin to pass through customs, a young woman was going to die on our operating table. They cleared the skin and we performed the grafts. Had it been a day – or maybe even half a day – later Turia would almost certainly not have made it.

Even the procedure itself was somewhat experimental. A lot of research had been done in America and I knew of a theory which posited that grafted human donor skin was capable of fighting the sort of post-burn contamination and infection that Turia had. But I had never tried it before – it was something I had only read about, heard talked about at various meetings and conferences. However, in the end I felt duty-bound to try it. Michael was always there in the background urging me to do everything in my powers to bring his girl back, so I felt I owed it to him.

The theory is that you use the skin to clean the wound – and frankly I was very sceptical. Though, as I now know, the theory appears to hold. It appears that human donor skin does have an ability to clear up infection.

There's no question that in terms of her family, their presence was as good as I have ever seen with a burns patient. One or more of them was present, by her side, every day she was in hospital. That was instrumental in Turia's recovery.

I remember quite early on in proceedings taking Michael aside and very clearly telling him that if Turia survived – and that was still a really big if at that stage – the same girl might still be there, but she'd be in a completely different package. I think he appreciated my honesty. I was always honest with him. I never tried to gild the lily. Here was a young man in the prime of his life, faced with a horrible situation. I had no intention of making his predicament any worse by making false promises or creating false hope. He never at any stage felt that I was embellishing anything – and I think that was important to him.

As a burns surgeon, I see pretty much the gamut of the human condition. The interesting thing about the burns population is that it is a very different population to that found in a general surgical ward. Normal people doing normal things very rarely get burned. More often than not, it is people who have set fire to themselves – people who have been involved in some nefarious activity, say burning a building or a car for insurance purposes; people under the influence of alcohol who have burned themselves falling into campfires or changing a gas bottle. People who are in control of themselves rarely get badly burned. And of course the backgrounds of these people are many and varied. Often what you might describe as colourful.

What I don't see a lot of are people who are burned simply because they were in the wrong place at the wrong time, through no fault of their own. And in my experience, it speaks volumes to the support those burns victims receive. Here was a girl who had an extremely interesting job, had her whole life in front of her, was taking part in an admittedly extreme but otherwise wholesome day of running, and she suffered this horrendous misadventure.

*

I remember, quite early on, we were forced to make the decision to amputate her fingers. From a clinical point of view, those decisions are made on quite reasonable, logical grounds. If the digit is dead, it's dead. But telling the patient – that's the difficult part.

At the end of the day it was begrudgingly accepted.

Again, Michael was extremely helpful in this regard. He was the guy who did all the hard yards with Turia. He was the one who was able to talk to her, to get the decisions that we wanted enacted. She wouldn't take advice from anyone in the same way she would take it from him. He was the one she would listen to, he was the one who would always sit with her and convince her that everything that was being done was being done for her own good. For her own survival. An investment in their future lives together. It was quite remarkable to watch.

Did it take a toll on him? I think absolutely it did. There's no way it could not have taken a toll. But the remarkable thing about Michael was how constant he was. I don't just mean in terms of his physically being there, but also in terms of his mood. He is one of those people who is calm and considered by default. He is extremely difficult to ruffle or upset. If you had to design a partner who was going to be good in a crisis like the one Turia was facing, Michael is the prototype you would come up with. Nothing seemed to faze him. Or if it did, he did a very good job of never showing it.

Celestine, Turia's mother, was also a constant presence in the hospital. She would arrive most mornings with an esky full of food. And Turia's father was here a lot. Each of them brought something unique to her recovery.

In burns victims, as much as the recovery is a physical one, it's a psychological one. Only the strongest of body and spirit prevail. The most common refrain from a burns victim is 'Why me?' – especially one like Turia whose burns came about through no fault of her own. But she never once demonstrated self-pity. Or if she did, I never saw it.

I always tell my patients that if they want to make the best recovery available to them – both physical and psychological – they need to adjust their expectations at the very beginning. They need to accept that their lives will never be the same, that their life going forward will forever be affected by the burns they have sustained, and the sooner they readjust the mental parameters in their head about what is and isn't possible, the more readily they will be able to lead a happy life.

It's a curious thing in Turia's case because though she accepts there are things in life she cannot do as easily as before the fire, there are so many things she has done since the fire that prove anything is possible if you put your mind to it.

One day she came in for a check-up. Her life was starting to return to its new normal and she and Michael came in to see me in outpatients. She sat opposite me with this straight face and told me she was pregnant. I know now she just did it to see the look on my face. Almost immediately, a mischievous grin spread across her face.

If there is one thing Turia has reinforced, it is how resilient the human spirit can be. In my experience, once she sets her mind to something, there's pretty much nothing that can stand in her way.

*

Something that is common to burns victims, especially if they have suffered burns to their face, is the adjustment that must take place to accept they will never look the same again. We can rebuild and repair – and certainly technology in this field is evolving every day – but there's little to no chance that someone who suffered burns to the extent Turia did will ever look like she did before the fire.

In terms of what might be considered conventional beauty, Turia was an extremely beautiful girl. She has never spoken to me about lowered self-esteem as a result of the injuries she sustained, but it's hard to imagine there haven't been moments where she hasn't felt deflated. Here again, I don't think we can understate how important it has been for Turia to have Michael by her side. I know that he would always tell Turia how beautiful she was: how she was as beautiful in his eyes after the fire as she had ever been before it. Having him stand by her throughout all of this has been an extremely important plank in the sense of acceptance that is necessary if someone is to go on and lead any kind of fulfilling life.

Having said all that, ironically enough, I think the accident has made Turia extremely independent. In the first few months, she was completely dependent on all of us here in the burns and rehab units, as well as on her family members who sat by her bedside every day or accompanied her to physio sessions. Then, when she went home to Michael's parents' place, she was completely dependent on Michael. Now, as she has gradually got back her own life, she has not only become independent of him, she seems to work hard constantly to actively assert that independence. As if every day she has something to prove.

I look at her now and I see this young woman who is determined to show she doesn't need anyone to prop her up anymore. And I don't know how Michael copes with it. I sometimes wonder what effect that has had on him. Because that's a massive adjustment for him to have to make: from being her primary carer, in a really fundamental, brush-her-teeth and wipe-her-bottom way, to being less vital with every day that passes. When you have dedicated five years of your life almost completely to your partner's rehabilitation, to then have to get used to the fact she doesn't need your 24/7 attention anymore, that can be a large adjustment to make. You have to once again get on with your own life.

Probably the thing that impresses me most about Turia – and there are many things – is the fact she has used her altered situation to great benefit. She has become this incredibly powerful force for good, motivating people on an almost daily basis, whether through her speeches or charity fundraising activities. It says everything you need to know about her. She was never going to be the burns victim who just sat back and moped. Almost from the very first day, she made a conscious decision to harness this tragedy and turn it into good. And for that, she has my utmost respect and admiration.

I remember the day, in fact, when she first became aware of the work I do for Interplast. Each year, I and other like-minded surgeons take ourselves off to countries – mostly in the Asia-Pacific and Africa – where the populations don't have access to the same health and medical facilities that we have here in Australia. And we spend a week or two every year performing surgeries in those countries – whether it be fixing cleft palates or operating on burns victims. Often these are really simple, straightforward surgeries – but they can change lives.

I started working with Interplast in 1998 and have done about fifty trips with them since. In my humble opinion, the organisation is one of Australia's best-kept humanitarian secrets. It's incredibly rewarding work.

Turia started to get curious about Interplast when she was recovering in hospital and she noticed I kept disappearing for two weeks at a time. I told her about the work we did and it was like watching a lightbulb go on in her head. I couldn't know it back then, but she would go on to become our charity's proud ambassador – and she has since raised more than a million dollars. And it's all done out of a sense of gratitude: she is grateful for all the work I personally did to help her recover; she is grateful that she lives in Australia where we have a functioning, world-class health and hospital system that is accessible to all; and she is grateful, I suppose, to be alive. And so she's determined to give back.

Is Turia my proudest accomplishment? Well, yes and no. I couldn't be more proud of her. She's made the sort of recovery that stands as a gold standard to all burns victims. And that's as much psychological as it is physical. But as her surgeon, I wish I could do more for her – particularly her nose. While her nose is a lot better than it was, I still think I could make it better still. I have spoken to one of the world's most recognised nasal reconstruction people, but there's just so little experience internationally in this sort of work. And I do look at my patients and consider them an advertisement for my skill as a surgeon, and professional pride compels me to want to keep improving on the canvas. So I am forever contacting her and telling her about new technologies being developed and new ways that skin can be rehabilitated. The fractional CO2 laser, for example, is quite new to burns but is proving efficient at softening up burned skin, flattening scar tissue and taking the colour out of it. Some days she is more receptive to hearing about it all than others. And that's perfectly normal.

Not that I would for a minute ever describe Turia as normal. Her level of determination when she sets her mind to something – it does make me wonder if perhaps she is addicted to endorphins. I have never seen someone who gets more joy out of pushing her body to its limits. She really does seem to enjoy punishing herself – it seems to make her feel good.

The thing is, I look at her undertaking Ironman competitions and the Kokoda Track and I think we haven't seen the half of it yet. She is still coming out of her shell. We are only just starting to see the transformation – there is so much more to come from this woman.

13

SET-POINT FOR HAPPINESS

Set-point theory is a scientific principle that applies to the mind. Psychologists talk about the existence in each of us of a set-point for happiness. Research has shown that lottery winners experience an initial rush of elation after winning the jackpot, but after this euphoria died down, they are often no happier than people who have experienced a catastrophic event. The point being that people get used to their circumstances; they become, in the scientific parlance, 'habituated' to their new normal and their happiness returns to its baseline level.

Geneticists suggest that our set-point is determined to a large extent by hereditary factors. If your parents were fundamentally happy people, you have a good chance of being happy too. Beyond that, the extent to which you veer from your set-point – either in a positive or negative direction – will depend on circumstances. A cataclysmic event in your life will send you careering away from your set-point. The bigger the catastrophe, the further off course you will be thrown, the longer it will take you to get back on track and the harder you will have to work to get there.

It's a simplistic account of a theory that is a whole lot more complex. And, certainly, it's all relative: one person's catastrophe is another person's walk-in-the-park. But throughout all of our lives, the theory goes, we will hover around our set-point for happiness. A relationship break-up, an accident or a career hiccup could send us into set-point deficit territory, but over time, we will rediscover our happiness equilibrium and life will go on as before. Likewise if our lives are suddenly touched by momentary elation – falling in love, moving into a dream home, getting that promotion – we will soar briefly, before eventually coming back down to earth.

Studies have shown that it takes on average a year for amputees to get back to their set-point. Lottery winners, the same – albeit at the other end of the scale.

It took me four years to get back to my set-point for happiness. And much of that has to do with winning back my independence. Up until then, I was pretty much reliant on Michael (to lesser or greater degrees, depending on the task and whether I was feeling lazy or small or on top of things on any given day). Now, though, Michael could go to South Africa tomorrow – which, to be honest, given his love of all things extreme and spur-of-the-moment, is not out of the question – and I would be okay. Sure, I wouldn't be able to do up a zip here or there, or manage a set of tricky buttons, but I just wouldn't wear the shorts with the tricky buttons.

For the first eighteen months, I wasn't able to do the most mundane tasks for myself. In medical terms, they call these things ADL – or 'activities of daily living' – and the professionals charged with your rehab use them as markers of how successfully you would be able to live an independent life. Can the patient prepare food themselves? Once food is prepared, is the patient physically capable of getting that food into their mouth? Likewise with liquids: can they turn on a tap or open a fridge door or hold a glass to ensure they remain hydrated? Then there are the essentials of personal hygiene: can they shower, toilet and brush their teeth? It can be as simple as whether or not a patient is capable of sitting upright. Can they walk 10 metres unassisted?

I remember vividly the first time I was able to wash my hair on my own. It seems like such a simple thing, but I cannot describe how ecstatic I was. Under the jet spray of the shower, with a bottle of Pantene in my hand and a crown of bubbles on my head, I felt like I had conquered Everest.

According to the ADL markers, I was classified as being 'capable of independent living' two years after my accident. But I still occasionally had trouble with day-to-day tasks, and while none of those things was essential to my survival, I used to get incredibly frustrated when I couldn't do them. It was almost as if, psychologically, I had tricked myself into thinking everything was back to normal. The achievement of sitting on the toilet without help would lift my mood immeasurably. Ten minutes later, though, if I couldn't open the milk to put a splash in my tea, I was plunged into a state of despair, railing against the injustice of the world.

Michael would just sit quietly in the corner, let me blow off steam, then offer a few gentle words of encouragement.

I still get annoyed at not being able to do things – especially when it comes to the physical activities I love so much. Like surfing, for example. I struggle to get into my steamer wetsuit without help – I just don't have the strength of grip in the three fingers I have left, or the coordination to pull it on. But when I'm in the water, when it all comes together and I catch a wave (which is admittedly less frequently than I would like), the feeling is like nothing else.

I also find surfing really spiritual. When I'm out there beyond the break and the sea is glassy and the sun is glinting off the water and I can taste the salt on my lips, I do feel at one with the earth. You see it in people's faces when they come out of the water. It's like a drug. Being in the ocean becomes an addiction and I suffer withdrawals if I don't do it every day.

When I ride my bike, because I only have one hand to grip the handlebars, getting up out of the saddle and climbing hills is a challenge. But then I focus on everything I can still do – and I marvel at what an amazing tool the human body is. It's incredible, when you think of it, how you can beat it to a pulp, break it, burn it, cut it, and it still bounces back and allows you to do the most extraordinary things.

A lot of people hate running. But not me; I've always loved it. I get a real high from pounding the pavement, and love the challenge of running faster or further than I did yesterday. That zone I get into when the endorphins kick in, the oxygen is coursing through my veins, my heart is thumping: it's a high that only a runner understands. Therefore, as much as being able to feed myself and dress myself was an important part of getting back to my set-point, so was being able to once again do all the things I loved doing. Going to the gym, surfing, Pilates, running and bushwalking.

If I had to describe my ideal day, it would be: wake up early, go for a surf, come back for breakfast, go for another surf, come back for lunch with friends, surf a bit more in the afternoon, go for a bushwalk to watch the sun set, and cap it all off with a romantic dinner with Michael – in bed by eight.

There is no question that the fire altered our relationship. We went from boyfriend and girlfriend to being carer and patient. And there's nothing sexy about that. You become really reliant on one person, and before long that reliance becomes dependence, so that even with small things that other people could easily have done for me, I only wanted Michael to do them. He was my security blanket, and there were times when he resented it. 'Ask your mum,' he would occasionally say in exasperation. 'But I want *you* to do it,' I would whine pitifully. It was like being a toddler all over again.

Why was I unreasonable with Michael? Because I needed to take my frustration out on someone. And also, probably because I knew I could be. Every morning he would set out clothes for me to wear. If I was in a particularly bad mood, I'd take one look and say, 'I don't want to wear that.'

Once he threw my entire wardrobe on the bed and declared, 'So, *you* decide what you want to wear. I'm done!'

Now Michael's and my life together is back to normal. I suppose as a couple we have made it back to our set-point for happiness. The space my independence has given us to develop elements that are vital to any successful partnership has been a balm all of its own. And he has found other things to do with his life. For the past year or so he's been building houses, and, as an ocean man through and through, doing some pretty impressive stuff with free diving. So now, if I want to hold my breath for longer, get bigger lobsters, pull in a fish, charge into the surf … Michael's the man to show me how to do those things.

14

BRIGGSY

I've known Kristen Briggs for as long as I can remember. She was one of the first people I befriended at school in Ulladulla, and from the moment we met, we hit it off.

She probably also knows me better than a lot of people. When you spend your school, teenage years and early twenties with someone, you tend to go through a whole lot of stuff together that bonds you for life.

It's important to me to have people in my life who remember the old me. They are like keepers of a kind of time capsule: witnesses to the Turia who was. It's also nice to have people around me with whom I can relax completely. There's nothing Briggsy and I don't know about each other or each other's lives, and that's comforting – if a little bit unnerving. If we ever stopped being friends, I would need to silence her. She knows too much.

Since the fire, and all the madness, all the amazing things that have happened in my life in the years afterwards, Briggsy has always been there, supporting me quietly in the background. It's hard to overstate how much the support of friends like her have meant to me during my recovery. Sometimes the love has been tough, but it's never been anything other than genuine and heartfelt, and for that I am enormously grateful. This is her story.

Kristen Briggs

I met Turia in high school – we became friends in Year 9. She came and sat with us girls at lunchtime and we gradually got to know her. She joined our basketball team, The Phattys – we called ourselves that because we thought we were cool, in that way fifteen-year-old girls think they are, when generally they're not.

Turia has always been the kind of girl who sits back and observes a situation – takes in all the people around her – and makes a calibration about exactly how much of the crazy she is going to bring. Because there's a lot of crazy in there: in some crowds, if she feels really comfortable, she will let it all hang out – and that has to be seen to be believed. In other situations, she will drip-feed the crazy.

One of the first really long conversations we ever had was walking home together after school one day, not long after we met. And it was just crazy enough for me to like her immediately. She was different to so many of the other girls at school – a little bit nuts, totally unpredictable and brimming with an enthusiasm for life. I knew straightaway we would be friends.

We played rugby union together and our coach called her Big Heart – because she mucked in and gave anything a go. She was fearless. Never scared to try anything.

But as much as she was sporty, she was also a bit of a bookworm. She had a definite touch of the nerd; she gave up rugby union in Year 12 to focus on her HSC. She and I shared a mutual love for chess. We used to have these massive competitions, some would last forever. When it comes to chess, Turia is really slow at moving. There were some games where one single move would stretch over hours. We even took a chessboard with us to schoolies.

She was crazy good at school. She was definitely one of those girls who did really well academically and so should have been a geek, but was also really popular. It's a maddening combination.

I remember she formed a band with a couple of other girls so they could play at the Year 12 farewell. The band was called Lunchtime Date – and they only ever learned and played one song as far as I can remember. Turia was the lead guitarist. At one point during their performance, she got down on her knees and belted out a solo. She's not exactly the shrinking-violet type. The spotlight has been something she's always been comfortable in.

When I got my licence, I would ferry Turia to school with another of our friends, Nicola, and the three of us became close. I suppose you could say we were considered to be the cool kids. Turia was a beautiful girl, and always really popular with the boys. We were a tight-knit group of girls and we're still close to this day. We used to go to the beach after school, go on hiking adventures on weekends. During the school holidays, we would practically live in each other's houses.

If we were at Turia's house, she would pretend she was a DJ; she was always DJ Pitty. She and Nicola used to compete and the rest of us used to sit there and judge them. Turia fancied herself as a gangsta rap and techno expert. The girl's definitely got rhythm, but, put it this way, she was never in any danger of being talent scouted by Dr Dre.

When school finished, Turia decided to take a gap year and she worked for a while at Civic Video in Ulladulla. We used to go in there and get free lollies! She left halfway through the year to go to New Zealand and work on the ski fields in Queenstown. Nicola and I decided we would surprise her for her eighteenth birthday by flying over and I remember sitting on her deck above the snow in Queenstown one afternoon with a couple of beers. When she came home from work she just dropped her snowboard and started crying.

Then Turia went to university in Sydney and I moved overseas for a year. I went to Scotland and travelled through Central America. After I got back, Turia and I decided to cycle across Cambodia together to raise money for charity. That was an experience that changed my life, and our tour leader on that adventure is my now business partner. I saw what a difference you could make in people's lives if the money we all spend as tourists goes to the right places. We raised $14,000 together on that ride, which went towards building a school there.

I remember before we left we worked our butts off to raise the money. We hosted a surf competition, we hounded businesses and friends and family all over Ulladulla, we threw a couple of dance parties. People look at the charity work Turia does now and they are impressed, but she has always had a really strong social conscience. She has always been aware of how lucky we are here in Australia and felt it's our duty to try to give back in some way.

Turia's mum, Celestine, was not happy at all that we were going to cycle across Cambodia. She thought it was too dangerous. But we went, and we survived. Even if it almost killed Turia for me to beat her almost every day on the ride – she's one of the most competitive people I know. In Cambodia, I had a racing bike and she was on a mountain bike. I always beat her and she wasn't happy about it at all. I think she gets her competitive streak from her brother, Genji, and from her dad. He was always making Genji and Turia compete with one another – racing across sand dunes and things like that.

I remember the last time I saw the old Turia. It was just before she moved to Kununurra. We decided to spend a day climbing The Castle, a mountain down on the South Coast. It's an eight-hour climb up and down the mountain. We took Turia's brother Toriki along with us.

She was leaving for the Kimberley the next day and I was supposed to be driving to Sydney. Even though we had spent the previous day together, I just had this weird feeling that I needed to see her again. I can't really explain it now. Looking back, it was probably nothing spookier than the fact that crazy things seemed to happen to people in our circle of friends and the community of Ulladulla. Out of the ordinary stuff. We had friends in the Bali bombings, for example; there were awful cases of friends dying of cancer, and car accidents that claimed young lives. Still, never in your wildest dreams do you think your best friend is going to end up in a fire. I remember dropping by Turia's place and her being surprised to see me. I gave her an extra-long hug and told her to take care of herself. That was the last time I saw the old Turia.

I had just arrived home from Thailand when I heard about the fire. I had taken on some volunteer work, looking after elephants, staying with a local family in the middle of nowhere. On my way back to Australia the night before the race I sent Turia a message on Facebook, telling her I was thinking of her, that I was proud of her and she was going to smash it.

I landed back in Sydney the next morning, went straight to my house in Enmore, turned off my phone and went to sleep. I woke up around 8 am the following day and checked my phone: I had something like fifty missed calls. I couldn't work out why everyone was so keen to speak to me – I had only been in Thailand for three weeks.

I walked out of my bedroom, still a bit bleary-eyed, and bumped into my flatmate, Dan, a fellow Ulladulla refugee in Sydney. I remember him telling me, 'Turia's been caught in a fire.' And in my sleepy haze, I don't think it quite registered. A fire? What was he talking about? I phoned Nicola. She was in Thredbo, snowboarding for the weekend. 'She's been in a fire running the marathon,' Nicola told me.

It scarcely seemed real. Details were so sketchy, no one seemed to know exactly what had happened or what the extent of her injuries were – if in fact she had been injured at all. Everyone seemed to be recycling the same three or four scant bits of information and adding a detail they thought they had heard from someone else. I became more and more panicked, although in some ways the not-knowing was a kind of relief. You couldn't freak out about news you didn't know. For as long as we didn't know anything for sure, we were able to believe that everything was going to be all right.

Nicola hopped on the next bus to Sydney and I started making plans to fly to Darwin. I didn't know what I was going to do when I got there, I didn't know if I was going to arrive to find she had sprained an ankle. And then we got word that it was serious – and that Turia was being medivaced to the burns unit at Concord Hospital.

*

Nicola got back from Thredbo the next day and we headed directly for the hospital. We didn't know it at the time, but Michael, Gary and Celestine were still en route from Darwin by the time we arrived at the hospital. Once the staff there had established we were Turia's close friends, the nurses let us straight into the intensive care unit. And there she was. Or rather, there on a hospital bed, with more tubes attached to her than I have ever seen attached to one single body, was a person they told us was Turia. She was barely recognisable.

Even talking about it now, remembering that moment upsets me. I try not to relive it for that reason. It's an image I will never forget. Nicola and I stood there in the hospital ward in a state of shock. We were speechless for the longest time. Neither of us knew what to say. Neither of us had any words. Eventually, we started talking to Turia: chatting with her as if she were conscious. 'It's going to be okay.' 'We love you.' 'Your family are coming.'

And then, one by one, the family arrived. Her mum hadn't seen her in Darwin, but was finally encouraged to go in and see her now. I think the feeling at that point was very much that no one could say with any certainty that she was going to survive, so family members were encouraged to spend as much time in her presence as they wanted. I'll never forget her mother's wail when she saw her little girl lying there in that state.

Yet, in spite of how awful she looked, in spite of the general air of uncertainty from the doctors and nurses, we were hopeful. 'She's tough, she'll pull through this,' we all told one another. We probably felt like if we said it enough times we might actually start to believe it.

We went back to Genji's apartment one evening and Michael pulled out his computer. He showed us an image of

Katie Piper, the young woman in England whose ex-boyfriend had thrown acid in her face. 'It will take time, but eventually she will look like this,' Michael told us all hopefully. 'If there's one person who can get through this it's Turia. I know how much willpower and determination she has.'

From the very beginning, Michael has never doubted her. He knew she would recover from the fire.

After that night at Genji's, we had constant contact with the family. I didn't see Turia again until after she came out of the coma and was transferred from intensive care to the burns unit; it must have been about three or four weeks after the fire.

Before I went to see her in the hospital, I met Celestine at Lavender Bay, near Genji's place. She took me for a walk and told me to prepare myself. She said that Turia had lost her fingers – and while that was shocking, there was always that enormous relief that she was alive.

Celestine told me that seeing Turia was going to be a shock – and I should try not to show it. 'She doesn't look like herself and never will,' she said. 'Be prepared.'

That morning I travelled with Michael and Celestine to the hospital. I walked into Turia's room – and passed out. I remember being outside in the waiting room and being told to put on a mask and gloves and a plastic suit to protect Turia from infection. Gary was there with us and when it came time we walked in together. It was really, really hot in the room. They keep the heating high, because burns victims typically lose their ability to regulate their body temperature. And there was a really overpowering smell. The heat and the smell and just the shock of seeing her was more than I could take. I had to sit down. And when I got up, I just passed out on the floor.

A nurse had to come in and tend to me. Obviously, I felt really embarrassed. I was supposed to be there to support Turia, I had been told by Celestine to prepare myself – and yet in the moment, I was completely overwhelmed. There she was. My best friend in the world. And I barely recognised her. She was purple and her hair had been shaved. Her face was drawn, like all the moisture had been sucked out of it. Her entire body was wrapped in tight white bandages. And the thing that struck me was how skinny and fragile she looked. She couldn't move or speak. She was conscious and clearly aware I was there. God only knows what she was thinking (of course, now she teases me heaps about this visit).

After me passing out, Celestine instituted a ban on friends visiting. I guess she figured, quite rightly, that it was unne-cessarily distressing for Turia to have her friends come to visit and then faint. I remember her gently scolding me: 'Darling,' she said. 'You need to be cool!'

Despite my performance on the first visit, I managed to convince Celestine to let me try to redeem myself a few weeks later with a second visit. I had been told that all Turia wanted whenever anyone visited was a cold can of Coke, so I took one along. For those first weeks out of the coma, she could barely speak. She would whisper, 'Coke!'

I was upset for a really long time. In the first month, it was the shock of it all having happened. Then came the gradual realisation of how it was going to change her life forever. And that was a sort of adjustment in itself. Getting used to the idea that Turia was going to live – but what sort of life would she have?

I'm not a super-emotional person, and certainly not prone to crying, but I did get very emotional about it. But because I'm more of a doer than a thinker, I did the only thing I could to help my friend. I swung into action and together with Nicola and another friend, Sarah, we set our minds to organising a masquerade ball to raise funds for Turia and what we knew were going to be a long series of ongoing medical expenses.

We settled on the idea of a masquerade ball because we knew when eventually she got out of hospital Turia would be in a mask, and we wanted her to feel comfortable. She loved the idea, so we set about getting up an online fundraising page, a ticket-selling mechanism, and started to spread the word. The response was almost immediate. Tickets sold out, local companies donated food and alcohol; we had more prizes donated for raffle prizes than we knew what to do with. The local community rallied like I have never seen it rally before. Everyone had been so affected by Turia's story. She was so well known and liked by all who knew her. One of Ulladulla's own had been damaged and the community was going to band together to try to make her better. It made me really proud of my little home town.

The ball was held at the Ulladulla Civic Centre in May, eight months after the fire. More than five hundred people packed the hall. Everyone had gone to great lengths to arrange their costumes and masks. Turia, who had only just been released from hospital and was not long home, came along on the night for about ten minutes. I think it was overwhelming for her to be there, with so many people. She was also really weak in those first months out of hospital. A walk to the bathroom was an effort in those days. I know she was touched, and I know she appreciated the show of community support, but it was just such a lot for her to process. It was the first time she had seen everyone publicly. Quite apart from anything else, it would have been an emotional, unsettling experience to be stared at by five hundred people.

That said, I think Ulladulla has been a really important factor in Turia's recovery. It's a small community and it has rallied behind her – closed in around her in a sense. The people down there feel very protective of her. It's a haven where she doesn't have to feel self-conscious each time she steps out the door.

Of course, Gary and Julie's place is another spot that was vital to her recovery. When she first arrived there from hospital, she was really weak. Occasionally I would drive her to the beach, just for a change of scene. She couldn't walk far, but the sight of the ocean and the sea air seemed to lift her spirits.

The recovery process was slow for that first year. The smallest things were celebrated as massive achievements – getting a spoon to her own mouth, being able to brush her own hair, finally being able to go to the bathroom by herself. These were all milestones. It made me appreciate how we all take the simplest things in life for granted. It's incredible to think about what your thumb actually does. And until you don't have a thumb anymore, you never stop to think how difficult life can be without one.

Removing the mask was a big step for her, too. Because I spent time with her at Gary and Julie's I had seen her with her mask off. She would only take it off for certain people, just to see their reaction. I remember making a point of only looking in her eyes – maintaining eye contact. It was the first glimpse, I suppose, of the extent of her burns. Her whole face had changed, and her neck too. But her eyes were still the same. They were the eyes I knew so well. Turia's eyes had always been the gateway to her soul – and that hasn't changed a bit.

I remember the weekend she took her mask off away from Gary and Julie's house. We went on a girls' weekend with Nicola and our other best friend, Shae. Turia wanted to thank us all for helping her recover. The weekend away was also to support Shae, who had just been diagnosed with cancer. So Turia took us all on a weekend down the coast to Tathra. It was the first time with me that she had ventured out and about without her mask.

We went to the local pub, drank way too much and had a real girls' weekend. Turia had bought Shae a muumuu – one of those oversized sack dresses for her to wear while she was having chemo. It was a tie-dyed job from one of those hippy shops. Completely hideous. We laughed a lot that weekend.

When I think about it, Turia's recovery was full of small steps like that weekend in Tathra – little developments or achievements that didn't seem much at the time, but all slowly worked to not only build her up physically, but also slowly prepare her to release herself back into the world.

If you have looked a certain way your whole life and then have it taken away – it requires a huge adjustment, and enormous inner strength. And I have no doubt it has made her stronger. People are always going to stare – first and foremost because she looks different, but then increasingly also because she has become quite well known. People stare just as much these days because she's a sort of celebrity – which I love hassling her about.

Something she has become really good at is putting it back on people. Not in a mean or confronting way, but if she catches someone staring, she will make a point of talking to them, of engaging them. 'How you going, mate?' she'll say. And it's usually enough to jolt them and make them speak to her. It must get tiring, just the same.

People are always coming up to her and wanting to hug her or tell her about an aunty they have who burned her arm on the stove. It's hard for her – because it's not like it's the only thing in the world she wants to talk to people about. But she is strong, and for the most part, she is tireless. Mind you, it does take its toll. There are days when she doesn't have the strength to face any of that and she will hide out at home.

As Turia and I have always loved to take on a challenge and raise money for a good cause, once she was strong enough I began to organise a charity challenge with her to raise funds for Interplast. Our first adventure was Turia's Great Wall of China Challenge. We organised a cocktail party, which raised $60,000. It took months to organise but we had some amazing prizes donated for the auction and raffle. After twelve months of fundraising events, our group of twenty-two women had managed to raise over $180,000 for Interplast and we tackled five days of trekking and a lot of stairs along the Great Wall of China.

Most of the women on the trip had never done anything like it before. People are inspired by Turia, and they want to be close to her. People sit around most of their lives not doing anything challenging or taking on anything that might be outside their comfort zone. Turia shows them what is possible.

She shows people that if you put your mind to it, anything is possible. And that's a really powerful message.

The trip itself was great. The Great Wall of China was everything we expected in terms of grandeur, but looking back, I wonder if it was the best choice of destination for Turia's first time leading a group like that overseas.

The Chinese have different ideas to us about what is appropriate in terms of outright staring at someone. I don't begin to know the cultural or social factors behind it – maybe they don't often see people who look different, maybe those people in China stay largely out of sight – but whatever it was, in the cities people stared at her wherever we went. It made the rest of us feel uncomfortable, so I hate to think how it must have made Turia feel.

Climbing the wall proved a lot harder than any of us expected, too. There are parts of it, away from the heavily trafficked tourist sections of the wall, where you have to clamber and climb and hoist yourself up. Turia was strong, at this point, but still working on her mobility and using her hands. There were parts of the wall we had to push or pull her over. That's the thing about Turia, though: it has taken her a while to accept there are things she cannot do easily and to recognise she needs to occasionally ask for help to do the simplest things – like unscrew a bottle top or do up a button. But she's got better and better at asking for that help.

About a year after the Great Wall, we organised another trip, this time on the Inca Trail in Peru. We had twenty-six women and two blokes.

It was the most breathtaking trek I have ever done. The Peruvian people are so humble and gentle and kind. It was a completely different experience for Turia than China had been. And walking the Inca Trail was a kind of medicine in itself. The scenery is just spectacular.

The thing that struck me about both of those fundraising trips was the sort of people Turia attracted. Some came along because they wanted to meet her and have an amazing experience while doing something good. Others were there for the adventure, pure and simple. But all of them came because of Turia: she's the drawcard.

And I have seen it at the talks she does around the country. People just want to be close to her, to be in the same room as her. They want to feel her energy and presence. She can walk into any room and command it. People listen to her now, which makes her a great motivational speaker.

After our China trip, I took a couple of months off work and went sailing around Tahiti with Turia and Michael. We sailed around the islands for about a month – just the three of us on the boat. Michael had taken sailing lessons before we left and he was more or less the captain.

There are some parts of Tahiti that are pristine paradise. We saw whales, went diving with lemon sharks and blacktip reef sharks. It was just amazing. It was healing time for Turia – something she and Michael had planned to do since her accident. We really didn't know how to sail very well. I seem to recall we spent a lot of time motoring from one place to the next, but when we did get the sails up we had a lot of fun.

It was nice to see where Turia came from, to see a little bit of her cultural heritage – being half-Tahitian is an important part of her life. It put so much about who she is into context for me. Turia would hate to admit it, because her mum can sometimes drive her crazy, but she's a lot like Celestine. They share a lot of similar characteristics. They have the same energy. Celestine can command a room upon walking into it. They are both driven and smart and quick-witted. Her mum is creative and Turia is analytical, but underneath the surface they both have the same energy and passion for life. And they are genuinely caring. It's that Tahitian warmth – it's so infectious. I love Celestine. She's the best. It's safe to say Turia wouldn't be the person she is today if it wasn't for her mum. How can you not feel happy and positive when you are with someone with so much positive energy?

Celestine especially is a very spiritual person, Turia not so much, but she's a proud Tahitian. And she's close to her family. Genji and Turia are close in age. When they would have parties when they were younger we all hung out together. Her younger brothers, though, were little kids when we were growing up. I remember them as babies, and now Toriki is studying engineering and Heimanu is studying and making music.

Both of them were kept away from Turia for a long time while she was in hospital. Genji would visit her all the time, but the younger boys stayed in Mollymook while their mum travelled back and forth to Sydney. They probably grew up more quickly than other kids their age. They were forced to, in a way. It's definitely had a ripple effect on the entire family, how can it not?

Then of course there's Michael. I'll never forget the night they got together. It was at a party thrown by one of Michael's friends. We girls had all gone to Shae's house earlier in the night, where Turia had got herself all dressed up and was saying, 'I am going to get with Michael Hoskin tonight.' She was only half-joking, as it turned out, because sure enough she did. She has always known what she wants.

She was living in Bondi at the time and he was in Maroubra. Pretty soon after that night, they became inseparable.

Why are they good as a couple? They balance each other out – she is crazy and he is calm. If she was with a hot-headed, impulsive person, it wouldn't have worked out. On a simple level, they love the same things. They are both really active and share similar interests, but they're otherwise completely different personality-wise.

Michael is a good man – pure and simple. He is quiet until he gets to know you. He tends to sit back and take everything in. He and I are similar in that regard. Turia is happy to walk in and own a room. Michael, not so much.

He changed, of course, after the fire. He didn't sleep much, lost a lot of weight, he was tired all the time. Your partner is on her death bed and you don't know if she's going to survive or not – it takes a toll. Yet there was never a doubt that he would stay with her. In the first couple of days after the fire, he went out and bought an engagement ring. It tells you everything you need to know about Michael. It's testament to how much he loves her.

Their love is a crucial part of why their story has resonated. His dedication has touched the hearts of so many Australians. At the end of the day, Michael is just an average Aussie bloke who was chucked into the most unusual circumstance and he has responded in a remarkable way.

I used to be one of those people who planned out every second of my life. Turia's accident taught me to be more flexible. If her experience has shown me anything, it is that you never know what's going to happen in life. Expect the unexpected; live life to the fullest.

15

THE MEDIA

Not long after the fire, I was presented with a choice: either I could make my recovery quietly, away from the spotlight, without public intrusion, or I could invite the glare of the news media into my life to document my story.

It was a decision I wrestled with. When you are laid up in hospital recovering from life-altering injuries; when you have no clear idea if you will make a full recovery (much less, how), it's a big thing to agree to let so many others come along for the ride.

In the days and weeks after the fire, Michael and the family were bombarded with media requests. In those first crucial weeks, when it wasn't even clear if I would live, the requests were routinely ignored. There was nothing to be gained at that point by laying bare my suffering – or the suffering of those around me, for that matter. But as things started to improve, and as the doctors' prognosis gradually started to shift from hopeless to hopeful, I started to take seriously the multiple media requests that continued to come in.

When finally I felt strong enough to meet one of the journalists who had been in contact, I had one very clear motive in mind: I wanted my story to be an inspirational one. Even back at the beginning, I was never interested in settling scores with the race organisers or wallowing in bitterness. Much more important to me was the chance to inspire people with my recovery.

Looking back, I wonder too if on some level I made the call knowing that having the glare of the national media trained on me would be the incentive I might occasionally need to push that little bit harder, walk that little bit further, do that extra hour of rehab, no matter how painful it might be. To my thinking, when people say, 'I'm going to get fit and then sign up for that marathon,' they've got it backwards. Signing up first gives you the incentive to train.

Ali Smith, a producer on *60 Minutes*, had been on Michael's and Mum's case from pretty much the day after the fire. And I don't say that in a critical, ambulance-chaser, heartless-journalist way. She had sent letters and kept up a respectful correspondence with Michael in the couple of months I lay in hospital. Together, Michael and I decided to meet with Ali – and then take it from there.

I was wary at first. When you've never before been exposed to journalists or the media, you tend to go into any encounter with them with pretty low expectations. But almost immediately upon meeting Ali, I felt comfortable with her. She had an easy manner, had spent time working in the Kimberley and seemed genuine in her understanding that I was only interested in participating in a story that was uplifting. I didn't want to be portrayed as a victim.

In the months that followed, Ali and I developed a rapport (which we enjoy to this day). In time, I got to meet the reporter

Michael Usher, whose compassion and determination to tell my story with integrity has never wavered. I know the media gets a bad rap – and certainly there have been more than a few instances where my run-ins with journos have been less than stellar – but for the most part I feel lucky to have met the people I have.

I wasn't the only one caught in that bushfire. I was just the only one who opted to make my experience public. I could never have imagined, during that first visit with Ali, how it would all snowball.

Ali Smith

I first met the incredible Turia Pitt in December 2011, just three months after the fire. At the time, Turia looked so close to death it was hard to comprehend that the young woman lying helplessly in a hospital bed was actually still alive. It shows Turia's strength and faith in her own recovery that she trusted *60 Minutes* to film her from such an early stage. She had pretty much been burned to the bone, so she was thin and frail, her skin looked painfully raw and she had no hair. However, she had these bright, big eyes that just stared at you with such optimism and somehow let you know that there was a very determined person fighting inside that badly damaged body. I knew from the moment I met her that she wasn't giving up in a hurry and I really wanted to be involved in telling her recovery story. I thought she was awesome.

Over the past four years, Turia and Michael have featured in seven *60 Minutes* stories. And every time, without fail, the response has been overwhelming. People can't get enough of them. They are a down-to-earth couple from the South Coast who, despite being dealt the toughest of hands, just keep striving for a better life together. I'm proud that their story has had such an inspiring impact on viewers. I once had a school teacher tell me that Turia's *60 Minutes* stories are shown in health classes to help teenagers overcome body-image problems and demonstrate how you should treat your partner in a relationship. I don't know if Turia and Michael could have ever imagined that they'd become such great role models when they first decided to share their story. It's pretty cool.

I'd been working as a junior producer at *60 Minutes* for six months when, in September 2011, a bushfire ripped through an ultramarathon being staged in the Kimberley. It made news headlines pretty quickly – 'Wildfire Traps Runners', 'Runners Race into Flames to Flee Fire'. It was a dramatic story – an Australian outback rescue, local heroes who went beyond the call of duty, courageous survivors including, as the media reported it, a model (Turia's modelling photos were always used in the articles, even though at the time she was working as an engineer) who was burned beyond belief. It was also, of course, an enduring love story.

60 Minutes first reported on the Kimberley ultramarathon about two weeks after the event. Michael Usher was the reporter, Stephen Rice was the producer and I was assigned to assist Stephen. I was particularly keen to work on the story because before starting at *60 Minutes*, I'd spent a short period working for ABC Kimberley and had heard from locals about the amazing chopper rescue to save Turia Pitt and Kate Sanderson. We'd heard Turia's family were happy with the story but no one from Turia's or Kate's family was interviewed for it. At this stage, very little was known publicly about the girls' injuries except that they were both in a critical condition.

A short time after the story aired, I sent Turia a letter via a mutual contact and asked if at some point down the track she would please consider meeting with me to discuss the idea of doing a story. I knew that suffering 65 per cent burns to her body was more than serious and doing media wouldn't have been at the top of her priority list. I didn't really expect to ever hear back but it was worth a try. An advantage of working for a program like *60 Minutes* is that we don't have daily deadlines – you can wait years to tell a good story.

I didn't hear anything for weeks, then one day I got a call from Turia's dad. In late November 2011, I had a brief chat with Michael Hoskin and Turia over the phone. Turia was so softly spoken in comparison to the loud, outgoing girl I'm now used to hearing on the other end of the phone. She said to me, 'I might want to do this because I want to show people that you can overcome hurdles.' I thought that sounded great and said, 'Let's meet!'

The lovely Michael Hoskin met me out the front of Concord Hospital in Sydney, a depressing old building that not surprisingly smells terrible. I felt sad that such a young couple were spending their days here. As Michael and I caught the lift up to the burns unit, he started to explain to me the extent of Turia's injuries. Until that lift ride, I had no idea that Turia's face had been so badly burned. Michael did a great job to prepare me before the meeting. He described where Turia had been burned, that they'd used skin from overseas to save her, she'd lost and could lose more fingers, and would need to wear a mask for two years but she wasn't wearing it today. It was a lot to take in. As we walked onto the ward, I started to get butterflies in my stomach. The last thing I wanted was to react in a way that was inappropriate or say something that might upset

Turia. I noticed that Michael seemed to finish every sentence with a positive statement. For example, 'She'll have to wear the mask but then her skin will get better over time.' As we walked out the lift door, I told myself to follow his lead – stay positive, and act calm. You're not the one with burns, hold it together! I think I did okay.

We had to put on plastic gloves and aprons before going into Turia's room due to the risk of infection. As I was putting the gloves on, I caught a glimpse of Turia's face through a window. I'd never seen a burns patient in such a bad way but her eyes stood out to me immediately. They just sparkled and looked so vibrant. In the early days, Turia's eyes were the main way I could tell what she was thinking. I stared at her eyes for the whole meeting except when I glanced up at the pictures she had stuck on her hospital-room wall. There were photos of her and her friends on adventures in the Kimberley. I immediately recognised a lot of the places she'd been to and decided that fishing and the Broome races were much better topics of conversation than the horrific fire that nearly killed her.

I think we got along well, I liked her sense of humour. She joked about her hair growing back and looking more like an 80s mullet. On a personal level, the fact that we were a similar age and had both lived cruisey, Kimberley lifestyles probably made Turia and Michael's story strike even more of a chord with me, because I genuinely felt that what was happening to them could have so easily happened to me or any of my Kimberley mates. I was in awe of Michael's maturity and how he supported his girlfriend. After the meeting he walked me back to the lift and said, 'If she decides to do the story you'll have crazy fun with her, she's mad.' He was right.

*

Over the summer holidays I visited Turia on several occasions while she decided if she wanted to do the story. I never left the hospital feeling depressed. It was uplifting to watch 'The Three Amigos' (Turia, Michael and her mum) in action, they were so hopeful about everything. Turia kept stressing to me that she didn't want the story to be sad or just an angry piece of reporting about the race organisers. She wanted to inspire people with her recovery. I told her she'd need to trust us to film the good and the bad parts of her journey so people could see the hurdles she was overcoming.

Initially we encouraged Turia and Michael to film themselves with a handi-cam; this way Turia could get used to the camera in her own time and, visually, *60 Minutes* wouldn't miss out on any critical stages if she proceeded with the story. There's a beautiful shot we always use of Turia and Michael holding hands in the hospital corridor. Michael has this proud, beaming smile and Turia is wearing a singlet that says 'Believe You Can Do It'. This moment was captured by their family on the handi-cam – I just love it.

Michael Usher also came to meet Turia in hospital. On this occasion she had just had surgery and still had a tracheotomy tube in her windpipe. We didn't want to stay long but she seemed to like talking to us; I think it was a distraction from the hospital routines and painful dressing changes. Michael Hoskin stood there next to her bed, holding her tracheotomy tube so she could speak to us. I think Turia and Michael Usher had a great old chat but to be honest I spent most of the time just captivated by Michael Hoskin's devotion. What a bloke. Michael and I left the hospital and agreed that, above all, this was a love story.

A few weeks later, Turia said she was happy to do a story with *60 Minutes*. I'm not sure how many other media requests she'd had, but I was stoked she had picked us. It's a huge call to let cameras into your life when you're still recovering and have physical injuries, but I think Turia's personality meant she was always going to tell her story. If there's a chance to make a positive difference, she'll take it. The senior producer, Stephen Rice, kindly let me take on the role as the lead producer. It was the first time I'd been given this opportunity and I was thrilled that it was for Turia.

We thought Turia would be in hospital for months, but sure enough her recovery rocketed ahead at full speed. In early 2012, she phoned to tell me she was moving to rehab. We needed to get cracking with the filming!

I reckon it's fair to say that rehab was one of the more depressing stages of Turia's recovery. I think that as time passed the adrenaline and thrill of surviving the fire was overcome by the reality that her and Michael's life had changed forever. She couldn't bend her elbows and needed help with pretty much everything. In between filming, she would often ask if I could scratch her back and ears – as her burns healed they became itchy but she couldn't reach them; it must have been so frustrating.

Michael was very honest and humble from the beginning. I've always called him 'the reluctant star'. On one rehab visit, I remember him saying to me that he'd been thinking, and had decided it was best 'if just Turia was in the story'. Eek, I thought – this from the gorgeous, caring man who was by her side day and night. I felt that not including Michael was not just a misrepresentation of his commitment to Turia's recovery but also problematic, in that how do you tell a love story if your Romeo doesn't want to be in it? As someone who works behind the camera, I understand being on TV isn't for everyone, but we wanted him included.

Over time Michael got more comfortable with us. Our crews are so experienced and have such a calming influence on people. I think they helped to make Michael feel at ease. One of *60 Minutes*' sound recordists still catches up with him to go fishing. Everything viewers see on the TV is real – his dedication, his love for her.

I feel that one of the reasons our viewers connected with Turia and Michael's story is because they were so open and honest in the interviews with Michael Usher about their personal struggles, how the fire had changed them and also about their relationship. They shared their highs and lows.

> **Michael:** We're not putting on a fake face here to say it's all smiles and happy days. There is probably one dark day in every week.
>
> **Turia:** In reality I looked like shit. Like, I looked really bad ... I saw my reflection and just lost it ... And I also felt silly for caring so much because I never considered myself to be vain.
>
> **Michael:** I thought, if she can walk in agony, and do all the physio that they're asking her, I can be there all the time. That's easy for me.

I think Turia lasted barely a fortnight in rehab before she decided to head home to Mollymook, so off *60 Minutes* went to Mollymook too for some more filming. We spent a lot of time in that friendly town, our cameras shadowing Turia pretty much everywhere she went.

In the early days, Turia didn't socialise a lot. She really only left home for rehab and medical appointments, so we did most of the filming at her mum's apartment and Michael's parents' place. They were so welcoming, and I enjoyed getting to know them. Some filming days were harder than others. Turia would get tired pretty quickly and sometimes I did worry if she was going to keep going with the story and if it was in her best interest, but then she'd ring and ask what we were doing next. She told me the filming helped her push herself and set goals.

Her surgeon, Professor Haertsch, was a great support, both to Turia and to me as I worked with her. As Turia got better, I learned pretty quickly that it was best to deal with her directly about filming plans. She wanted to be involved, she's very organised and loves a list. Turia may have lost some physical abilities but her brain works just fine and she likes to use it.

I recognised from the outset that she had always been a very independent woman, which I admired. Turia didn't want to be treated like she had any type of handicap – who would? Even though she looked fragile, I had to learn to ignore her scars because I knew she appreciated me being straight with her about what shots I thought we needed. I don't think we would have got along if I'd treated her like a victim.

She was great to work with, and we had a lot of fun planning. Early on we'd sit in her mum's living room under piles of blankets (because she was always cold) discussing things to film while munching on her mum's homemade slice. It wasn't the most professional set-up but it worked for Turia and

Wearing traditional Tahitian clothing that Mamie (my Tahitian grandma) made for me

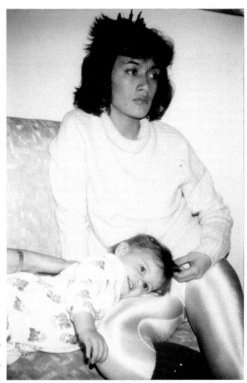

Mum. Wasn't she a stunner? And that little white grub on her lap is me.

Heimanu, Genji and me on one of Dad's infamous camping trips. Camping in our family was not a relaxing pastime – it was more like a boot camp. As soon as we arrived at the campsite, we'd be issued with our evening tasks: Genji had to put up the tents with Dad; I had to pump up all the air beds; and Heimanu, being the youngest, had to collect kindling for the fire. The only one who got out of his chores was Toriki, because he was six months old.

Mamie, me, Virginie (my Mum's sister), Mum and Dad. The two kids are Heimanu and Toriki. Mum would visit Tahiti every two years, and sometimes her family would come and visit her. Look at Dad's face! I think he found the invasion of the Tahitians for a few months just a little stressful.

Michael and me on Lake Argyle after a swim

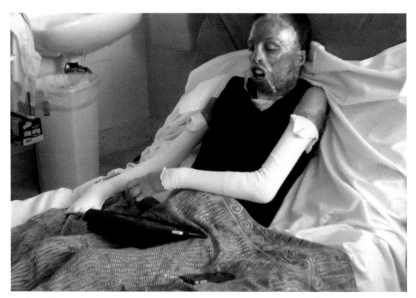

Early early days of my recovery. I'm rocking a skinhead, and Mum thought it would be a good idea to 'decorate' me with a sarong for the photo. I've got my mouth splint in, which I absolutely detested. I'm reading to distract me and keep me happy.

One of my heroes! Professor Haertsch. Nothing is ever a problem for this bloke.

Prof Maitz. Another one of my heroes. This man realised I loved to be challenged.

Is it a bird, is it a plane, is it Superman? Nope, it's just Turia. Even though I had major wardrobe restrictions, I still liked to make an effort with what I was wearing.

On holidays with Michael. In retrospect, it was probably way too early for me to go anywhere, let alone to Lord Howe Island! But it was great to have something to look forward to.

My beautiful, generous and kind second set of parents. I love you, Julie and Gary!

Briggs and me up to mischief. Again.

In Antarctica doing an ultramarathon or at the North Pole doing an ultramarathon? Hully's done both – kinda hard to keep up with all his escapades!

How hardcore is this woman! Kate doing a casual 250-kilometre ultramarathon in the Sahara Desert. Oh, and see that woman next to her? That's Bronwyn Hull, Michael Hull's wife.

Anthony Robbins and me. A photo definitely taken after the firewalk – look how relaxed I am!

Princess Kate and me having a chinwag.

I pull some hectic facials when I'm speaking.

Getting ready for another run. I've had to get used to doing a lot of things with my three fingers. At first when I started trying to do my shoelaces, I'd get really frustrated. Now I just do them without even thinking about it. Practice makes perfect, and I try to remember this whenever I'm struggling with something.

No wind machine required here!

Michael is in the zone.

I love diving with no gear – no weights, no fins, no sled.

My first fundraising adventure for Interplast. I was stoked because ten girls from Ulladulla (including my best mates, sister-in-law and personal trainer) did this with me. Ulladulla has always taken care of me. Stoked to be from this little town!

INTERPLAST

We've reached Machu Picchu.

DAVE ZWOLENSKI

My ghostie and me. Bryce was so dedicated to this book that he decided to come all the way to Kokoda to get 'up close and personal'. That's him there, squatting in the mud of the Kokoda track.

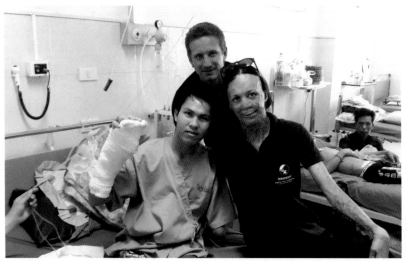

Meeting Keo in Laos. He had an electrical accident and lost one of his hands, and his other hand is dead. It's people like Keo who remind me how important Interplast is. He is just one of the reasons I work with the charity.

Ironman training. I'd take my bike with me whenever I did a speech or went away for work. This was in Kalgoorlie.

GRACE MCBRIDE

NATHAN EDWARDS/NEWSPIX

At the start of my first Ironman, in Port Macquarie. At this stage I was shitting myself nervous, but I also just wanted to get it over with.

That feeling! No amount of money can buy that feeling of crossing an Ironman finish line and hearing the words, 'Turia Pitt: you are an Ironman!' All the sacrifice and hard work culminated in this moment.

DELLY CARR

Middle of the bike leg during Kona Ironman. It's hot hot hot, and at this point I'm seriously doubting my ability to get across the finish line.

Another feeling of absolute joy and elation! This race was nothing like Port Mac. Not sure if anything could've prepared me for the tough conditions in Kona. I was really proud of myself, though, because all day I kept fighting that urge to quit.

A special hug from coach Bruce, the man who got me to the Ironman finish lines.

Check out that bling! The night Michael proposed.

In the States, on the DonateLife float, rocking the lei like I was born to do.

Excited to spend the rest of
my life with Michael.

My little boy,
Hakavai Hoskin.

that's what mattered. One day we locked in a date to film her running 50 metres on the beach. It seems such a short distance now she's completed an Ironman, but at the time it was a huge goal and a huge achievement. It's one of the most iconic shots from her first *60 Minutes* story. We all cheered when she did it and then laughed when cameraman Greg Barbera asked her to do it one more time so he could get another angle. Turia was exhausted but she did it again – she loves a challenge and is living proof that you get back what you put in.

About a week before Turia's first *60 Minutes* story went to air in May 2012, she travelled to Perth for the parliamentary inquiry into the bushfire. Up until this point, no pictures of her had been in the media since the fire. The day after the inquiry, Turia, Michael and I read the newspapers on our way to the airport. She did a great job of giving evidence but she was not happy with the articles. She didn't like being described as 'frail', and she took exception to one report, which said she'd arrived in a disabled taxi – this was true, but Turia sighed, 'It's not because I need a disabled taxi, it's because that's what was available.'

I tried to stress to her that, like me, the journalists were just doing their job and reporting what they saw, and that they hadn't spent as much time with her as *60 Minutes* had so they didn't know how well her recovery was going. I tried to lift her spirits by telling her that everyone would see her *60 Minutes* story on Sunday night and be inspired by how quickly she'd gone from her hospital bed to running on the beach. She said, 'I hope so.' Hell, I hoped so too! I really wanted Australia to love Turia and Michael.

I was nervous, but of course the response to their first story was amazing. Australia loved them. Peter Harvey's mailbag was full to the brim with fan mail:

'Turia, you are an inspiration to us all. You are a triumph to the human spirit against all the odds.'

'Well done to The Three Amigos.'

'Wow. Turia Pitt, absolute champion. Makes us all look like a mob of bloody whingers! You are a true winner!'

'Michael, you are one in a million. Most blokes would have run a mile but you have stuck through the thick and thin.'

'My heart breaks for Turia and what she has been through. She is an absolute legend, what a big heart!'

'You deserve the very best out of life, love to you and Michael, may your life together be truly happy and the past left behind.'

Our viewers were so generous and full of admiration. Children sent Turia drawings, and viewers wrote about how they'd been inspired to do everything from join a gym to quit smoking. There were parcels of health foods and creams for her skin.

Most importantly Turia, Michael and their families were happy with the story. Michael said to me that not long afterwards they'd gone on a trip to Dubbo Zoo and people didn't stare or ask questions about Turia's mask because they knew what had happened to her from our *60 Minutes* piece. In true Turia fashion, after the program aired she said to me, 'So, mate, what should we plan for the next one?' She's always on the move.

There was always going to be a next one. A defining moment in Turia's second *60 Minutes* story came when she took the mask off. It was her trip to a clinic in France that prepared her to do this. For two years, she had worn the mask to help heal her scars but she was also self-conscious of being seen in public without it. I'd only ever seen her without it in hospital or the privacy of home. The psychological impact the France trip had on Turia was profound. As I sat and listened to Michael Usher interview her, I was gobsmacked by how philosophical Turia had become. She was always honest in interviews but had never seemed to deeply reflect on things. I got goosebumps when she told Michael, 'There's a little piece inside of me which the fire didn't get to ... It may have taken away my body, but there's still a piece inside of me which is still that independent woman, who's very determined ... I'm actually still Turia. I may look different but I'm still me.'

Turia has a pretty clear-cut way of looking at life. I feel that once she has overcome something there's no looking back and it's almost as if it was never an issue. I believe this way of thinking has helped with her survival. An example came when she, Michael and I were heading to an airport in France, and Turia was starving. Eating with her mask on was very difficult, and as we were parking the car, she said, 'I think I'm going to just take my mask off and just eat lunch at the airport.' Michael responded casually, 'Do it.' I thought it was always best never to make a big deal about anything with Turia and just let things unfold. This was the first time I'd sat in a public space with her when she wasn't wearing her mask and I was super-proud. We didn't talk about it, we didn't make a big deal about it, nobody stared: it just happened. After all this time it didn't even seem like a huge moment of empowerment. She was hungry and the tight mask was bloody annoying. I asked her about this moment recently and she agreed – that in France she got to the point where she felt that any downside of being seen without the mask didn't outweigh the inconvenience of wearing it. When *60 Minutes* put the 'mask off' story to air, we did the 'reveal' right at the start of the story. We didn't want to have a big build-up: her recovery was remarkable enough to hold the audience's attention and we wanted to use the vision that we had of her 'mask-free' in hospital and physio to show how hard she'd worked and how far she'd come.

The reaction after this story was even bigger than the first. Social media went crazy for Turia and Michael. I had so many emails from different media outlets around the world asking if they could be put in touch with Turia. Most of the subject lines in my inbox read 'Turia Pitt'.

Of course, after this story a huge moment came when she landed the front cover of the *Australian Women's Weekly*. I remember seeing it on the supermarket shelf and thinking, *Wow – that's the same girl who never wanted to leave the house without her mask on.* I was so proud. Turia is a self-confessed tomboy, but what chick doesn't like having their hair and make-up done? I went to the photo shoot for that cover and she worked the wind machine like she was Beyoncé. Turia really does show that confidence is beauty. I was out with her and a friend one evening for drinks after she first stopped wearing the mask. A group of guys started chatting to us but Turia had her back to them. I'm a bit protective and was concerned that when she turned around they might react to her scars. Silly me, they didn't, the crowd thought she was great. I never think twice about it anymore.

Another thing about Turia's strong mindset and pragmatic brain is that she doesn't dwell on things. Sometimes it's been hard for me to read her emotion because she is so tough. She has only cried twice on *60 Minutes* and it was never about her own heartbreaking situation. She cried happy tears in Laos when the Interplast doctors helped a farmer who had been burned, and then again at a *60 Minutes* forum as she listened to the stories of families who had lost their children.

Turia never looks back, she's always going forward. She has a special bond with the other surviving runners and *60 Minutes* has enjoyed filming with them too. In 2014 they all went back to the Kimberley to take part in the Lake Argyle swim. The other runners were returning to the fire site. Understandably, everybody copes differently, and Turia had zero interest in going back to the gorge where she had been caught by the bushfire.

Reflecting on her decision, it's typical of Turia to return to the Kimberley to do something positive, like an adventure swim, but to avoid the fire site. When I told her that Michael Usher would probably ask her in the next interview to explain her emotions about not wanting to go back, she responded, 'Yeah, no worries, I'm sweet with interviews.' She then changed the topic of conversation to trying to set me up with one of her friends. This was classic Turia. She doesn't sweat the small stuff.

Months after the *60 Minutes* stories and the *Women's Weekly* cover, I was still receiving requests from people who wanted to contact Turia. She was the 'it' girl of the moment, and everyone wanted a piece of her. I didn't want to rain on her parade but some of the requests were a bit odd. As her friend, and the producer of the stories that had helped boost her profile, I did feel an obligation to warn her just how fickle the celebrity world can be, to tell her that it doesn't last forever and remind her the most important things in her life were Michael and her support crew in Mollymook.

It might sound clichéd but I truly believe that Turia was saved by the love and support she received from Michael, Michael's family and her own family. *60 Minutes* spent a lot of time with them over the years and it was remarkable to see them all rally behind her and build her up every day. I said to her, 'Not everybody has those kind of people in their life.' She looked at me and said, 'I know that, mate, that's why I like being down here.' I do feel a bit silly now about my little speech because years later, she's still got 'it' and people still want to get in contact with Turia Pitt. And of course, I know she knows what's most important in life.

I still smile when I see her popping up on different TV shows and in magazines. She has come such a long way and developed such a positive public profile. There was a point when people started to interrupt us during filming because they wanted a selfie with her. When we travelled to Laos, the *60 Minutes* team was invited to the Australian embassy because Turia was giving a speech. She has sell-out crowds for her speeches and I'll often send her an 'OMG!!!' text when I discover she's won another award or got to meet the royals or Brad and Angelina. It's crazy, but she deserves every good thing that comes her way. What I am most impressed with is how Turia and Michael have used their profile to help others and do charity work. They're very generous.

I'm not sure I will ever produce another story quite like Turia and Michael's. *60 Minutes* followed them for such a long time and through so much – from hospital, to France, to Laos and back to the Kimberley. I'd be lying if I said it wasn't challenging at times – it's impossible not to take a story like hers home – but it was a great privilege that they let us into their lives and trusted us to tell their story when they were at their most vulnerable.

I pursued a journalism career because I believe good storytelling has the power to make a difference. I hope the *60 Minutes* stories made a difference to Turia and Michael's life. I definitely know it changed the lives of lots of our viewers, and mine, for the better. I learned there's always a positive. Sometimes you need to fight tooth and nail to find it, but it will always be there. Never give up.

16

TESTING MY LIMITS

It's 3 am. I'm on a bush track somewhere between the Hawkes-bury River and Manly, in Sydney. I'm flat on my face, having just tripped over a tree root, and am swearing more loudly and more obscenely than I have for at least six months.

'Bloody stupid shit of a tree root!'

I'm not happy.

We're about nineteen hours into the Oxfam trail walk – a 100-kilometre fundraiser in which teams walk all day and through the night on an unlit, barely maintained bush track. Whoever came up with the idea is clearly a sadist. There's nothing good about it at all. I've done some extreme sporting events in my time – and on paper a 100-kilometre walk doesn't seem all that challenging – but as I pull myself back to my feet, wipe the mud from my hands, arms and clothes and adjust my head-torch, I start to silently curse the day I ever agreed to do this.

My head is down, my eyes trying to make out in the pitch black exactly which part of the uneven terrain in front of me I will place my foot next. Images of my bed flash in my mind – my beautiful, big, soft, king-size bed at home in Mollymook – and I want to cry.

My feet are in agony. At the last checkpoint, Michael removed my shoes and spent a meticulous fifteen minutes popping all of the blisters. Now I can feel liquid from the open wounds seeping into my socks – making my every step feel wet and uncomfortable. It's got to the point where I can feel blisters form as I walk, then burst under the constant rubbing and pressure – forcing me to walk through ten minutes of agony before the searing pain subsides and the process starts all over again on another part of my foot.

And then we come to steep rock face. The only way is to go over it. The rest of my team scramble up on all fours as I stand at the base, holding back tears. I'm done. As if the walk hasn't been hard enough, here now is the ultimate indignity: a rock face I cannot possibly get up because I DON'T HAVE THE FUCKING FINGERS FOR IT!

I start to cry and, despite the flurry of physical activity around me, I suddenly feel alone and vulnerable.

'Turia!' I hear a voice from above. 'Turia, up here!'

I look up and through my tears, I see a hand. And it looks not dissimilar to my own. Mottled, scarred, the tell-tale signs of a burns injury.

'Turia, give me your hand.'

It's my friend Kate. She's lying on her stomach, her arm outstretched towards me.

'Come on. Give me your hand.'

Seven hours later, I stumble across the finish line in Manly – delirious with pain and exhaustion. The walk has taken twenty-nine hours, five pairs of socks and every ounce of fortitude I have. I collapse into Michael's arms and let him carry me to the car. He takes me back to our hotel, lays me on the bed and leaves me to sleep – in the same clothes I have walked in, with my shoes still on – for the next fourteen hours.

About two years after the fire, when I was starting to regain my fitness and my public profile was beginning to take off (thanks largely to my *60 Minutes* stories and a subsequent flurry of media interest), the trickle of requests I had received up to that point from charities asking me to help them out started to become more of a flow.

One of the first requests came from Variety – an organisation that does great stuff for under-privileged kids all over the country. They were staging a fundraising bike ride from Sydney to Uluru – a distance of 3000 kilometres – and invited me to take part, as one of several 'celebrity' bike riders. At the time, it sounded like a good idea. It was the first major sporting event I had signed up for post-fire, and I didn't feel ready for it at all. But I know that no one ever feels ready, and sometimes you just need to take a leap of faith. It was a 'softer' sporting event as well, in that a bus followed the group, and I knew that if I ever got tired or sore, I could get on the bus. I had never ridden a road bike before the fire, but thought this was a great 'stretch' goal, right in the sweet spot of the sort of extreme sporting challenges I had always loved to do. Two years' worth of physio and weights and cardio training had left me feeling strong and ready to get back among it.

So I donned my Lycra and helmet and joined the thirty other racers at the start line one overcast morning on the outskirts of Sydney. For the next three weeks, I cycled an average of

100 kilometres a day, through outback New South Wales, across the top of South Australia. Up hills, down dales, along long, lonely, featureless stretches of highway through long, boring patches of nothing. Michael rode alongside me the whole way. Not exactly a romantic getaway, but special in its own way.

I was saddle sore as I had never been before. Each night, we would pull into a small town and invade a motel where I would collapse and wonder how I was going to muster the energy to wake up the next day and do it all over again.

This, I discovered, was a whole new discipline. Multi-day events that require you to back up and repeat the following day whatever amazing physical feat you had achieved the previous day are hard. One-day events require you to put in one massive effort – after which you can curl up in the foetal position and take as long as you need to recover. But once you get into the realm of a physical challenge that interrupts your sleeping and eating patterns, you are in a whole other world of pain. I soon realised that I wasn't at the fitness level required to ride 250 kilometres day after day, so I decided to ride fifty a day instead.

Looking back, it was easily as remarkable an achievement as any I have ever undertaken. Only two-and-a-half years previously, I had been lying in a coma in hospital. My body, though well on the road to returning to full strength, was still fragile. You know how you sometimes look back on things you've done and wonder what you were thinking and how you ever managed to do it? This was one of those.

At the end of each day, I was sore and exhausted – but exhilarated. And there were plenty of moments when I wanted to give up. But whenever I did, I only had to summon the memory of that doctor back in my early days of rehab telling me to manage my expectations and come to terms with the fact I might never run again, and the fire in my belly would be reignited. I had resolved back then that I would complete an Ironman. This bike ride was just the start. A taster.

Barely three weeks after the ride, I found myself on a plane to Darwin. The annual Lake Argyle relay challenge was taking place and we had formed a team and entered. Me, Kate, Hully, Hal Benson: four mates whose friendship had been forged in the most unusual of circumstances. The Lake Argyle swim takes place each year on the large, man-made lake adjacent to the Argyle diamond mine, where I had worked when Michael and I lived in Kununurra. It's a 20-kilometre swim completed by teams swimming in a relay. Our team was a rag-tag bunch of fire survivors. We were there to finish more than we were there to win.

I can't speak for the others, but the thought of returning to the Kimberley for the first time since the fire filled me with no small amount of anxiety. I'm generally not the sort of person who spends too much time overthinking stuff. Life, for the most part, is just a series of one day after the other. The mind is an instrument you can train to deal with pretty much anything. Melodrama is not my thing. And yet, as the plane banked and the red earth appeared below us, I'd be lying if I said I didn't feel a small knot in my stomach. Senses, I realised, can be powerful invokers of dormant feelings. In the same way a whiff of a certain aftershave or the smell of a certain meal can bring back memories, here I suddenly was, surrounded by red earth and those unmistakeable sights, sounds and smells of sun-baked northern Australian scenery, and that day started to come flooding back. I remember looking at Michael and saying I wasn't sure this was such a good idea. He just pulled me into him, gave me a squeeze and said, 'You'll be right, darl.'

Because it was the first time any of us had returned to the Kimberley since the fire, and because I had allowed myself to be talked into another *60 Minutes* story, we were ghosted on our trip by a camera crew.

We did the swim, and though we came last, it didn't matter. We'd all had a laugh together, and we all knew how significant it was for each of us. No words were exchanged on the subject, because none had to be.

Afterwards, *60 Minutes* invited us all to take a helicopter ride back to the gorge – back to the scene of the fire. I knew it was coming. It had been mentioned in phone calls and conversations I'd had with the producers prior to the trip, and I had always remained non-committal on the subject. I had done enough media at that point to know it was the pivotal scene of the story they were shooting. The burns victim returns for the first time to the scene of the bushfire. But I was determined not to do anything I thought was going to make me uncomfortable.

I remember looking at Michael and saying, 'I'll go if you want to go.'

On the plane from Sydney, I had thought about how hard the past two years had been for Michael. How his entire life had been put on hold by this freak fire in a gorge in the outback. How his entire existence for two years had been defined by this place. Maybe I owed it to him to visit it.

Michael looked at me as if I were crazy. 'I don't want to go,' he said. 'Why would I want to go there? We've worked so hard and come so far. Why go back?'

And with that, my mind was settled. I felt a huge weight lift from my shoulders. He was right. Nothing was going to be served by going back there. I had spent two years rebuilding the life that had almost been snatched away completely by that gorge: why would I want to be there again? People talk about closure – and the importance of facing your demons. But going back to that place was only going to bring to the surface a whole lot of negative emotions I had worked hard to process and eliminate.

Still, the others took up the offer of a chopper flight. Hully, Hal and Kate hopped aboard the helicopter and apparently had a wild old time, joking and laughing their way through the entire enterprise; I'm not sure they gave the 60 Minutes crew the poignant, tear-jerking footage they were hoping for.

Later that day, we came together for a barbecue. The idea was for all the locals who had either been involved in the race or in our rescue to gather for us to talk to them and offer up the thanks we'd never had a chance to properly express. I was psyched about meeting up with Paul Cripps – the helicopter pilot who'd risked life and limb to rescue Kate and me from the side of the gorge. And in person he was just as kind and humble as I had expected. The 60 Minutes cameras were there to capture the reunion, which made things slightly more awkward than they might otherwise have been. With the cameras rolling, I felt a bit restrained: not wanting to make a public spectacle of myself, self-conscious enough in the first place to be seeing all of these people again (or meeting some of them for the first time) and hyper-aware of how the presence of the TV cameras was making everyone feel. It was almost as if the more acutely aware I became of the reaction the TV cameras wanted, the more determined I was not to give it.

Even so, the reunion was a lump-in-the-throat moment. When Paul, so shy, so unassuming, so quiet, shuffled over and said hello, at first we made small talk. But it was never going to be about the words. He came in for a hug and it was all I could do not to break down. Two-and-a-half years of rehabilitation seemed to melt away, and suddenly I was back in that chopper, drifting in and out of consciousness, my life in the hands of this quiet, stoic man.

The ambulance officer, Bonny, who had been first on the scene after the fire and who – despite us having been friends and volunteer ambos together – had not recognised me as she administered first aid, was invited to come along too. I scanned the crowd hopefully, sipping my beer, but I couldn't see her anywhere. I learned later she had wanted to come, and had wrestled for days with the prospect, before finally deciding it was going to be too much for her to handle.

It was a reaction I would encounter again some twelve months later at a speaking engagement in Perth. A couple of girls who had taken part in the ultramarathon and not been caught in the fire had sat up the back of the room as I delivered my talk but had not been able to bring themselves down to speak to me afterwards. They spoke to Michael and told him they had wanted to meet me but weren't sure what to say – how they had been so profoundly affected by my story and struggled for a while afterwards to come to terms with how close they had come to possibly suffering a similar fate. And it left me feeling frustrated. I remember thinking: *What am I supposed to do with that? How is what I have been through even remotely about you? And why is it up to me to make you feel comfortable?*

I get it. People react to things in their own way. I can't begin to know how deeply someone has been affected by something or what impact an event like that fire has ultimately had on their life. But what I do know – only too well – is the effect it's had on my life. And that, in order to make the recovery I have made, I've had to be selfish. Sometimes, just sometimes, it's had to be about me, and what's best for me. So my reaction can sometimes be a bit extreme.

Ever since I cycled across Cambodia with Briggsy when I was back in uni, I had seen the transformative power of charity fundraising. The small efforts that people like me make can have an enormous and sometimes lasting impact on the lives of people who, simply by an accident of birth, live lives much harder and more poverty-stricken than my own.

I've always had a strong social conscience, so when I started to think about how I might most effectively use the profile I was starting to build, the obvious choice was to give back by way of charity work.

Briggsy, as it happened, was working at the time for a tour company that specialised in organising charity fundraiser group tours. So the plan was hatched to organise a rolling series of Turia's Challenges. The Inca Trail had always been on my bucket list, and it seemed like the perfect combination of physical challenge and cultural exposure. The idea was for Briggsy to put together a tour and advertise it to the general public with me as the drawcard. The problem was, with the World Cup unfurling in Brazil, flights to South America were prohibitively expensive, so we decided to look elsewhere on the map.

The Great Wall of China seemed like a good idea. An iconic wonder of the ancient world, a country steeped in history, and all the beef-and-black-bean a girl could eat. So Turia's Great Wall of China Challenge was launched.

Within a month it had sold out. We were a group of twenty-three. And, in what would prove to become a trend, not only was the group all women (my story seems to resonate most powerfully with women), but because this was the first charity event I'd organised, heaps of locals in Ulladulla came, and heaps of my good mates.

Decked out in all our hiking gear, we arrived in Beijing, and almost immediately I was out of my comfort zone. Different concepts of what is socially acceptable, plus what I believe is a general lack of exposure to anyone who might look a little different, meant that the Chinese were not averse to having a good old stare. Some locals even thought it was okay to come up next to me and pose for photos. It made me realise how comfortable I had become in my new skin back in Australia. How nurturing, generally, Australia is. And how much I had come to rely on Ulladulla as my little cocoon: the place I could go to and feel utterly protected.

Then there was the noise, and the crowds, and the smog and the traffic and the constant bustle of waves and waves of people. By the time we got to the Wall, I was relieved to have left Beijing behind us.

We walked 70 kilometres in just over ten days – and raised about $200,000 for Interplast in the process. It certainly wasn't the most arduous physical feat I had ever taken on – even if on day one there was a moment when I wondered if I would make it at all. On our first day we had to climb over a section of the wall in order to start trekking. It was a steep, wide section, and as I looked at it I thought, *I don't think I can climb that.* I just didn't have the grip to get any purchase as I scrambled up. I got to the top, thinking, *If I can't do this one simple climb at the very start of the challenge, how am I going to get through the next seven days?* As it happened, there was little climbing to be done thereafter and I managed just fine. I think perhaps I was jetlagged after arriving in China and a bit rattled at being stared at so openly.

The rest of the walk was just as I expected: equal parts stunning and dramatic. The scenery is beautiful: a series of undulating hills and mountains, over which crawls this most awesome human construction. There were moments during the walk where I would pause, look up from the path in front of me and stare out across the landscape. It bowled me over how even in the most populous country in the world, there were still pockets of sublime serenity.

For a lot of the women on the trek, there was a real sense of purpose, and we shared a camaraderie, a feeling of girl power. Everyone had their own story, their own personal mission. There was a girl who had suffered extreme emotional trauma as a child, and a woman who was really scared of heights. As I got to know each member of the crew and started to hear their stories I began to understand something of their motivations. I suppose it was the first time I started to understand that by virtue of what I had been through, I had become a lightning rod for people determined to change their lives. It was too early for me to properly grasp the significance of that.

A year later I signed on to do another charity walk. In July 2015 I found myself on a plane bound for Peru, en route to the Inca Trail challenge we had had to postpone twelve months earlier. Once again I had a crew of charity fundraisers in tow – a team of some twenty-six this time, with a couple of blokes thrown in for good measure. After a flight that felt like it was never going to end, we arrived in Cuzco and almost immediately the altitude sickness kicked in. A dull, persistent headache and a slight feeling of drowsiness; it wasn't pleasant. Not only that, but Cuzco left me cold: a really touristy place with not much to see. So it was a relief to get to the start of the Inca Trail.

The Inca Trail is one of those iconic tourist treks that attracts thousands of pairs of hiking boots every year. Winding through a tiny stretch of the Andes, it takes in some of South America's most stunning scenery – along an ancient route that leads, ultimately, to the ancient Inca city of Machu Picchu. The Incas were an ancient, scientifically advanced society that built their cities in harmony with the sun and its movements. To enter Machu Picchu by the so-called Sun Gate, just as dawn is breaking, is supposed to be one of those adventure bucket-list things. So it was with no small amount of excitement that we set off.

The trail itself is only 40 kilometres in length – stretched out over four days, it was an easily manageable 10 kilometres a day. That said, stretches of the trail are really tough: steep ascents that, when combined with the altitude, made for hard going. Often I would find myself gasping – taking short, shallow breaths in air that was thinner than my lungs were used to. The altitude took its toll on the team, too, knocking one or two of them for six. But we started as a team and we were determined to finish as a team.

Of course, it would be an out-and-out lie to pretend we were roughing it. Yes, we were camping, and no, the meals we had at the end of each day weren't exactly gourmet, but the fact we each had a *waiki* – or porter – to carry our rucksacks and to run ahead each afternoon and set up camp so that all we had to do was tumble into our tents, certainly made things much, much easier.

As with China, the group comprised a collection of people who had each been motivated to tackle the Inca Trail for a different reason. Once again, it was clear I was a rallying point for people who had overcome adversity. One of the team was walking to deal with the grief of having recently lost a grandchild. One had been a victim of domestic violence. Another couple of women were struggling with not being able to have children. Each of the stories were gradually revealed to me as we walked. Not that I ever had to probe. Most times, all I had to do was ask one or two questions of people and their story would pour out. It's amazing how infrequently we ask questions and really, properly listen to the answers. But everyone has a story to tell.

By the end of four days' trekking – and sharing the experience of spectacular mountain vistas and tumbling mountain streams cutting through lush meadows – we felt like a little unit. A walking, talking, self-healing, mountain-climbing unit.

Day four of the trek was my birthday. I remember waking on a mountain top and watching the sun inch its way up into the sky. And I felt happy. So very happy. I thought about how far I had come, the pain I had been through to be sitting there, in that tent, on a mountain top in Peru.

Happy birthday to me.

At the end of the day, we walked through the Sun Gate, and the emotion of my birthday, the physical exhaustion I felt and the sheer beauty of the place moved me to tears.

Later that evening, the guides who had led us across the mountains made me a cake. A relatively basic cake – but a cake nevertheless. I was so grateful. One of our guides in particular copped a lot of attention. A hot Inca. And he seemed to know – or at least pretend to know – a lot about the way of the spirits and the land. We called him Mr Jungle Man. He was a really lovely man. He would often make us stop and look at a tree and give us a mini lecture on the flora and fauna of the local area. 'Look,' he would say, pointing skywards. 'That is a condor. You know, in Quechuan history …'

We never really listened to what came next – we were too busy swooning.

It was a pleasant relief to find myself in a country where I wasn't stared at. My experience in China had rattled me so much, I had been apprehensive arriving in Peru, but the locals could not have been warmer or more welcoming.

I almost forgot I looked different – until we visited a local school. On most of these trips, we try to spend at least a bit of time interacting with the communities we visit: so a visit to a school was organised. The kids are always shy at first – who wouldn't be with a swarm of loud foreigners descending on them – but they eventually warm up. The teachers had arranged for us to do a traditional dance all together: to break the ice and encourage, oh, I don't know, five seconds' worth of cultural interaction. So the kids were all told to pick one of us from the trekking group to be their dance partner. I stood and watched as, one by one, my fellow trekkers were all taken as partners, leaving me standing alone, and feeling conspicuous. It felt like school all over again. Eventually, a timid little girl came over. I put my hands out for her to take and she screamed and ran away. I tried to laugh it off and pretend it didn't matter – but in that moment, I was devastated. I felt small. I felt different. And it hurt.

But another little girl had seen me standing there and rushed over. She saw I was adrift, and held out her hand. It was a perfect illustration of humanity.

*

The morning after the Oxfam Walk, I wake up and almost instantly everything hurts. It takes me a while to register where I am, and why every cell in my body is in protest. I'm in the hotel room in Manly – and it all comes flooding back. That bloody torturous 100-kilometre test of endurance that almost broke me. I have no idea what time it is. The room is blacked out. Night? Day? It's impossible to know.

I lie there and let my mind wander. It keeps coming back to Kate – and especially how hardcore she is. She has basically done this trek on one foot – half her left foot was amputated after the fire. There had been a moment at dusk on the track as the light was fading and it was hard to make out the trail when everyone in our team turned on our headlamps – everyone except Kate. A smile creeps at the corners of my mouth as I recall how she had compiled a hit-list of teams that were pissing us off on the track. How she wrote their team number down and kept track of them throughout the walk, and rejoiced when we overtook them, and how that list got longer the further we walked. And then at the end, how she was determined to check the race stats and triumphantly text me that we had beaten everyone on her hit-list.

Of the all-female teams, we finished in twenty-nine hours and came tenth. A reasonable effort, all things considered. Before the fire, Kate did the same walk in thirteen hours and came third. And I know how much of a letdown that will have been for her. I know, also, that I was probably a drag on the team at the end. My legs had stopped working. I couldn't climb stairs – at one point I had to drag myself up a set of stairs by my arms alone.

Kate and I don't see each other all that regularly, but when we do, we talk about the fire. We don't sit around deconstructing the day or anything. But we do talk a lot about how it has changed our lives. Sometimes we wonder, if we could, would we go back? I say, Well, I can't change what happened. So I can either dwell on the what-ifs or I can channel that energy into something positive. We talk about body acceptance, too. I probably have more than her – I wear midriff tops and don't try to hide my scars. But it's not like I jumped from wearing long sleeves and jeans to running around in a bikini, I've done it bit by bit over the last five years. Kate was a jeans kind of girl before the fire, and she still feels more comfortable in clothes that cover her up, which is her prerogative. That's the sort of stuff we discuss. Stuff that only we can understand. Even Michael doesn't really get it sometimes. No one else is able to relate the way she can.

The day after Oxfam, Kate sent me an email asking if I was keen to join her on the Brisbane Oxfam walk. Um, no. Not so much.

17

KATE

I wouldn't be friends with Kate Sanderson if it wasn't for the fire. That's not to say she's not a top chick and lovely person – because she is. It's just that we have almost nothing in common apart from a love of extreme sports and pushing our bodies to the limit.

People forget there were others in that fire. Other people whose lives were irrevocably changed. Because of the path I have chosen to take – and all the different factors that have made my story the media-worthy story it is – people aren't aware, by and large, that when that bushfire ripped through the gorge, it swept up more than just me.

I think about it a lot. And when I do, I sometimes feel a little guilty because so much of the attention after the fire was heaped on me. But mostly I feel grateful: grateful that none of us was killed. And grateful that out of this incredibly traumatic experience, I have gained a handful of friends for life.

It's funny when you think about it. What were the factors that meant I happened to be in that gorge at exactly the same time as Kate? The same time as Hully, Hal, Martin and Shaun? It's all so random. But from that one (admittedly quite significant) moment in our lives, we have formed a little club. I wouldn't say they are people to whom I am very close, but we have a bond. And we understand better than anyone else we know how one moment in a person's life can change everything.

Kate and I have become friends in the past five years. She lives in Melbourne, so we don't see each other all that often. We're not on the phone every other day, but when we do catch up, it's like seeing a long-lost sister. A slightly daggy, introverted and shy big sister, but a sister all the same. There's a sense of having one another's back and an unspoken understanding of what it's like to live with burns injuries. We know that there's another person out there – at the end of a phone line if we need – who will understand when we are having a bad day.

If you think I'm hardcore when it comes to sports, you should see Kate in action. She is something else. She competed in the Marathon des Sables in Morocco this year. She walked 257 kilometres across the Sahara!

There's this perception that, out of the two of us, Kate hasn't recovered as well after the fire as I have. But that's not true at all. She's just a lot quieter than I am. She is way cooler than me – so humble – and does more amazing things. I'd say she is easily harder and tougher than I am.

But I want to let her tell her story in her own words. This is my friend, Kate's story.

Kate Sanderson

I had never met Turia before the race. I only vaguely remember her from when we were all bused to the start line around 6 am. It was a picture-perfect morning on the Kimberley. The sunrise was spectacular.

When the race started, I remember watching Turia overtake me at the first corner and thinking what a gorgeous girl she was: tall, tanned, beautiful. Off she jogged into the distance.

The next time I caught sight of her was in the gorge. I had just run into it and stopped dead when I saw the fire approaching from the other side. I could see Turia up ahead, running along the track through the shoulder-high grass. She had her head down and her earphones in. She was running straight towards the fire. I was yelling at her to stop, but she couldn't hear me.

She looked up, saw the flames and came running back to where a small group of us had gathered and were weighing up our options. The flames were getting closer, I could hear the dull roar and the crackling of grass as it burned. We were all starting to panic. Turia looked across at me. This girl I had never met before met my gaze and said, 'I'm scared.'

I was scared too. I'd say we all were. But I did my best not to sound scared.

We couldn't go back either, because of the extreme heat behind us by now. But our way forward was blocked by flames. We had a pow-wow and decided our best option was to try to outrun the fire by scrambling up the escarpment to our right. So we started climbing. There was smoke everywhere. I could hardly see where I was going. The dull roar was getting louder – it had turned into a rumble and seemed to be sucking all sound out of the air. I could feel the heat building behind me as I ran, which is when the adrenaline started to kick in.

About halfway up the hill, I realised Turia was scrambling up beside me, tears streaming down her face. 'We'll be right,' I said to her. And at that point, I actually believed it.

I must have known at some level that I wasn't going to outrun the fire, because I stopped briefly to pull my merino jumper out of my pack and fumbled to put it on and then poured water on my head – all the while desperately looking around me for somewhere to shelter, a little hidey-hole to crouch in and hopefully let the fire pass over me.

I remember vividly the moment the fire reached me. In the seconds before it hit, I crouched behind a rock, but it got so unbearably hot I stood up and started to run. I slipped and fell backwards into the fire – back down the side of the gorge as the fire tore up it. The sound was just so terrifying – like twenty massive road trains about to drive over the top of me. And I distinctly remember thinking, *This is how I die*. I screamed as the flames engulfed me and I realised I was on fire. A couple of seconds later, I heard Turia scream and knew in that instant that she had been caught by the flames too.

Then, just as suddenly as it had hit us, it was gone. I stood up in shock. All around me was black and charred. Wisps of smoke were rising everywhere. It was eerily silent. I looked around me in a daze and could make out others from the group coming towards me. Everyone was covered in soot.

It was only when Hully and Hal materialised out of the haze that I became aware of Turia. She was a little further up the side of the gorge, lying face down, her face in her hands. She didn't seem to be moving. She wasn't making any noise. Even so, I remember thinking she was all right, because from where I was standing she looked as if she hadn't been too badly burned at all.

When the others tried to move her, we got a sense of how badly she had in fact been injured. Chunks of skin came off in the hands of anyone who touched her. And I remember Hal walking towards me, and I must have attempted a smile. You know in that way when you are in shock and your instinct is to keep up appearances? I just recall the look of horror on his face when he saw me – that was the first hint I had that something was seriously wrong with me, and then the pain started to kick in.

As we sat in that burned-out gorge, things weren't made any better by the midday heat – we actually suffered sunburn to our burns – or the flies.

Hal and Hully and the boys did their best to make Turia and me comfortable – gave us what water and medicines they had, rigged up a kind of shelter by stringing space blankets between trees.

I've spoken since to Paul Cripps, the pilot of the helicopter that rescued us. He's told me that it was the end of their working day when they got the call that there were a bunch of runners stuck and injured in the gorge. His company did tourist flights out into the Kimberley. He and his co-pilot mates had just finished for the day and were sitting down to have a couple of after-work beers. They can't fly if they've had even a tiny amount of alcohol. Paul says he remembers pulling the top off a beer – but then being distracted by something he had to do, which is when the radio call came through. One sip of beer and he might not have been able to come to us.

Turia and I were taken together to the hospital at Kununurra and put in separate rooms. I remember lying on the stretcher, being aware that my bum had been burned and worried that the doctors weren't aware, telling them I had been 'badly burned on my bum'. And I was worried about my shoes. 'Can you save them?' I remember asking the doctors. 'They're brand new.'

That's the last I remember. I was put into an induced coma and transferred to the Alfred Hospital in Melbourne, where I woke up a couple of weeks later.

I suffered burns to 60 per cent of my body. Half of my left foot had to be amputated. I had saved my face by covering it with my hands, but as a result, the tendons in my hands were exposed. Doctors amputated half of my right index finger. The fingers that were left were fused together by the fire, meaning I now can't do a lot of things as easily as I used to. Doing up buttons or holding a pen. Touch typing is out of the question. Those sorts of little daily things. But you work out ways to get by.

At the time, I was fixated on my foot being amputated. It was devastating. I had competed in about ten ultramarathons; I was in two hockey clubs; on weekends I would do 50-kilometre mountain-bike rides with friends. Sport was my life. The thought of never racing again or being able to play any kind of sport almost broke me. As it turns out, I now have a brace that allows me to walk. I can't run anymore, but I can walk. Anyway, it's the functionality of my hands I miss the most. Until all those micro skills you take for granted are taken away, you have no idea how reliant you are on them.

Altogether, with the burns, the amputations, the operations and infections, I spent about a year of my life in hospital – between the Alfred and then the Caulfield Hospital burns unit. The hardest part wasn't the physical pain of recovering and rehab. The hardest part was the mental thing: I couldn't see the end. People would say, 'You will get over it and life will get better.' But I couldn't see it. I couldn't see how life was going to get better. I was just going to get out of hospital eventually and my life was going to be shit. I wouldn't be able to do all the things I loved doing, my foot was fucked, my hands were fucked, I had burns to 60 per cent of my body. How exactly was my life going to get better?

It was frustrating because I had such a long road ahead of me and couldn't see how I would get back to how I was before.

Did I ever want to die? To chuck it all in and check out? No, not really. It never got to that point. But I was certainly at the lowest I have ever been in my life.

I remember one afternoon, after I had got out of ICU, the nursing staff put me in a wheelchair and wheeled me out of the hospital to a big park across the road. And they were all expecting me to be ecstatic, just happy to be out of the hospital and out in the fresh air – but I was angry. I was a complete bitch to them. 'Just take me back,' I snapped as soon as we got there. I didn't see the point of being there. I was only going to have to turn around and return to the hospital. To my twisted way of thinking, it was cruel to give me a taste of the outside world only to then wheel me back inside.

I had the same reaction on Christmas Day. I was granted day leave to go home for Christmas lunch, but I didn't want to take it. I remember the guy I was seeing at the time, Brett, who had been by my bedside from the beginning and was so supportive throughout the whole thing, was really upset that I would rather spend Christmas Day inside the hospital than be outside it with him. But I just couldn't face leaving the hospital knowing I would have to return twelve hours later.

Brett was another casualty of the fire. We broke up almost as soon as I left hospital. We had only started to see one another two months before the fire, and he had been such a wonderful support during my recovery, but it wasn't meant to be. The pressure put on the relationship proved too much in the end. It was just bad timing for us. Like me, I suppose, he was in the wrong place at the wrong time.

Then of course there was the whole two-boyfriend thing that he inadvertently got caught up in. For the first few months after the fire, wherever I went in the hospital or rehab system, nurses would greet me with, 'Oh yeah – you're the girl who got caught in the fire and had two boyfriends.'

The newspapers also reported at the time of the fire that I had two boyfriends on the go at the same time. The truth – as is often the case – wasn't nearly as exciting. It all came about because when I signed up to do the race, some eight months before it, I had listed an ex-boyfriend as one of my emergency contacts. So, when the fire happened, both Brett and my ex showed up at the hospital and apparently this Mexican standoff took place. My poor mum and family didn't know Brett, because we had only just started seeing one another, and I was in a coma so I wasn't able to explain any of it to any of them. I was pretty mortified when I came out of the coma and found out what had happened. It's funny when I think about it now, but back then it was anything but funny.

About a month or so after the fire, I got a friend of mine to write a card to Turia and send it to her at Concord Hospital. Just to say hi and to let her know I was thinking of her. We kept in touch, vaguely, but we were both so focused on our own recovery it wasn't like we were talking every other day.

We finally met about a year later, and it was a meeting I remember well. I was shocked to see her in her mask. The last time I had seen her, on the side of the gorge in the Kimberley, waiting for the helicopter to arrive, she had seemed okay to me. Now, here she was wearing a compression mask, and it was confronting. I began to understand for the first time just how extensive her injuries were.

She was quite meek – almost quiet. The same personality that she has today was still there – and so was the potty mouth – but it was all subdued.

Not long after, Turia made her first proper public appearance, at the government inquiry into the fire in Perth. It was the first time the news media had got a glimpse of her, and in many ways it was the launch of the Turia the country has come to know and love today. She was on all the front pages. I think it was the shock factor. From that moment, people have had this insatiable interest in her – people have been invested in her story. And it's only grown and grown from there. As she has gained more confidence, she has done more things, so in turn the public and the media's interest in her only continues to grow.

It's funny, because people have sometimes asked whether I mind that she gets all the attention and I am relatively unknown. After all, we both went through the same ordeal; she sustained burns to 65 per cent of her body, I sustained burns to 60 per cent of mine. But I couldn't be happier for her – not least because I absolutely hate the limelight. In that regard, we are polar opposites. I would rather be strapped in a chair and made to watch infomercials all day long than have to stand in front of a room full of people and make a speech. Turia was probably always destined to be famous. I just don't suppose she expected it to be for all the reasons that she is.

Turia and I are so different; if it wasn't for the fire, we would never have crossed paths or been in the same friendship groups. We are complete opposites – yet because of this experience we share, we have this incredible bond.

I'm not exactly the world's biggest extrovert, and Turia is so upfront, so direct. I remember I had a fundraising event here in Victoria back in 2013, which Turia flew down to take part in. Now, I am not much interested in fashion, as any of my close friends will tell you. To me, clothes serve a function. I'm not interested in wearing the latest this or the trendiest that. So for the fundraiser I had just thrown on a top and a skirt, and walked out into the living room where everyone was waiting. Turia took one look at me and said, 'Kate. You look like you work in Target.' And there was a sharp intake of breath from everyone else in the room and none of them knew where to look, and I just burst out laughing. 'Come on,' she said. 'Let's get into that wardrobe of yours and pick something more suitable.' And so we started going through my wardrobe together, and she pulled out coathanger after coathanger, saying, 'Jesus, there's nothing in here!'

And I love that about her. One thing you can say about Turia is that you are never in any doubt about where you stand with her. She pretty much says what she thinks, there's not much in the way of a filter. That sometimes shocks people when they meet her for the first time. They have this idea that she's going to be all proper, but she has a potty mouth on her like no one I know. When she did the Lake Argyle swim, *60 Minutes* were in the boat next to us and had put a microphone in our boat. And Turia was swearing like a trooper until eventually Michael Usher had to shout out to her, 'Turia, you have to stop swearing! We can't use any of this.'

Then there was the night more recently when we did the Oxfam walk together. Twenty-four hours of walking a coast bush-track north of Sydney. At one point in the early hours of the morning we had to cross a sort of boardwalk, over a kind of swamp. Turia slipped and her foot went into the water. All you could hear for a good minute or so, ringing out across the bushland in the dead of night, were loads of swear words! Luckily it was so dark that no one could make out it was her.

Michael is the complete opposite to her. It's like he is the pacifier – he is just so amused by it all.

I remember mentioning to Turia that I had been invited to climb Mount Kilimanjaro. She was annoyed because they hadn't invited her, and she said something like, 'Shit, you get all the interesting stuff.' I replied, 'Are you kidding me? You walked the red carpet with Brad and Angelina. You met the Duchess of Cambridge.' And she shot back, 'Yeah, but that's not as cool.'

Because for all the glamour of those sorts of celebrity encounters, she isn't dazzled by all that. She would much rather spend a week walking Kokoda or climbing Mount Kilimanjaro for charity than meeting princesses and movie stars. She's down-to-earth like that.

She's also got a very short attention span. She's just this ball of energy and perpetual motion. It's like, we did the Lake Argyle relay swim, she rode her bike to Uluru, she did the Inca Trail, she took on and conquered Ironman, she walked Kokoda. It's almost as if the world is soon going to run out of challenges for her.

But she has definitely grown in the past few years. It used to be red carpets and fame and stuff, now it's all about Michael and starting a family. And that will be a whole new chapter in her life. Sometimes I wonder if she gets tired of being dragged from pillar to post. Speaking to groups of people all over the country has its upsides, for sure, but I think she gets tired sometimes of always being on show. In some respects, she has become a commodity – and often that means people want more of her than she has to go around. And I think that wears her out a bit.

I remember when we all travelled back to the Kimberley together to do the Lake Argyle swim: Turia, Hully, Hal and me. *60 Minutes* came along to film it – to take us back to the gorge. I was happy enough to go for the sake of the free heli-copter ride, but Turia didn't want any of it. I was asked for the cameras what it was like to fly over the gorge, and I replied that it was good to have closure: but I didn't really mean it. I don't need closure. It happened, my life has been completely changed because of it, and now I just get on the best way I can.

The funny thing was, from the helicopter we looked down into the gorge and straightaway I spotted a perfect place we could have run to and avoided the fire completely.

It will be five years ago in September. It hasn't gone fast, but it seems like a long time ago. Does that make any sense? I guess I just mean a lot of stuff has happened.

I was never haunted by the fire and I am not to this day. A friend last year phoned me and invited me to his bonfire, and I told him I couldn't come. And he rang up a day later saying, 'I am so sorry, I should have thought! I feel really stupid.' I just laughed and said, 'It's cool – I just have a dinner date with a friend.' I'm not traumatised at all.

I'm now studying for a criminal justice degree and just did a three-month internship at the Coroner's Court. I haven't really had a significant relationship since I left hospital, and that's okay. I'm in a foster group for dogs and have collected three dogs along the way – Millie, Twistie and Sadie. They are my number one. Twistie and Millie are whippets and Sadie is a Staffy Ridgeback crossed with a boofhead. I rescued Sadie from a puppy farm. She has special needs, and I'm a sucker for a lost cause. I also figured, what is one more basket-case in the house?

18

HULLY

Hully is one of those blokes who, when you meet him for the first time, seems familiar, like you've known him forever. He's a little bit older than me. He has three adult daughters and a beautiful wife, Bronwyn. But he's possibly younger at heart – and more adventurous – than I will ever be.

The extreme-sports community is small and tight-knit. It takes a special kind of person to want to run a marathon across the Sahara or trek to the peak of Mount Everest or run an ultramarathon through the Kimberley. It's four parts crazy, two parts adrenaline-addiction and two parts just wanting to wring everything possible out of life.

I count Michael Hull as one of my dear friends now – and it's funny, because were it not for the twist of fate that meant we happened to be in the same gorge at exactly the same time a fire was tearing through it, we would so very easily have missed each other completely. He would have run his race and I would have run mine. We would have been lucky to exchange three words on the day. Now I cannot imagine my life without him in it.

Hully has been a faithful friend for years now. He and Michael get on like a house on fire, too. Hully lives every moment to its absolute fullest. He takes on wild adventures for the simple reason that they're there. He figures he's only got one life so he might as well test how far he can push his body.

All of us caught in that gorge on that day were given a wake-up call a year or so after it. Martin Van der Merwe, the lovely man who was running the race that day with his son, Shaun, and whose kindness in the gorge when I was terrified I will never forget, was hit by a truck a couple of years after surviving the fire. He was killed almost instantly. It was so terribly sad, and yet another reminder that you just never know what lies in wait around the corner. Life is a gift, and you have to tell yourself that each and every day. Just like Hully does.

This is his story.

Michael Hull

I clearly remember the time and date I first met Turia. It was 1.10 pm on Saturday, 2 September 2011. The exact moment fire swept into that gorge. I remember running through shoulder-high spinifex grass and suddenly becoming aware of a rumbling noise. I looked up and saw fire tearing across the floor of the gorge.

I started running back, which is when I came across Turia. She was in a sort of a huddle with Hal, Martin, Shaun and Kate in a small clearing. There was no time for pleasantries or any formal introductions, that's for sure.

I remember Martin suggesting we all turn around and get out of the gorge, but as we looked, the fire had already swept up around and encircled us – blocking our exit. The main wall .

of fire was coming at us from straight ahead. It was getting hotter and hotter, the sky was getting darker from the smoke, and black ash and red embers were flying about us on the wind. We had no other option but to scramble up the side of the gorge. All I could think about was escape. I kept thinking that if we just stayed together, everything would work out.

By the time we all clambered up onto an escarpment, the flames were practically on top of us. We were only on that escarpment for a minute or so before the fire was on us.

It was so loud. Just so loud. I couldn't get over the sound. It was a deafening roar. As the flames started to lick over the edge of the escarpment, Kate crouched down behind a large rock and curled into a ball. For a split second, Turia stood there. That was enough time for her to be engulfed by flames. She had nowhere to go.

If you've ever seen one of those action movies when the main character is filmed running away from a fireball or an explosion – that was Martin and me. We just turned on our heels and started sprinting (at least we thought we were) along the side of the gorge, running for our lives, literally. Hal and Shaun must have taken off in another direction completely. Behind us, as we tried to escape, I could hear the screams of the girls as the fire engulfed them.

At a certain point, and I'm still not sure why, both Martin and I must have realised separately that we weren't going to outrun the fire. And without saying a word to one another, we both turned and faced the wall of flames and ran back towards and ultimately through it.

In some part of my brain I must have reasoned that if I was able to jump back through the flames, I'd be safe. I might get burned in the process, but surely on the other side of that wall was relative safety. I remember thinking: *I don't want to die like this*. I did what I had to do . . . on pure instinct and adrenaline.

Somehow, by a miracle, I got through. And as I looked up and took my bearings, I realised I had stopped at a point directly between Kate and Turia. Martin had also jumped through the flames and fallen as he crashed through to the other side.

Turia was lying on the ground to my right, and Kate was standing up. I remember looking at Kate and seeing burned flesh. Her clothes had burned off completely and I was looking at her burned arse. The skin was just hanging off her. We joke now that I don't recognise her when she is wearing clothes!

She looked around at me with this expression of bewilderment – as if she didn't quite know where she was or what had happened. And then I heard Turia say, almost apologetically, 'Guys, can you come and help me?'

Kate just looked at her and said, 'I can't.'

When Kate saw my face as I took in her injuries, she knew she was in trouble. I couldn't speak. I suppose I was in shock. But I also just didn't have the words to describe what I was looking at, or to offer anything in the way of comfort. It all seemed so unreal.

Hal appeared a few minutes later. I went and sat down. But then for about ten minutes Martin was unable to find Shaun and thought his son had died. We were blowing whistles, shouting out for him, and although everything around us was in an eerie silence, we couldn't seem to rouse him.

For his part, Shaun had thought *we* were all dead. He couldn't imagine how anyone else could have survived. When he found us alive, the reunion between father and son was quite emotional. I will never forget that moment.

Martin and I had sustained burns but we were okay. Shaun and Hal were relatively unscathed and they then quickly assessed the girls and went into tending to them.

It became obvious pretty quickly that there was not a lot that could be done for Kate or Turia. They kept going in and out of consciousness, which was probably a saving grace. They would both have been in acute pain and discomfort. We were out there in the middle of nowhere, in the desert in the middle of the day, completely exposed with no protection from the sun and suffering severe burns. All we had was a few Panadol and some water bottles.

The only thing I remember Turia saying in the time we waited for help was, 'Can someone get the ants off me?' The poor thing had sat down on top of an ant's nest and had them crawling all over her.

I was wearing compression socks made of Lycra, and they had been burned into the skin on my legs. I also had on a pair of Lycra shorts under my running shorts. In all, there was probably only about six inches of exposed flesh on my legs. As I ran back through the fire, I must have pivoted to the right, because my left arm was burned worse than my right arm. I was wearing a buff around my neck, which I'd thankfully had the presence of mind to wet. I pulled that up over my face as I charged through the wall of flames and I think that saved my face.

Turia and Kate lay where they had fallen. Shaun and Hal tried to move them at one stage, but their skin was coming off in their hands when they touched them so it was decided not to proceed.

They weren't moving or talking. They were both too far gone to feel any pain. They were just trying to remain conscious.

My burns were not nearly as bad as the girls', but I was still in a bit of pain. I kept repeating a mantra in my head: *It doesn't hurt, it doesn't hurt. It's all mental.* The parts of me that were burned the worst actually gave me the least pain. I only discovered later that's because with deep, severe burns, the nerve endings are so damaged you can't really feel pain. So the parts of me that were burned less were causing me more pain – but I knew the girls were much worse off and they weren't complaining. Anyway, the worst part of the whole ordeal was knowing they were both hurt and there was absolutely nothing we could do to help them. I felt useless.

To tell you the truth – I couldn't bring myself to look at Turia after I had seen the extent of Kate's injuries. Apparently Turia had spoken to Shaun in the first few minutes after the fire. The first thing he remembers her saying was, 'Is my face burned?' He told her it wasn't.

I suppose the first time I really understood the extent of her burns was when we all got back to Kununurra Hospital. We had been brought back on separate choppers. I was well enough to walk into the hospital. I remember looking to the left as I went into intensive care and there she was. They had removed all her clothes and were bandaging her up. She didn't appear to be conscious. I just walked straight past.

I sustained burns to 20 per cent of my body. I had to have skin grafts to my arms and my legs. I was flown by the Royal

Flying Doctor Service to Perth Hospital. I was extremely fortunate to be under the care of Dr Fiona Wood and her team – the famous burns surgeon who treated so many of the Bali bombing victims. My wife Bronwyn flew over from Sydney and stayed with some very supportive family friends while I spent three weeks in hospital in Perth.

After my surgery, rehab started on a daily basis. I was transferred to the Royal North Shore hospital in Sydney after three weeks. From October until May the following year, I had to come down to the Royal North Shore from our home on the Central Coast to have my dressings changed. At first, it was every second day, then every third day. Then eventually I just stayed home and did them myself.

In the beginning, the doctors talked about wanting to do my skin grafts again. They reckoned they could do a better job, but I wasn't having a bar of it. I thought they were fine. Afterwards, the science of how and why I escaped with relatively minor burns compared to the girls was explained to me. Because I ran through the fire, I created a kind of vortex around me that protected me a little bit, instead of being stationary as the flames passed over.

The crazy thing is that when the fire had passed, Turia and I were barely two metres away from each other. It was like one of those scenes you see after a bushfire passes through a neighbourhood, where three houses in a street are burned to the ground and one is left untouched. Why? It's just luck.

I didn't have any contact with Turia in the months after the fire. I guess I was focused on my own recovery as she was on hers. And I didn't exactly know her. I just got snippets about what had happened to her from media reports.

My mate Hal had made contact with Kate, because they had known one another prior to the race. Hal had Hosko's number. I knew it was delicate stuff, so I waited a while until I called him. I think it must have been the February after the fire when I finally phoned and left a message. He called me back a couple of days later and we had a really good chat. It was good for him, he said, to speak to others who were there, to try to piece together exactly what had happened. He struck me as a really nice bloke. We got on really well.

It was in about April that I finally got to see Turia. She was coming up to Sydney for some treatment or operation and I went to meet her in the hotel she was staying at. I remember seeing her and being shocked. She was just so thin and looked so fragile, like a stick person. She tired really easily, was still unsteady on her feet – but there was still that sense of relentless positivity.

It was awkward in the beginning. Hosko was there with his mum, Julie. There was a bit of small talk to begin with, then silence. Finally Turia broke the ice by asking, 'So, what do you remember about the fire?'

A few weeks later, we were together again for the inquiry in Perth. It was Kate, Turia, Shaun and myself all in the same room, together for the first time since we had sat in that gorge. It was strange, and emotional. It turned out that while we each have little unique things we remember specifically about the fire, we all had the same recollection of what had happened. We all went through the same thing.

The inquiry was run very professionally, I thought. And the people running it were really supportive. I came away from it feeling guilty, though. Guilty that I had survived relatively unscathed and both Turia and Kate had been so badly injured. I was in my mid-forties with teenage children; the girls were both so young and had their whole lives ahead of them. I used to wish that I was able to trade places with them.

Seven months after the fire, while I was still wearing my compression garments on both my arms and legs, I took part in an expedition to the North Pole. It was something I had agreed to do with an American mate of mine, Frank Fumich: probably while I was under the influence of painkillers. When I was in hospital Frank would ring me every night from his home in the United States. 'Let's trek to the North Pole,' he said one night. 'There are no fires up there.'

So apparently I had agreed. I had no recollection of the conversation, and it took Bronwyn to remind me. But once the idea took hold, there was no distracting me from it. Just like Turia had her Ironman to inspire her recovery, I had the North Pole.

Bronwyn, being the sensible one, said I had to check with my doctors, because at that stage I was still undergoing treatment for my burns. So I said to the doctor, 'Would it be okay if I didn't come back to see you for three weeks?'

And he said, 'Why?'

I said, 'I want to go skiing.'

The doctor said, 'That's fine. Skiing is fine – just keep your injuries covered and make sure you dress them every day.'

So I went home, feeling very smug, and saw Bronwyn standing there with a knowing look on her face.

'Did you ask the doctors?' she said.

'Yeah, of course. They said it was fine.'

'But did you tell them what you were planning to do?'

'Sort of.'

So I flew to Norway and we made our way north to a temporary Russian research station and airstrip. There were three of us and a guide. We skied the last degree on earth, a distance of about 100 kilometres, pulling our gear behind us on a sled. It was minus 27 degrees every day. I thought it was going to be flat, but there were a lot of pressure ridges and hills. The sled I dragged behind me weighed about 50 kilos. It took us ten days to do. We averaged about 10 kilometres a day. But because you're skiing cross-country across a series of floating ice shelves, you could pitch a tent at night and wake up to find you had been pushed back a couple of kilometres in your sleep. On the flip side, there were a few days when we had tail winds that pushed the ice shelf, so we were closer to the pole.

When we finally got there, it was all a bit of an anti-climax. There's absolutely nothing there. Nada, zip. There are no landmarks. The only reason you know you have reached the North Poles is because your GPS tells you. That said, it was still a pretty emotional experience for me.

It had been a tough seven months.

I suppose each one of us set our goals as we lay in our respective hospital beds. Maybe it has something to do with how well both girls have recovered, that we are all such goal-oriented people who love doing stuff that challenges and tests us.

For Kate, it was the XPD adventure race, in which teams of four trek, mountain bike and kayak, day and night, over a

550–600 kilometre course; and the Marathon des Sables. Both of which she did.

Hal and I did the XPD race with Kate, and Bronwyn and Hal did the Marathon des Sables with her. That girl is hardcore. For Turia, it was Ironman. And I've been there for both of them as they ran across the respective finish lines. Because we have a bond. You can't go through something like we went through and not come out of it feeling like you are connected in some really fundamental way. We are all totally different people, but on this one level, we are bound together. And despite being completely different, we all get on so well.

I've done a few Ironman triathlons, and Turia and I used to talk about them heaps. About eighteen months before her event, she called me and asked whether I thought she could do it. I told her of course she could, but she needed to train. So I put her in touch with an old coach of mine, Bruce Thomas. He's really measured and methodical, a complete professional. She was impatient – she wanted to smash it every day. She wanted to go at it like a bull at a gate. So it was interesting to watch those two interact.

Bruce is based in Sydney and obviously Turia is down on the South Coast, but they worked out a rhythm. She did a couple of his training camps; she came up to the Central Coast and we did some cycling together. She wasn't confident on the hills. I knew she could run and her swim was always going to be okay. As long as she did the bike ride without falling off, I had no doubts that she could do it.

There's nothing physically wrong with her legs or her feet – and mentally she's tough as an old rusty nail. And anyway, if she didn't finish, I told her I was going to heap shit on her for the rest of her life.

At the start of the race, she was shitting herself; every first-timer feels like that. But she set herself a realistic goal and she eclipsed it.

Watching her come across the finish line was great. I was extremely proud of her, actually. Welcome to the club, Turia. But you know, there were about fifteen hundred other people out there that day running that race. And while they might not all have had her journey, there were hundreds and hundreds of other inspiring stories being played out. That's what makes Ironman so special.

Kona is Port Macquarie on steroids in terms of people and atmosphere. Turia has the media spotlight on her, which will add to the pressure. But more than that, the conditions for Kona are just so tough. It's so hot and windy over there. She is going to have to be really conscious of the heat and manage it. But with the right mindset and race plan she's going to be fine. She now knows what she has to do to finish an Ironman. At the end of the day, it's all about mental toughness – and she's proven already that she has that in spades. Her mental strength is her number-one quality. That and her determination. Once she sets goals, she is very driven. She is a competitive little thing – everything is a race.

Even before the fire, she was always very goal-focused. I guess she is just doing different stuff than she would have been doing if we had never been caught in that gorge. Now she has this story, and her journey is inspirational to a lot of people. And then there's the not-insignificant fact that she is not even thirty. She has so much of her life ahead of her. She'll get married, and she and Michael will have kids, and once she has a family, her priorities will shift. That's just what happens. But in Michael, she has the best guy possible. He's so perfect it's annoying. You just have to meet his family to see where he gets it from. He's just your normal South Coast bloke: he loves surfing, fishing and knocking a nail into a wall. And that has been so important to her recovery.

I love catching up with Turia and Hosko; we have a few laughs and generally too many reds. There is no filter when it comes to Turia. She is always on her best behaviour when she is in the public eye – but get her after a few red wines and all bets are off. But they are private moments.

At the end of the day, she is just a little South Coast surfie chick. You can take the girl out of Ulladulla …

19

THE COACH

Sometime around May 2015 I made the decision that I was going to contest the Ironman in Port Macquarie in twelve months. I put the feelers out among my extreme-sports friends, and the one name they came back with as the man who would help me reach my goal was Bruce Thomas.

When I met Bruce, he had competed in thirteen Ironman events and been the first Aussie across the line for three consecutive years from 1994. Over a thirty-year competitive racing career, Bruce completed the original (and still the hardest) Ironman in Kona, Hawaii a staggering four times. Kona is considered the grand-daddy of all Ironman events: if you complete even one of them, you have demi-god status in extreme-sports circles.

Bruce's lovely wife, Chris, is herself a champion triathlete. Together they run Energy Link Training from their home in the Hills District of north-western Sydney. Each year they prepare fifty-odd people for triathlons and Ironman-style competitions.

I remember my first meeting with Bruce. Michael and I made the trip to Sydney to sit down and talk about what I wanted to do and why. There's a wonderfully calming aura about Bruce. He's one of the most accomplished athletes I know: and you don't get to be the champion he was without steely determination and a fierce desire to be the best. And yet, somehow, that super-competitive athlete is packaged up in a humble, quietly spoken package.

I don't remember the particulars of our meeting, except that we were both checking each other out. He was doing his due diligence on me, to make sure I wasn't a flake. And I was doing my due diligence on him, to make sure he was the real deal, and also to make sure I was taking on a trainer I got along with.

We must have both liked what we saw and heard. Within weeks I was signed up to train with Bruce and on the receiving end of a series of emailed training programs. Every hour of every day was accounted for – including down-time and rest days. It was strict. It was tough. It was exactly what I was looking for.

If there were times I was interstate or travelling overseas or just too busy with the rest of my working life, Bruce would be understanding and encourage me to take a break. Or if I simply didn't have the passion, or felt worn out by the grind, he'd give me the week off until I felt I had re-found my mojo. As much as he was my physical trainer, he completely understood how to manage me mentally. I came to thank my lucky stars that Bruce had come into my life.

Here's his side of our Ironman journey together.

Bruce Thomas

The first contact I had with Turia was about a year before the Ironman event in Port Macquarie. I got a message on my voicemail from a woman saying she wanted to do an Ironman and could she talk to me about it. I didn't catch her name, or, for that matter, really understand the message, so I passed the phone to my wife, Christine.

She heard about the first three words of the voicemail and looked at me, wide-eyed. 'I recognise that voice! That's Turia Pitt! You have to call her back!'

I did and we had a bit of a chat. It sounded as if she knew what she was about, so we organised a meeting. She and Michael came to visit a week or so later and we sat down together to talk about what was involved in training for an event like Ironman.

Looking back, I wasn't nearly as well educated as I might have been about what had happened to Turia and where she was at – physically or mentally. I knew she had been in a fire, but that was pretty much it. I had no idea that it had only been three years before. For her to have come that far in such a short period of time is quite incredible.

When I work with someone I always look at where they are at in that moment, not where they have been. I knew Turia had some fitness, but I didn't know how much. I asked her how far she could run without stopping. Around five ks, she replied. As I emphasised to her, the hardest part of Ironman is not, however, the physical toughness required but the mental strength. The biggest part of Ironman is in your head. With twelve months until the race, we had plenty of time to get her ready physically, but in the end it would be her mental fortitude that would get her across the line. And when I stopped and thought about what she had been through, her recovery, I concluded pretty much on the spot she had this in the bag.

That's not to say it was going to be easy for her. The first thing you have to remember when thinking about Turia doing Ironman is that she has a few physical disadvantages that the rest of the field are unlikely to have to contend with. Swimming 4 kilometres in open water is tough enough, but imagine swimming that distance when you don't have any fingers. Imagine jumping into the sea and closing your hand into a fist and swimming non-stop for an hour and a half. That is what the swimming leg of the Ironman was like for Turia. Plus she has some other physical disadvantages. She can't breathe through her nose, which does limit her oxygen intake. Her resting heart rate is permanently elevated due to her injuries, not to mention the extra work her body does trying to maintain a constant temperature. It's incredibly hard, no matter how effortless she makes it seem.

So in designing her training regime, we had to factor in a few physical restrictions. The sorts of devices and training aids I would normally use with other clients we weren't able to use for Turia. A paddle in the hand for swimming training, for example: we had to abandon that. Then there was the whole bike thing. She's not able to operate a bike like most people: she can't grip the handlebars, she can't brake quickly. So we had to make adjustments.

But, as I said, I knew it was the mental toughness that was most important in the Ironman and she had that in spades. All the rest we could work on.

With twelve months to get her ready, I devised a training schedule that started out easy and ramped up as the months progressed. I started out by giving her something physical to do each day. At first, she would have two rest days every week, which we eventually scaled back to one. As her fitness levels improved, I started to up the ante.

In a big week, as we approached the peak of the training schedule, she was running anywhere up to 100 kilometres, usually broken up over a couple of days, and taking anywhere between six to seven hours to do it. On the days she wasn't doing long runs, I had her doing short bursts of intensity training – sprints or stair climbs.

When it came to the bike, at the peak of her training, she was riding about eleven hours a week, covering somewhere in the vicinity of 350 kilometres. And for the swimming training, at the peak she would do about four hours a week, covering anywhere between 8 to 10 kilometres. On top of that we did Pilates, yoga and core workouts.

She did a lot of training on her own in Ulladulla. Being out on your own on your bike for six, seven hours is not much fun. It takes enormous discipline to keep backing up day after day, to follow the training schedule to the letter and not cut any corners. It would be so easy to slack off – to only ride your bike for five hours instead of seven, to swim for one hour only instead of two, or to run 35 kilometres instead of 42 – but she never compromised.

I knew pretty much straightaway that the faith I had in her mental toughness was going to be well placed. Watching her train, she put me in mind of an Ironman champion called Dave Scott. He won Ironman in Hawaii six times. He used to set up his bike in his garage and hang a black sheet in front of him and cycle for hours and hours with nothing but that black square to look at, because he knew it would toughen him up mentally for the race itself. Turia has similar tenacity.

About six months into the training, she headed off to Forster to do a half-Ironman. The idea was for her to get a taste of competing alongside a large group of people. Michael went along with her and ran beside her. At the back of his mind, he had always thought that he might do the Ironman with Turia as well – to be there in case she needed back-up. But after Forster, he decided Ironman was something she was capable of achieving on her own. And that it needed to be her accomplishment and hers alone.

In the weeks leading up to the event, we all went up to Port Macquarie to check out the course and do a dry run. I think it was sobering for her. I think she thought it was going to be easier than it was. The bike course especially freaked her out.

After that, we spent a fair bit of time chatting over the phone. I would ring her up to make sure her head was okay. We talked a lot about expectation management. How her focus needed to be on finishing. Not breaking any records, not setting a time – just getting across the finish line. I told her to resign herself to the fact she was going to be on the bike a long time. It's going to take as long as it takes, I told her. And the important thing was not to psyche herself out of the race before it had even begun. When you get to the run, I told her, that's your zone. That's the part of the race she likes and can control. She knows the strategies she needs to keep going. By the time you start running you are going to be passing people hammer and tong, I said. And she was good with that. I think she felt a little better about it all.

When race day finally came, I was worried about her. In the days leading up to it, the organisers had involved her in a lot of media and publicity work. She couldn't walk down the main street of Port Macquarie without waves of people coming up and wanting photos with her. And while that might be nice at first, after a while it can get tiring.

One of the big things I said to her about the whole day was: you are going to have to be a bit selfish. Everyone is going to want a bit of you, but you have to keep as much of yourself in reserve as possible. Don't feel you need to say thanks or acknowledge everyone who wants to wish you well. Get in your head space and stay there. You can thank people after the race.

As she milled her way towards the start line with the thousand or so other competitors, the organisers started whipping the crowd into a frenzy, pointing her out and yelling her name over the loudspeaker. All she wanted at that point was to be anonymous: to be just another first-time Ironman competitor in the crowd.

When finally she got into the water, she was away. She did the 3.8-kilometre swim in one hour and sixteen minutes, which was faster than either of us had expected. She came out of the water feeling calmer, I think. It gave her a real boost.

Next came the bike. As you ride south out of Port Macquarie, the road snakes up and down a nasty little section of hills, which can take it out of you. There's a nice flat section at Lake Cathie, which runs for about 30 kilometres. The last 15 kilometres is up and down. Then you turn around and come back again. For Turia, going uphill is easier for her. She is better able to control the bike than when it is going at speed downhill.

There was also the whole problem of what she would do if there was some kind of mechanical failure: if she got a flat tyre, for instance, 45 kilometres out from Port Macquarie, in the fading light, with the rain starting to fall. Most other competitors would jump off, change the tyre and keep going.

But changing a tyre was never an option for Turia. At first, I'd suggested to the organisers that I be allowed to ride along behind her – to be there in case anything happened. But they weren't keen on the idea. So they gave her a mobile phone to carry in the event of any misadventure. She was told to call them if anything happened and they would despatch a rescue crew. She was nervous about it. She hated the thought of not being able to compete if something happened that was beyond her control. When the rain started to fall, that didn't help matters. The road became really slippery and the potential for wipe-outs became even more real.

She was fine, but by the end of the ride she was really starting to flag. I could see she'd had enough. There's a particularly nasty little hill on the way in, about 400 metres of steep pitch on the Matthew Flinders Drive. It's been the undoing of plenty of Ironmen. I told her not to try and ride up it, but get off her bike and walk up the hill. I knew she'd be better off conserving energy. I think she rode up it both times.

In the end, she completed the 180-kilometre bike ride in seven hours and thirteen minutes. It was about fifteen minutes faster than I anticipated. She was in good shape. And she only had her favourite part of the race to come.

Remember that Turia had either been swimming or cycling for nine hours by this point – non-stop. The body goes into a kind of autopilot, you are so far beyond tired. Most people will never run a marathon. To run a marathon after you've already swum 4 kilometres and cycled 180 is nothing short of remarkable. This is the moment when you need your mental strength to really kick in: you're asking your body to do things that it long ago stopped thinking was a good idea, so you've got to override every instinct and just keep pushing.

We had talked about this third leg beforehand and the plan was for her to run between the aid stations, which are spread out along the running course at 2-kilometre intervals, walk the 80 metres or so of each station, take in whatever food or drink they were offering, then run the 2 kilometres to the next one. It's called the run-break method, and pretty widely practised in these sorts of events.

In the end, it took Turia four hours and forty-three minutes to complete the run. It was maybe a little longer than I thought she would do, but only by about ten minutes. Otherwise, the race went exactly as we planned it.

I remember standing at the finish line when she ran across it. It was around 9.30 pm. She had been going since 7 am. She ran across the line with her arms in the air and danced a little jig. I'll never forget the smile on her face.

How was that moment for me? It was really emotional. The hardest thing about coaching people is that you can give them advice and train them as much as you like, but on the day it's completely up to them. There was one lap of the run on which I missed her when she came past, and I started to worry something had gone wrong. But then she reappeared on the return and I was overcome with emotion. Just to think about what she has gone through and achieved. To have played even a small part in that is just so rewarding. But the thing about Turia is that once she sets her mind to achieving something, there's not a lot that can stop her.

20

IRONMAN – PART I

Five am and the sun has yet to rise over Port Macquarie. It's the morning of Ironman. It's unusually warm for this time of year – it strikes me as a godsend as I make my way to the marshalling area. I'm nervous enough without having the added shakes of an early morning chill.

The scene is a strange combination of excitement and silence. Never have I seen fifteen hundred people collected in one place making so little noise. Everywhere I look, scattered about the scene, are my fellow competitors – eating a banana, jogging on the spot, lost in their thoughts – focusing on the challenge ahead.

We're gathered in wetsuits in a large, open car park alongside a small arc of one of the tiny bays that make up Port Macquarie. It's floodlit, casting an orange glow across the scene. One by one, participants are psyching themselves to take part in the toughest physical competition in the world.

My coaches, Bruce and Chris, have been by my side this morning for over an hour. Together with Michael, they form a protective huddle around me. I listen, but distractedly, as Bruce mutters the last of his instructions to me. Twelve months of training and it has all come down to this. Michael is here – as he always has been. I see him looking at me, a mixture of pride and anxiety on his face.

'She's done the work, she's a clever girl. She's got this,' he says to the steady flow of well-wishers who file past and pat him on the back.

I seem incapable of speaking. I'm in the zone. With each minute that the clock ticks closer to my 7 am start time, I go deeper into myself. Shut out the noise. Focus on the silence. Listen to my breathing. I also start to psyche myself out. 'Why am I doing this? Stupidest idea ever. Wish I hadn't told everyone in Australia that I was doing this ...'

There is a rolling start, so when you enter the water depends on the time you're expected to finish in. Fifteen hundred barefoot people in swimming caps, goggles and full-body wetsuits shuffle nervously from foot to foot. My wait in the queue to start seems to last forever. And then, before I know it, the clock strikes seven and we are summoned to the start line. This is it. I shuffle alongside a wave of fellow racers towards a wide stretch of red carpet that passes under the starting arch and disappears into the water ahead.

'Ladies and gentlemen! Turia Pitt!' I hear my name over the loudspeaker. There is a roar from the crowd. A couple of slaps on my wetsuited back from fellow competitors; a flash of cameras; the outstretched arms of well-wishers, reaching out to high-five me as I jog into the bay. It's all a blur. I hear nothing but the beat of my own heart. I see nothing but the inky blackness of the water in front of me. With a dive and a sharp breath, I throw myself headlong into the sea.

And into the second-biggest challenge I have ever faced in my life.

My road to Ironman began, of course, in the burns unit of Concord Hospital when I was told by a succession of physicians that I needed to be realistic about how my life would look after the fire. I remember lying in my hospital bed listening to all of these people tell me what I would *not* be able to do. It was a succession of negatives. You should *forget* about this, you need to *let go* of that. It's important you accept that from now on your life will be a whole series of things that you *cannot* do.

And as broken as I was, it still managed to light a fire in me. The fire had burned me on the outside, but it hadn't touched me inside. I was still the same Turia who had set out to win the physics medal. The same Turia who had taken on a double degree and entered the male-dominated work space of mining engineering. The same Turia who had cycled across Cambodia and signed up for an ultramarathon. If I set my mind to something, I generally achieved it. And nothing, but nothing, spurred me on more than someone telling me what I *couldn't* do.

From my very first tentative, incredibly painful steps in Concord Hospital, there was always one goal in mind. Ironman. I would prove them all wrong and complete one: the toughest physical test on the planet.

For months, as physios coaxed my limbs back into working order; as I learned to walk again; as I conquered a staircase, one step at a time – the one thing that kept me going was the thought that it was all leading to the Ironman.

When finally I got out of hospital and returned to Ulladulla: that first ocean swim where I was knocked off my feet by a tiny wave; those sessions pulling a tyre around Gary and Julie's backyard with only the parrots for company; the times I would scramble back onto my surfboard and paddle into an oncoming set, fresh from being dumped again – it was all in preparation for this.

Looking back and thinking about the hunched, barely mobile skeleton that I was in the first months of my recovery, it's almost laughable that I thought I would ever be well enough to compete in an Ironman, much less do so only five years after my accident. Certainly, if I'd known back then how utterly gruelling the race is, I would definitely have given up on the spot. Back then, walking up three consecutive steps without collapsing in exhaustion and pain was an achievement. But as it turns out, what you don't know can't intimidate you.

I'm in the water, focusing on my stroke, concentrating on my breathing, reaching for all the lessons Bruce and Chris have taught me. The bay is a mass of limbs and churning water – a great shoal of wet-suited humans moving slowly westwards. I try to move into a patch of clear water, but there are arms and legs flailing everywhere. I think to myself how lucky it is that I don't suffer claustrophobia: this would be a definite trigger for a panic attack. I try to simply keep my head down and concentrate on my stroke. It's weird – even though I was in a negative mindset before I started, as soon as I kick off, I know I'll be fine.

This 3.8-kilometre swim is crucial for setting the pace for the rest of my day. I need a good time as a springboard for the 180-kilometre bike ride that will follow, which in turn will impact how fast I manage to run the 42 kilometres before reaching the finish line at some point, in about fifteen hours' time.

I try not to think about the race ahead. Even though I have trained for it, even though I have psyched myself for fifteen hours of constant, gruelling physical activity – I try to stay in the moment. Concentrate on my breathing, break up the coming hours into little chunks. How do you eat an elephant? One mouthful at a time.

Here in the water I feel safe. Unseen. For the first time since we arrived in Port Macquarie, I am anonymous and it feels good. The organisers of Ironman are excited to have me in the race, they've made a huge media fuss about my presence. For the last two days, I have walked around Port Macquarie and been approached by well-wishers, stopped for selfies. And while the support from strangers has been very much appreciated, it was also overwhelming. And a little embarrassing – journalists were asking me if I was going to win and I didn't even know for sure if I was going to finish!

I used to be a gun swimmer, and could slide effortlessly through the water with maximum efficiency. Now, with barely any handspan and hardly any fingers to speak of, my ability to pull myself through the water is limited compared to most, so I rely heavily on my kick. Nonetheless, as I reach the halfway buoy at the 2-kilometre mark and turn to make my way back to the bike-marshalling yard, I glimpse the clock and I'm making good time. The adrenaline and excitement have spurred me on to my best swim time split ever. It lifts my spirits no end. I'm feeling good. The lungs are sucking in and expelling air, the blood is pumping, the muscles feel primed. I put my head down, and keep swimming.

As I emerge from the water and run to my bike, I allow myself to feel a small surge of excitement. For the first time in the race, I let some of the nerves slide off me. I've finished the swim in one hour and sixteen minutes. I can hardly believe it. It's at least fifteen minutes faster than Bruce and I had planned.

All around me, people are stripping out of the wetsuits, pulling on their Lycra riding kit and strapping on shoes and helmets, with volunteers helping everyone get changed.

It's coming up to 8.30 as I mount my bike and pedal off through the start of the course, along the streets of downtown Port Macquarie. The bike ride is the part I have been least looking forward to. The fact I will be in this saddle for the next eight hours or so, riding down to Laurieton and back ... twice – 180 kilometres of cycling – is intimidating enough. The fact that, of all three sections of the Ironman, the bike is the one which I feel in the least control of, fills me once again with nerves. I can pedal as fast and as hard as the next person, but with less dexterity in my hands than most, I don't always feel like I have complete control over the bike. Downhills at speed are especially scary. I try not to think about what will happen if I come off the bike as it flies down a hill, as has occasionally happened during my training. And then there's my fear that, 60 kilometres out and a long, long way from any assistance, I could get a flat tyre or encounter some other mechanical problem.

But Bruce has told me there's no point focusing on stuff like that. If it happens, I'll deal with it. The important thing is to stay in my head, to be completely in the moment, listen to my breathing, take each kilometre as it comes – and whatever I do, don't focus on the enormity of the task ahead.

As I cycle past a block of holiday apartment buildings, down a hill, past a high school and up a rise, I hear a loud cheer erupt. There is Michael and a small group of our friends. He is jumping up and down, shouting my name – a smile from ear to ear. I grin back, but try to stay focused on the job at hand.

'You're going great!' I hear him shout as I pass. 'You are going to smash this!'

Riding out of town, southwards along the coast line, I glance to my left out to sea and see the sun trying to push through a heavy bank of clouds. The ocean is still, the rain clouds are gathering. The temperature will hover around 16 degrees all day, thanks to the cloud cover – perfect conditions.

During the cycle past Lake Cathie, the road flattens out and a light drizzle sets in. It will be good, I think, to keep me cool, but the road has just got a whole lot more slippery. Focus on the bitumen in front, concentrate on my breathing, just keep pushing the bike forward.

We're riding in small, separate clumps now. Everyone has found their speed and rhythm. For the first time, and with hours and hours of cycling ahead of me, I start to take in some of my fellow competitors. It's amazing, the range of different people who are racing. Men and women of all ages and body shapes. There's a seventy-year-old woman among us, undertaking her eighteenth Ironman. There are plenty of professional athletes, sure – who look every bit the picture of fitness you would expect – but there are also grandmothers and young women and weekend warriors and middle-aged men who frankly look as if they just stepped out from behind their office desk and whacked on some Lycra. I've got plenty of time to reflect, and I find myself wondering what everyone's story is. You don't enter Ironman on a whim. It's not something you do without a pretty good reason.

With every kilometre of bitumen we churn up on this otherwise sleepy little coastal road on the mid-north coast of New South Wales, fifteen hundred inspirational stories are coming closer to their conclusion. I am but one of them. And there is comfort in that.

In the end, I'm on the bike for just over seven hours. Seven hours and thirteen minutes, to be exact. I started the bike ride around 8.30 am and as I coast back into Port Macquarie at around 4 pm, it's starting to get dark. I've ridden up and down hills, through pouring rain, on sometimes extremely slippery stretches of road. I've been in a bike saddle for nearly every daylight hour this day has to offer and my legs are in agony. All things considered, though, I'm in okay shape. Twelve months of training has paid off: train hard, race easy. That's the Ironman motto – and it couldn't be truer. To say I feel buoyant would be a massive overstatement. Every fibre and cell in my body feels depleted, my brain is fuzzy, my muscles are burning and my inner-thighs are red raw. All I've ingested are gels and electrolyte solution and water.

I dismount the bike. It feels odd to not be pedalling anymore and to be back on *terra firma*; it takes my legs and balance a moment to adjust. Another quick change and it's into my running gear. My bum is so saddle-sore I can barely sit down to put on my trainers.

The run is my favourite part of the competition. Without a doubt, it's my comfort zone – the one part of this event that I feel completely in control of. I've been running almost as long as I can walk. Even so, the prospect of running 42 kilometres (a full marathon!) after seven hours on a bike and more than an hour of swimming is pretty daunting. So Bruce and I have reframed it. I know I can run a marathon. I am saving the best for last. Every time someone overtook me on the bike, I thought, *I'm going to catch you on the run.* I try not to dwell on what's ahead as I set off. One foot in front of the other – focus on my breathing, keep up my fluids.

The course takes me through the streets of Port Macquarie – still lined with spectators and well-wishers – out along a path that hugs the contours of the bay, up the hills on the outskirts of town, south down along the coast road and back again – in four loops of roughly 10 kilometres each. It's dusk, and a magnificent pink and orange sunset has lit up the sky in the west. As I run up one of the first little hills in town, there's Michael and a bunch of our friends. They're standing in the rain, screaming my name as I jog past. It gives me a lift, but it's all I can do to look up and acknowledge them with a smile.

The road winds out of town and down along the coast road, the buildings peel slowly away, the crowds dissipate and it's just me and my fellow competitors in the fading light. Some are flagging – barely shuffling. Others are run–walking: jogging in little bursts and walking in between. The strain is etched onto everyone's face. Faces look drained – but at the same time, there's the tiniest frisson: a sense that we are close now. Just four or five hours to go.

As the lights and the buzz of Port Macquarie gradually recede behind me, the only sound is the dull slap of waves on a beach nearby and the steady thud of my trainers on the bitumen. With each person I overtake, I feel a surge of confidence.

The course for the run brings us back into town; cruelly, we're brought past the finish line on three occasions before we're able to run across it. Three times I glimpse the end and have to run past it. Three times, I watch as those in front of me – some way, way ahead of me in the race – sprint the last 100 metres down a long red carpet, through cheering crowds and across the line. A large digital clock ticks dutifully above the finish. Watching all of these people finish while I still have a race to run could have the effect of demoralising me completely, but the crowd is behind me, and the prospect of actually finishing an Ironman is now so tantalisingly close, I find a reserve of energy and power on. I think, *Only a couple of hours until I'm an Ironman! I've trained for fifteen months for this day! I'm going to be an Ironman!*

All around me, people are fading – their step faltering, their run turning to a shuffle and then eventually a walk. Bruce's advice was to employ the run–walk method. There's a man who has inadvertently become my running buddy on the course. We've been running at a similar pace, using one another as a benchmark, silently acting as one another's time-keeper and pacemaker. 'I'm going to walk for a bit,' he'll say at intervals, so we'll slacken the pace and catch our breath. Nothing else is spoken between us. I don't know his name, and as far as I know he doesn't know mine. We're just two people in the dark, feeding off one another's fast-fading energy levels.

As I make my last swing past the finish line and prepare to run along the bay foreshore out of town for the last time – with only 4 kilometres left to run – I make out Michael's face in the crowd. He's there, willing me on.

As I run back into town, the crowds lining the race track seem to build on either side with every step I take. Through the

Norfolk pines, I can make out the floodlit finish line. Music is pumping, a man on a microphone is commentating the last 50 metres of every competitor. I feel a surge of energy. I'm so exhausted that it almost feels as if I have left my body and am watching it from above – but I pull focus, determined to remember this moment. I run towards the finish line, and the pair of bleachers that line it, packed with people screaming my name.

'Here she comes, ladies and gentlemen,' booms the MC. 'Turia Pitt! The most inspirational woman you will ever meet, about to complete an Ironman!'

The feeling in my limbs is strange. I feel empty, but energised. I'm running now on pure adrenaline. There's a roar from the crowd, the dance music is thumping, lights are flashing – it's all quite surreal. With ten final steps, I run across the finish line, my arms held aloft in victory.

I glance up at the clock: 13:24.

I can scarcely believe it. It's at least forty minutes faster than I anticipated. Hell, I can scarcely believe I've finished.

'Turia Pitt!' yells the MC. 'You are an Ironman!' There's another roar from the crowd and I feel elated.

The flashes of a bank of cameras greet me as I cross the line. I stand gasping for breath, suddenly aware of a great wave of people building where the bright lights meet the darkness. Beth Gerdes, the winner of the women's race, steps forward with my medal, hugs me and places it around my neck.

I gracefully accept the congratulations from strangers and do my best to answer the questions from notepad-wielding reporters, but I am distracted. My race isn't complete until I find him and share this moment with him. And then I spot his smiling eyes. They're wet with tears of pride and moving slowly through the crowd towards me. I push towards him and throw my arms around his neck. I want to collapse then and there into Michael's arms – to have him lift me gently and carry me away. Away from the noise and lights and people. But this is my moment: the moment I – and everyone else, it seems – has been waiting for. I wipe a tear from my eye and turn to face the cameras.

With the interviews, photographs and fielding of well wishes done, I'm still looking for Bruce. True to his humble self, he's quiet on the sidelines, swallowed up by the crowd. When I find him I give him a hug. Then I finally go to the recovery tent. Suddenly I've lost the ability to walk. My legs are wobbly and everything hurts. I'm hungry. So ravenous I could eat a horse. I want to sit, but I'm scared I won't get up again. I pause for a few minutes in the recovery tent, uttering my well-worn lines of gratitude to the steady stream of well-wishers. But I just need to be back in the hotel now – horizontal on a bed, with Michael next to me.

Four weeks will go by, during which the adrenaline will subside and the pain will set in. Yet I'm walking on air. I feel invincible. Almost immediately after Port Macquarie, I feel I could do it all over again. I know how nuts that sounds, but the sense of achievement is so great, the endorphin hit is so intense, the hole that is left in my daily life now that I no longer have an Ironman to train for is so enormous, I find myself wishing I could have the day again.

Then again, barely three weeks will pass and I will be on a plane bound for Papua New Guinea to trek the Kokoda Track. And when I return, there will be a letter waiting for me.

A letter from the organisers of Ironman in Hawaii inviting me to take part in their annual race – the Ironman World Championship! I will open that letter and dance with joy. And the first phone call I make will be to call Bruce. 'Bruce,' I will say. 'We're back in business!'

21

KOKODA

They say Eskimos have fifty different words for 'snow'. I can't profess to have researched it in any great detail, but it wouldn't surprise me if the people of Papua New Guinea have at least as many different words for 'mud'. Never in my life have I seen, nor studied in greater detail, as much mud as I did on the Kokoda Track. Brown, oozy mud; black, gritty mud. There's even a mud that when stepped on gives off a foul odour. There's not a kind of mud in the world that isn't present on the track. I know, because for two weeks after I returned, I was still scrubbing it out of my clothes.

What is there to say about Kokoda? It's one of those experiences that, once done, is hard to put into words. Epic is the closest I have been able to come to describe it properly. It is vast, it is sweeping. While you are there, and for a long time after you come back, it defies description. It overwhelms the senses. Physically, it is draining and unrelenting. Mentally, it takes a toll. Like few experiences I have had before, it demands that you are in the present, You step into the jungle, and as the canopy closes over the top of you, the world you left at home is shut out.

And there's a release in that: no email, no phone, no possibility of being involved in the workaday minutiae that otherwise fills all of our lives. But there's also a sense of free-fall: as if the intricate web of ropes and strings that keep you tethered have been cut and you are left out there in the middle of nowhere, floating without anchor and so very isolated.

It's primitive, it's primal – and it strips you back to your very essence. It's dirty and hot and every step is uncertain. And the mud! Walking in it up to your ankles is one thing, but trying to make your way down a 60-degree slope in it, during which with every footfall the ground seems to slide from underneath you, is just plain exhausting.

But walking that track is also one of the most rewarding things I have ever done. And – without wishing to blow my own trumpet – that's saying something. It's funny. Before I left, and even after I got back, various well-meaning people referred to my Kokoda trip as a holiday. But you certainly don't undertake Kokoda because you want a break. You build up to Kokoda. You train for Kokoda. And when it comes, you tackle Kokoda with all the mental and physical strength you can muster.

The timing of the trek was unfortunate, being, as it was, so close to the Port Macquarie Ironman. Originally I'd planned to enter the Melbourne Ironman in March, which would have given me time to recover for Kokoda. But it was cancelled, for the first time in its history, so instead I set my sights on Port Macquarie's a couple of months later. And obviously by then I couldn't change the date of the Kokoda challenge – because everything had been booked and twenty-seven excellent human beings were busily planning, training and fundraising for it.

So, there was nothing else for it but to buckle down and accept that after I had competed in the most gruelling physical challenge I had ever undertaken, I was going to double-down a few weeks later and take part in another relentlessly gruelling physical challenge.

In the intervening weeks, while I should probably have been training and wearing in my boots and testing myself on early morning ascents of Pigeon House Mountain, I was instead kicking back and discovering what it was to have a life again. The months of training for Ironman had added up to a year of discipline. Carefully watching what I ate, training up to eight hours every single day, never having a weekend off – feeling guilty every moment I sat still because it wasn't a moment I was on my bike or swimming the length of the Mollymook beach.

In the weekend before I left for Kokoda, my three brothers came to visit Michael and me in Mollymook. It's a rare enough thing for all four siblings to be together. On this particular weekend, the universe seemed to be smiling down especially on us. The weather was perfect, in that late-autumn, South Coast, sunny-with-a-chill kind of way. We spent the entire weekend hanging out: surfing, eating, laughing, paying out on one another in that way siblings do. I remember sitting around the table with my brothers – all grown men now – sipping on a glass of red wine and thinking how nice it was not only to share this moment with three men who are dear to me, but also to have my life back. It's a small thing, having a glass of wine without feeling bad about it, but it meant the world.

Still, before I could get too carried away, Kokoda had to be conquered. So the backpack was pulled out and a last-minute packing frenzy was undertaken.

In the weeks leading up to our departure, the tour company organising our trek, the Brisbane-based Backtrack Adventures, had been bombarding all us prospective trekkers with list upon list of the things we would require to tackle Kokoda. Boots, poles, backpacks, socks (lots and lots of socks), malaria medicine, mozzie repellent, foot powder (lots and lots of foot powder), wet-weather gear, water bottles, water-purifying tablets, sunscreen, thermals, sleeping bag, sleeping mat and two rolls of toilet paper per person (the toilets along the track, if in fact you could call them toilets, had to be seen to be believed. But more on that later ...).

Any sensible person would spend a good month or so preceding a Kokoda adventure gathering together all the stuff they need. I'd had a few things on in the lead-up, so, as it was, the final few days were spent madly scrambling to get my proverbial shit together.

When the morning of our departure arrived, I woke at 2 am and drove the three hours to Sydney Airport to meet up with the one half of my trekking colleagues who were similarly flying to Port Moresby out of Sydney.

Once in Moresby, we merged with the remainder of the crew, who had flown in from other Australian capitals, and sat around the pool of the Holiday Inn as our guides, Jason and Ray, explained how tough the next ten days were going to be, how intensely we were going to have to concentrate on our every step (so treacherous was the walk we were about to undertake) – and how imperative it was to go back to our hotel rooms and empty our packs of at least half of the clothing and other unnecessary items we had stuffed in there.

Small talk was made, introductions were exchanged, and with a call-time the next day of 3 am for our flight up into the Owen Stanley Range, beds were duly retired to. I'm not sure anyone slept all that well. The next morning, bleary-eyed and full of nervous anticipation, we made our way to the airport.

The plan was to fly up into the mountains and walk back out, following the 96 kilometres of track from the village of Kokoda to Owers' Corner – a point at the base of the Owen Stanley Range some 40 kilometres to the north of Port Moresby. In so doing, we would trace the footsteps of the Australian soldiers who had so bravely served on the Kokoda Track during the Second World War.

The flight over the Owen Stanley Range to the town of Popondetta took barely an hour. Staring out the window of our twin-prop Air Niugini plane at the mountains below, I couldn't help be struck by two things. The first was how beautiful the country was. Row after row of undulating mountain ridges and valleys, all covered in a lush blanket of green jungle canopy, unfurled beneath us, marching to the horizon as far as the eye could see. The second was the mounting realisation that every kilometre the plane flew and every mountain it passed was a kilometre we were going to have to walk back over, and a mountain top we were going to have to climb. I'm sure I wasn't alone watching the ridges unfurl below willing the plane to land sooner rather than later.

Kokoda has loomed large on my to-do list ever since I ready Kurt Fearnley's amazing autobiography, *Pushing the Limits*. Born without the lower portion of his spine, Kurt propelled himself along Kokoda with his arms only. When he undertook to tackle Kokoda in the company of his brothers and cousins in 2009, crawling his way along the track – hauling himself up sheer mountain faces and hurling himself down the other side – he set a precedent for one of the most iconic walks in the collective Aussie psyche, which I don't believe has ever been beaten. You want to talk about grit and determination? That man has it in spades.

So Kurt's conquering of Kokoda seven years previously was a major reason I wanted to do it myself. I also knew it would be the sort of challenge that would help raise much-needed funds for Interplast. Furthermore, I realised that there was something missing from previous trips: we'd put ourselves through all these gruelling challenges to raise money for Interplast, but we'd never actually seen them in action. In PNG we'd meet a local surgeon, an Interplast volunteer surgeon, and a local patient, whose future had been changed as a direct result of the work of the organisation.

I knew me doing the track would capture the imagination not only of the Aussie media (who would help raise awareness of the work being done by Interplast) but also attract a hefty number of participants keen to take part, allowing them to tick an item off their bucket list while raising money for a worthy charity. As well as spend ten days in the jungle without a shower. In the heat and humidity. Clambering up and down mountains by day and sleeping in tents by night. Who wouldn't want to do that?

Twenty-seven foolhardy folk, as it turned out, signed up to walk with me. The composition of the crew was similar in some ways to the make-up of the groups who accompanied me on the Inca Trail and Great Wall of China fundraising trips: namely, mostly women, with a handful of brave guys.

They came from all walks of life: stay-at-home mums from Sydney's well-heeled north shore, an investment banker from Hong Kong and his two young-adult children, a nurse-turned-funeral-director from Adelaide, a teenage life-saving champion from the New South Wales Central Coast and her aunty, a petrol station attendant from Darwin.

One of the men was walking to honour his adopted grand-father who had served on the Kokoda Track with the Australian army. One of the women undertook the trek carrying her father's ashes in her day pack. It was, she said, her dad's lifelong dream to walk Kokoda – and she was determined to do it in his memory. To a person, every single one of the people on our trek came with a laundry list of life matters to sort out while they walked. Some had come to mull over a career move, others had determined to use the time to sort out a relationship issue – everyone expected the ten days in the jungle would be the perfect opportunity to press the pause button on their life, shut out the noise that otherwise fills their daily existence, and make some long overdue decisions about their future.

But as it happened, we were all just so busy concentrating on not falling to our death, we didn't have time. From the moment we woke each morning at 5.30, until the moment we crawled into our sleeping bags around 8 pm, the vast majority of our brain space was occupied with the pressing business of basic survival.

At first, that was disconcerting. I too had come away to take stock. Yes, I was there first and foremost to raise money for Interplast, but the plan was also to take a moment to breathe – to use the meditative act of putting one foot in front of the other on a ten-day wander through the bush to set a course for the next twelve months of my life.

After Ironman, my body, miraculously, had bounced back without too much of a hangover. Away from the email and the phone and the speaking engagements and the rushing from one place to another, I was going to use the time to think about what was next for me. Physically, I knew Kokoda was going to be a challenge. But mentally, I expected I was going to be able to put my brain on auto-pilot and spend the time roaming those corners of my mind that rarely get visited. The long-term-planning corner and the big-life-decisions corner.

Alas, it wasn't to be. Yet there were other rewards. Reaching the top of a mountain I didn't think I could possibly ascend. Finding humour in the least funny of circumstances. Meeting new, like-minded people and walking with them together to raise money for a good cause.

When the going got really tough, as it did at least three or four times every day, each of us dug deep and called on whatever reserves were at our disposal to take one more step, to pull ourselves up onto one more ledge, to navigate our way gingerly down one more steep incline. All but one of us on the trek had opted to engage a porter – one of the many sure-footed locals who make a living accompanying clumsy foreigners on the track, carrying their backpacks and other-wise hovering close at hand to stop them from plunging to their deaths. Our very own fuzzy-wuzzy angels.

As we collapsed at the top of one particular ascent one day, struggling to catch our breath, baking under the midday sun and sucking deeply from the water bladders in our backpacks, one trekker told me he had been close to collapse – to stopping dead in his tracks, unsure where he'd find the strength to keep going. Then, he said, he looked over his shoulder and saw me struggling up behind him. And he thought of me three weeks previously competing in the Ironman. And he thought of me in hospital five years ago, being told that while I was lucky to be alive, I ought not to expect to ever walk again. And he put his head down, stuck his walking pole into the track that rose up at what seemed like 90 degrees in front of him, and hauled himself forward.

I'm not prone to shows of emotion, and I certainly don't cry easily; but it was an admission that came out of the blue and straight from the heart, and I found myself tearing up. I felt humbled.

I learned later that one woman on the track – who wasn't as fit as the rest of the crew, was carrying more weight than most of us and whose 'friends' at home had laughed dismissively when she told them she had signed up to walk Kokoda – had spent the first two nights alone in her tent crying after everyone had turned in for the night. Exhausted after a day spent struggling to keep up, tired of being the one everyone was waiting for at each scheduled stop, she had seriously considered dropping out: pulling the pin and orchestrating a helicopter evacuation.

But she didn't. She woke up each day at 5 am with the rest of us, packed up her tent, laced up her boots, put on a brave face over breakfast and steeled herself for another ten gruelling hours of trekking. Towards the end of the trip, she became our talisman. Whenever she would crest a mountain ridge, a huge cheer would erupt. In so many ways, she was the embodiment of the spirit of the diggers who had trudged the track (in admittedly far more horrific circumstances) seventy years before us. There was an against-the-odds quality to her achievement that made the completion of the track all the sweeter not only for her – but for everyone who walked alongside her.

Not that evacuations were really an option. And here's the thing about Kokoda. The reason it is such a life-altering experience is because turning back or stopping is not an option. Once you step onto that track, the only way off it is to go forward. You are compelled to finish what you have started – because there simply is no other choice. And in an age where our lives are cushioned by any number of conveniences designed to provide an easy out, that is perhaps Kokoda's greatest lesson.

Having said that, certain circumstances sometimes mean opting out is the *only* option. As we found out on day two. This was a day when we were all starting to get to know one another, and each of us was trying to find our Kokoda feet. After a morning spent walking through some gorgeous scenery – entire sections of the trail that weaved through landscape that made it seem as if we had wandered onto the set of the Sigourney Weaver movie *Gorillas in the Mist* – we paused for lunch in a small village called Deniki. After lunch in the sun, we set off again, climbing a ridge and finding ourselves traversing a section of track that seemed to have been barely scraped into the mountain side. It was treacherous, but no more or less so than countless other sections of track we would walk in the week to come. On our right, the ridge reared up almost vertically. To our left was a ravine that dropped away precipitously.

Jess, the woman from Adelaide whom I had met and befriended at the Tony Robbins seminar in Sydney the year previously and had since signed up to join me on Kokoda, was walking behind me. We had been chatting happily for a good twenty minutes. Looking back, I suppose I noticed that the chat became less animated as we each turned our attention to the trail in front of us, which seemed to deteriorate with every step. We began to walk in silence, careful to place our feet in the footsteps of the porters who seemed to hop effortlessly along in front of us.

In the hours after it had happened, Jess would recall how she placed her left boot in the very footprint left by her porter Nomi not five seconds before her. She would recall how she felt the earth shift under her foot and how, for one gut-churning moment she was suspended in space – grabbing pointlessly at thin air in front of her, her arms flailing as she desperately tried to regain her balance. Before anyone knew what had happened, and with barely a noise, she fell backwards into the void. Hearing a gasp from behind, I spun around to see a tumble of limbs being swallowed by the thick undergrowth. She fell 25 metres, cartwheeling her way down the cliff, thankfully having the presence of mind to curl into a ball and cover her head with her arms.

Without hesitating, Nomi threw off his backpack and launched himself down the ravine after her – closely followed by no fewer than three other porters who leapt, without a second's hesitation, off the side of the track.

As we watched in horror, Jess's fall onto rocks below was only broken at the last minute when her legs became entangled in a series of vines. And there she hung, motionless for what seemed like forever. When finally she let out a scream for help, it was the sweetest sound any of us had ever heard. Against all odds, she had survived. Jess would later recall how she watched, hanging upside down, as Nomi tumbled past her, somehow managing to stop himself before reaching the rock-strewn creek bed just 15 metres below. Within seconds, Jess was surrounded on all sides by porters, one supporting her head, another taking the weight of her body, a third working to gently disentangle her legs from the vines. Nomi even managed to right himself and pull himself back up to Jess's side, frantically checking her for serious injury.

Back up on the track, we stood in shock. The porters who remained with us swung into action, working out the logistics of getting Jess back out of the ravine. With no idea of the extent of her injuries, it all had to be done gingerly. When finally she was lifted back onto the track (and I still don't know how the porters managed it), it was clear she had severely injured her right leg. She couldn't stand on it. Miraculously, that seemed to be the extent of her injuries.

Within minutes, another team of porters had disappeared into the jungle, machetes held aloft, to chop down a couple of saplings to create a makeshift stretcher. Lashing the frame together with vines, then stretching a couple of hessian bags between the supports, a bush stretcher was created and·Jess was hoisted upon it and off they set. A team of six porters, running at a trot along the track, taking shortcuts over ridiculously steep rises, nimbly passing a prostrate Aussie trekker from one set of hands to the other.

'Is it okay if we stop and put you down for a moment?' the leader of the pack humbly requested of Jess twenty minutes into their mammoth effort.

Upon arriving at the small village that surrounds the war memorial at Isurava, Jess was tended by her friend, Sally – who, as fortune would have it, was a trained nurse. As the shock wore off and adrenaline subsided, the full extent of Jess's injuries became clearer. There was no way she was going to be able to continue. Despite her protestations, a satellite phone call was made, requesting an emergency evacuation.

With cloud closing in and night fast approaching, it was decided to stabilise her overnight and evacuate her by helicopter first thing the next morning. As she lay in wait, dosed up to the eyeballs on painkillers, we pitched camp for the night. A pall hung over the group that evening. The initial flush of excitement at being on the Kokoda Track had been replaced with a glaring reminder of how dangerous a place it could be. Everyone retreated early to their tent. Sleep came only fitfully.

The following day we rose as normal, breakfasted and bade a sombre farewell to Jess. She'd had a rough night. Sally cried as she strapped on her boots, picked up her walking poles and donned her day pack to join the rest of us as we trooped quietly out of the village.

The sun was brilliant that morning as we set off again along the track, a blue sky over some of the most dramatic and beautiful mountain vistas. About an hour into our walk that morning, a helicopter flew overhead. Through the thick jungle canopy, we could just make it out. We all walked slowly, extra carefully and largely in silence that day.

In our group, whether you were the woman who cried in her tent at night or one of the super-fit who were always at the front of the pack and seemed practically to jog the track, we all did it tough in our own way. Hardly a person wasn't touched by a virulent stomach bug that seemed to pass through the group like wildfire. The toilets – when we encountered them each evening or lunchtime in the string of villages that are scattered along the track – were a harrowing enough experience when you were feeling well. Six-foot deep holes dug into the ground, with only a flimsy bamboo lean-to with a hessian-sack door flap for privacy, it was all you could do to use them without dry-retching. To be compelled to use them because of an upset tummy – or having to duck into the bushes mid-track to answer a pressing call of nature – shredded whatever last vestiges of pride you had brought with you to New Guinea. It was not for the faint-hearted.

Nor was the smell. Of both the long-drop toilets or of ourselves. Ten hours a day of walking in the heat and humidity of a tropical jungle meant we sweated more profusely than ever we had sweated before. Clothes would be wet through with sweat from dawn to dusk. Attempts to dry them out overnight usually failed – meaning by the end of ten days, we were all waking in the chill of the early morning to don wet underwear, wet shorts, wet T-shirts and – if we were really unlucky – wet socks and boots. We all stank to high heaven. There are no showers along the track, save for the occasional pipe in the occasional village, diverting a stream of freezing water from a mountain stream. If we were really lucky after a full day of trekking, we would arrive for the night in one of the few villages that had a makeshift shower. We would all queue to take our turn under the flow of cold water to scrub the mud from our legs and indulge in a rare splash of soap. Or we'd hope to get to a village that, while it didn't have a shower, was at least happily located next to a creek, whereupon we would all fall, fully clothed, into the ice-cold water in the hope that the passage of liquid through material would wash away at least some of the sweat stench. There were nights, too, when there was no shower or stream – and we simply had to clean ourselves as best we could and put on what dry clothes we had to huddle around the campfire and eat dinner.

Of course, sweating was a problem I wish I had more of. One of the main functions of our skin is to regulate our body temperature: we sweat when we're hot (cooling us down) and when we're cold we get goosebumps (heat is trapped in our hairs and that makes us warmer). A lasting consequence of my burns is that the sweat glands and pores that once helped me regulate my body temperature are no longer able to do so. With much of my skin permanently scarred, there are limited areas of my body that are able to sweat: my armpits, groin, back and head. And that means I have to be extra careful not to overheat. I would often reach the top of a steep mountain climb in Kokoda and while everyone around me was sweating buckets I was as dry as a bone. So every time we crossed a stream, when my trekking buddies paused to fill their water bottles, I would douse a neck scarf in water and drizzle the water down my back, around my neck and across my forehead to try to cool down.

The thing I had learned from the Great Wall of China and Inca Trail challenges was that I tended to feel a sense of responsibility for each of the trekkers who had signed up to walk with me. Responsible not just for the safety of each person on the trip, but also for their enjoyment of the experience.

On Kokoda, I did my best to move from the back of the troupe – cajoling, joking and generally making a clown of myself – to the middle of the pack, to the front, where the serious walkers marched purposefully each day. More of my time, truth be told, was spent down the back, because that was where I figured I was needed most, and also because it gave me more time to stop and smell the proverbial roses.

The thing about Kokoda that few people who have done it seem to talk about is the sheer physical beauty of the terrain.

From the top of a mountain at the Isurava Battle Memorial looking down into the valley far below, to wandering through one of the many magical stretches of rainforest where butterflies of the most vivid blues, yellows and purples flit about your head, to the truly breathtaking Myola (a flat, vast, dry lake bed in the heart of the Owen Stanley Range that appears suddenly out of the jungle and makes you feel as if you've stumbled suddenly onto the African savannah), the place is just breathtaking.

And the local people are among the warmest I have met. Our porters – all male – were kind and unassuming. At first I felt self-conscious at the thought of having someone carry my backpack – even if I knew, long before starting, that attempting the track without a porter would make the feat ten times harder. After only one day of trekking, I came to understand that carrying my belongings was only part of the porter's gig. For the most part, they were employed to shadow their charge, one hand hovered above the handle on our daypacks, ready to grab us and pull us back from the brink of any number of potential disasters. Lose your footing and slide precariously close to a cliff's edge and you'd feel the hand of your porter. Struggle to climb a section of track that seemed to rise at 90 degrees in front of you, and you'd see the friendly hand of a porter proffered, ready to pull you up.

Quiet, gentle and unfailingly generous, my porter, Noel, spoke only a little English. But just by watching where I put my feet or the angle at which I leaned going down a cliff face, he was able to anticipate my every misstep long before I had taken it.

One of the great amusements of the Kokoda Track – it occurred to me as I watched the porters nimbly hop from one vertiginous part of the trail to the other – is that while we visitors trekked with every piece of hiking equipment known to man – state-of-the-art boots, poles, backpacks and clothes – the porters wore shorts, T-shirts and thongs. The really experienced ones walked barefoot. And, carrying our packs, our food and our tents, they skipped along the track at twice the pace we could muster. It was, I thought, more than a little embarrassing.

One day, when one of the porters slipped on a downhill section of the track and fell on his bum, the other porters laughed at him, teasing him in their local dialect.

'What were you saying to him?' I asked Noel.

'We told him he walks like a white man,' Noel grinned back at me.

Midway through our trek, we stopped for a day of rest in the village of Naduri. Up in the mountains the locals are pious when it comes to the Sabbath, so we pitched camp for a day and attended a local church service.

The singing from the choir – melodic, pitch perfect and almost haunting in its beauty – rose up out of the large shed that served as the community's church hall and soared across the valley. It was a rare privilege to sit in the congregation and watch these people exercise their faith.

During the service, I was invited to come forward and introduce myself. I was a little nervous, but the village elder ushered me to the front of the congregation, describing me as 'someone who is very special to us'. And though I had never met any of the villagers before – and I couldn't be sure how many of them knew who I was or how I came to look the way I do – they certainly made me feel special.

After the church service, I challenged a bunch of the local kids to a running race on the airstrip above their village.

(Every fifth or so village along the Kokoda Track has a helipad or an airstrip – the latter are little more than 100 metres of flat grass carved into the side of the mountain. Definitely not any airstrip I would ever want to have to land on.) Their English was minimal, my grasp of their local dialect was non-existent. But it didn't matter. With the sky above and the mountains rising on either side of us, the wind in our hair and air filling our lungs, in those moments we were all just a big bunch of kids, running and laughing together in the Papua New Guinean jungle. If I was any different to them before that race – be it because of my nationality, my age or the way I looked – we were the same at the end of it. It felt good.

If I had to choose a word to describe the locals we met along the way – and especially the porters who became like family to us (albeit not very talkative family members) – it would be 'humble'. This led me to one of the few epiphanies I had on Kokoda. After three days in the company of my porter, Noel – which often included extended periods of walking together in silence through the rainforest – it dawned on me how much the porters reminded me of Michael.

Quiet and unimposing, Michael is the last person in any room to blow his own trumpet, even though he is usually the most impressive. There's a quietness to him to which, I realised on Kokoda, I am unconsciously drawn. Dependable, trustworthy and, most of all, humble.

Kokoda also taught me that it is okay not to talk; that sometimes you don't have to fill the silence with noise. Sometimes the silence is noise enough.

*

Of course, no visit to Kokoda takes place without the spectre of the Second World War campaign waged there by Aussie soldiers against the Japanese in 1942. It hangs over each step and gives every inch of the track's inhospitable terrain a heavy sense of history. Some days, we would divert briefly off the track to visit the site of an important battle – invariably another spot in a land far from their homes where a rag-tag bunch of Aussie diggers routinely distinguished themselves in the face of staggering odds. Other days, we would stop briefly at an overgrown spot of jungle where a collection of rusting Japanese helmets, grenades and mortars lay in the undergrowth. With the passage of time, nature is gradually reclaiming the Kokoda Track. Sometimes it was hard to reconcile how this simple dirt track, which was so overgrown in some places that it seemed almost not to exist, could have assumed such massive importance in our national psyche.

Then we would sit at dinner and listen as our guide, Jason, read excerpts from Kokoda history books recording the campaign. Acts of selfless bravery, displays of mateship, courage and sacrifice in whose presence we were humbled.

As remote and inhospitable as the Kokoda Track is, because it is steeped in meaning to only Australians and Japanese – and because the Japanese choose not to commemorate their loss there – it's mainly only other Aussies who tackle it.

One morning, as we stood just outside a village catching our breath after a relatively gentle climb, a man came into view. He was preceded by a couple of porters who waited patiently as he caught up to them. His name was Tony. He was a veteran of the Vietnam War and had lost a leg in a car accident twenty-five years previously.

We all of us stood amazed as he explained his determination to walk the track on a pair of crutches to raise money for returned servicemen suffering from PTSD (post-traumatic stress disorder). I had been hanging at the back of our group as he told his story to a rapt, gobsmacked audience. Mid-sentence, he caught sight of me and stopped.

'Is that Turia Pitt?' he asked. I flushed. 'Oh, wow. I can't believe it. It really is Turia Pitt.' He seemed suddenly over-whelmed. Choked up, even. I didn't know where to look. 'I heard you were doing this,' he continued as he fumbled in his daypack for his camera. 'Do you mind? I'd love it if I could have a photo with you. You're my inspiration.'

I was touched, and a little embarrassed. Here was a man who had served our country at war, who had lost a leg in a car accident and was somehow making his way along the Kokoda Track on a pair of crutches. How he thought there could be anyone on the trail at that moment more impressive than himself just didn't make sense to me. But I posed happily for his photograph, gave him a cuddle and sent him on his way.

The following morning, just as we were leaving our camp-site, a snowy-haired gent strode into the village. He was, I overheard him explain to a couple of members of our party, a seventy-seven-year-old Sydney man called Col Reynolds who was walking Kokoda to raise money for research into kids' cancer. He had founded the Kids' Cancer Project twenty-three years earlier when, as a tourist-coach driver – with no links to kids with cancer at the time – he stopped his bus near the former children's hospital in Camperdown, in Sydney's inner-west, to let a couple of kids with bald heads cross the road. Moved by the spectacle, he parked his bus, went inside the hospital and started a conversation with a paediatric oncologist that led to the creation of a charity that has raised more than $27 million since its inception.

Col's story moved me profoundly. That on a whim, this man had dedicated the past twenty-five years of his life to helping others. That he was here, now, walking the Kokoda Track in his seventies to raise more funds for his charity. Once again I hung back, content to listen, when he stopped mid-sentence upon catching sight of me. 'You are an incredible lady,' he said, as I tried to disappear under the nearest rock. 'I am so honoured to have met you. Would you allow me to have a photograph with you? This is a highlight of my trek.'

I felt humbled and honoured to be photographed along-side Col, just as I had felt being photographed with Tony. But for the four days I had been trekking with my crew, I was just Turia: another one in the crowd. No one treated me any differently from anyone else. And it was nice. Don't get me wrong: being an inspiration to people is an honour and a privilege. And it's a responsibility I take seriously. But occasionally – just occasionally – it's nice to get lost in the crowd.

Two weeks after I got back from the jungle, everything still felt a bit weird. I spoke to some of the other trekkers and we all felt the same. We were pining to go back. And none of us could work out why. Because it was hot and cold and sweaty and bloody hard. And the food was bland and the showers were cold and the toilets were a whole world of disgusting. But there was something so wonderfully simple about our daily existence: wake up, eat, walk, laugh, eat, walk some more, laugh some more, eat, sleep. And somewhere along that track, twenty-six strangers forged a little family. Completely cut off from the rest of the world and utterly dependent on one another – for company, for encouragement, for amusement, for support – we forged a bond.

At home, people kept asking me if it was a life-changing experience. I wouldn't say for certain that it was. Did I change as a person? Nope. Did I stumble across a life-altering revelation? Not so much. But something definitely shifted. And that's a good thing. At the end of the day, it's good to be taken out of your life and challenged like that. And that's lesson enough for me.

22

GIVING BACK

It's hot, sweaty and humid. There's a strange smell in the air. I feel like I'm going to pass out and hit my head on the concrete floor. Overhead, a fan hums listlessly. The cry of a child, a soft cough, murmured conversations in a foreign tongue.

The ward is packed with people of all ages with a variety of injuries. It is so crowded that families are sleeping on the floor in the hope that their loved one will be the next to receive surgery. One man has been in an electrical fire and lost both his hands. A young girl's chin is stuck to her chest, saliva is leaking out of her mouth. A kid's face is completely distorted by a huge cyst. In a corner bed lies a young farmer – a father of four. The burns to the back of his knees are relatively minor – only 5 per cent of his body surface area – but sustained as they were five years ago and never having received treatment, bit by bit they have contractured (when skin is burned, the surrounding skin begins to pull together). As a result, he can't walk. We are told he has spent the past couple of years pulling himself along by his hands, while his atrophied legs dangle behind him. Without the use of his legs, he cannot farm. Without farming, he cannot feed his family.

As Michael and I stood in this hospital in Laos, it struck me (not for the first time) how very lucky I was. Lucky to have been born in a country like Australia, with a first-world hospital and medical system that means if, like me, you have an accident, you will be attended to by some of the most highly qualified doctors in the world.

It's fashionable to knock our medical system – and for sure, there are things it could do better or more efficiently – but until you have seen first-hand how many relatively minor afflictions go untreated in countries like Laos, and thus have a disproportionate impact on the lives of the people who suffer them, you don't truly appreciate how good we have it. Or at least I didn't.

Of course, Dr Peter Haertsch first introduced me to the work of Interplast, the charity I have mentioned before. And the more I learned about the life-changing work this group of Aussie and Kiwi surgeons did – and have been doing, on a volunteer basis, for the thirty-odd years that Interplast has existed – the more I became determined to do something to help them out.

Interplast has a relatively narrow focus. Their mission statement is to perform reconstructive surgery in developing countries in the Asia-Pacific. Their work is tangible and straightforward: is it a physical disability that can be fixed with surgery, like a cleft palate or burns scarring? If so, Interplast gets involved. And in my opinion, that is way better than having too broad a scope (save everyone in the world!). As with everything, the more laser-like your focus, the greater your chances of success. That's not to say that Interplast have a 'fly in, fly out' mentality. In fact, their goal is to do themselves out of a job. A huge component of their work is to train up local surgeons and medical staff in the countries they visit. This means that the whole community keeps benefiting from the surgical skills and knowledge being passed on to local teams. I really respect that about the organisation.

I think that the doctors and nurses who volunteer for Interplast are unsung heroes. People like Peter Haertsch, whose life in Australia is dedicated to helping patients in the public system (he could make much more money if he worked in a private hospital) and whose holidays are then spent volunteering in places like Nepal, Bangladesh and Laos.

It's not the best-known charity in the country, and it certainly doesn't have the advertising or marketing grunt to be a household name. But in terms of impact on the lives of those whose work it touches, it punches far above its weight. It's a privilege to be its ambassador.

So why did I start supporting Interplast?

I think often we can become too introspective (why has this stuff happened to me? Why is my life like this?). Helping others shifts our perspective. And, looking back, one of the most important factors in my recovery was gratitude. By working with Interplast and travelling to places like Laos, I gained perspective on my own circumstances and was grateful. I wouldn't go so far as to say that it made sense of what had happened to me in the Kimberley as I'm not one of those people who believe that things happen for a reason, but working with Interplast was an awesome unforeseen development in my life, which would probably never have come about had I not been caught in that fire.

The generosity of others has been a pillar of my recovery. I could work all day, every day raising money and awareness for Interplast and I still wouldn't come close to balancing the ledger of all the kindnesses that have been shown to me. Plus I only have a certain amount of hours in any given day, so I want to make sure the work I'm doing has both meaning and impact. And I'm a firm believer that if you're going to do something, you have to commit to it 100 per cent. When I'd go surfing with my dad, and I'd go to catch a wave, but wasn't fully committed, I'd either not get the wave and cop a disappointed look from Dad, or get dumped. Dad would say, if you want a wave, you have to go for it, come hell or high water.

So that's why I dedicate all my charity work to Interplast. I could support multiple charities and not really make a meaningful impact with any of them, or I could throw my full weight behind this one and actually make a difference.

My previous interactions with other charities sometimes left me befuddled. Why, I asked myself when I was in Mongolia, are we building houses for these people when quite obviously they just want a new ger? I remember being the guest speaker at one fundraiser and watching with bemusement as a guy handed over a $200 novelty cheque (one of those big, oversized cheques). It costs at least $100 to make a novelty cheque. How is that an efficient use of time or resources?

The only charity that I've seriously thought about setting up is an education charity. My mum broke out of the cycle of poverty because she won a scholarship to a prestigious school. But if I ever started an education charity, it would need to have a specific focus. People also ask me why I don't start my own foundation. And it is something I've thought about. But then I consider the reasons why I'd do so. Would

I actually be helping to solve a problem? Or would I just be another one of the 50,000 registered charities in Australia? Besides, Interplast already does what I want to do. And they are great to work with. All my work is voluntary, I choose what I can and can't commit to, and they really respect that and never act like they own me. And they're happy for me to fundraise for them in whichever way I like. So I walk the Kokoda Track and the Great Wall of China, do the Inca Trail, and soon I plan to climb to Mount Everest base camp. How awesome is that?

The impact I'm making with Interplast is tangible, too. Say it costs $250 for a cleft lip operation. Multiply that out, and with the $1 million I have raised since 2011, I've potentially changed a lot of lives. And that's the best feeling of all.

23

THE THINGS THAT MATTER

It's a sunny autumn afternoon and I'm standing in the sun-drenched northern foyer of the Sydney Opera House. I'm one of about 300 people who have gathered here, all of us dressed to the nines, making small talk, looking at our watches, shuffling awkwardly from foot to foot.

We're in a kind of reception line, snaking its way from one end of the foyer to the other. A seemingly random collection of sports stars, charity workers, school kids, media personalities and me.

A cheer rises up from outside – a large crowd has gathered on the Opera House forecourt. They're waving flags and craning necks to get a glimpse of the Duke and Duchess of Cambridge – otherwise known as William and Kate.

I'm not a royalist by any measure – which is to say, I'm kind of indifferent to the whole monarchy thing. But when I received an invitation to join the official reception welcoming the royal couple to Sydney, I figured why not.

I see Catherine, the Duchess of Cambridge, as she enters the foyer. She knows my story before she gets to me. She's clearly done her homework. As she gets closer, speaking earnestly to the group of people to my right, I can't help but stare. So many magazine photo shoots, so many appearances on the TV: does she really look in real-life as flawless as she appears in the media? Pretty much. Every movement is considered. Not contrived or forced: just graceful and elegant. Her hair is long and luxuriant, her skin has a sort of English rose translucence. (Though I do notice that she has pimples underneath her make-up, which reassures me – after all, these royals are just like the rest of us.)

She's wearing a bright yellow dress – and she looks good in it. For some strange reason, I am feeling nervous. I feel my heart beating as she moves in front of me, takes my hand and shakes it.

An aide introduces us. Do I curtsey? Do I bow? What is the appropriate royal protocol? Is it hello? G'day? How do you do? In the end I cock it up royally and do a stumbled curtsey, before she holds out her hand to shake mine. I manage to spit out, 'Hi, nice to meet you.'

We talk for what seems like a split second, and little of which I can remember afterwards. She is engaged, she is nodding politely. She's either the most sincere stranger I have ever met, or she's just very well-practised at appearing to be interested.

As she goes to move on, she takes my hand in both of hers, looks me in the eye and says, 'You have tremendous spirit!'

One of the stranger by-products of the fire – the injuries I sustained and the very public manner in which I undertook my recovery – has been the funny sort of celebrity I now have.

It's rare these days that I can walk through an airport or go to a restaurant and not be approached by someone who recognises me. Do I mind? It depends. Mostly it depends on what people say when they recognise me. 'You're the chick that got burned in the fire' – I hate that. 'You're the chick from the TV' – that's not so good either. But when people come up and tell me I've inspired them to actually *do* something – whether it be to run a marathon, quit smoking or leave an abusive partner – I'm really proud and pleased I can have that influence. I went into Concord Hospital the other day and saw a nurse who had looked after me. She told me I had inspired her (actually, I think 'given her a kick up the ass' were her actual words) to start her Master's degree. I was stoked.

So for the most part, I appreciate the celebrity status I have, use it for as much good as I can, and – at the end of the day – am grateful I am famous for having rebuilt my life after a terrible tragedy, rather than for making a sex tape or embezzled lots of money!

The only bad thing about it all is that I am rarely 'off'. Every time I step out the front door, I feel obliged to be on show. But I normalise it – we all run into someone at the shops when we're not feeling sociable, and we just have to fake it. I also remind myself: I don't have to be a public figure – I have chosen to be a public figure. This is a path I have actively pursued. This, for the time being, is my job. And besides, every job, no matter what it is, has its pros and cons.

The pros are that I can get a lot more done in a shorter space of time than most people. Doors open more readily, meetings are taken more willingly. And that usually means funds can be raised for the charities I choose so much more easily. Working with Interplast and undertaking the various charity events and overseas challenges, I'm really proud of the money I've raised.

One thing I have learned is that the media can be fickle. When you are the new item, everyone wants a piece of you. At first, I was simply really pleased that anyone was interested in my story. But then, once it got out there and my profile took off, I started to realise I was as much use to these media outfits – and indeed the various charities, companies and organisations who would soon start to line up to seek my involvement in their activities or endorsement of their products – as they were to me. Far from being a one-way street, the benefits whenever I did a story for a media outlet flowed in both directions. And the more media I did, the more I came to appreciate that fact.

Which is not to say the media I engaged with most regularly were only involved for purely cynical reasons. I've become friends with many of the journalists I've got to know along the way. The vast majority of them are empathetic and considerate. But there are always those who just don't get it. They're too interested in the cheap laugh or want to push and prod you until you give them something new or fresh. I remember one radio journalist interviewing me purely for the purpose of provoking me.

I understand they want the best story, but that's not necessarily what I want. And besides, I have to be careful, for my own sanity if nothing else, of only giving away as much of myself as I want to. So after an initial burst of saying yes to everything, I've now scaled it back.

But of course it's been far from all bad. I wouldn't be where I am if it wasn't for the interest *60 Minutes* took in my story at the outset. And appearing on the cover of the *Australian Women's Weekly* was one of the proudest moments of my little celebrity life.

Sometimes I think it's weird – the fact I am well known because of a random accident. A few seconds of my life that have changed everything. But then I don't think I am famous because I was burned but rather because of what I have done since. I am famous because of my resilience, my optimism and my attitude.

As bright as my little star might be shining on the national scene – as many appearances as I might make on TV or shoots I might do for magazines – the one, wonderful, vital constant is the indifference with which it is largely treated by my home town of Mollymook. It's my safe place. It's also the place I retreat to when the speed and whir of this new world I have suddenly found myself in proves too much.

As much as I have carved out an independent existence now – I travel all over Australia and all over the world by myself – I can still manage to feel vulnerable when I am out in the big wide world. I read a *National Geographic* article recently about a killer whale that was injured after a run-in with a boat. And the other killer whales in the pod would kill fish for it and bring them back for the injured whale to eat. How beautiful is that? And sometimes I feel like that injured killer whale – with Mollymook as my pod.

One time when I was out surfing recently, the waves were really big and I was struggling to get my flippers on, and one of the boys put them on for me and held my hand to get me out to the back. Another time I was surfing out at the Bombie and it was seriously massive – even Michael was a bit scared. I got smashed by a set and my leash got ripped off, and I was just getting hammered by these waves. One of the local boys saw me copping a beating, paddled over to me, wrapped me in a big bear hug, talked me through the waves and helped me get washed back to shore. We ending up drifting in to another beach entirely.

People here have my back – and that's reassuring. And it doesn't matter how many princesses or movie stars I meet. To everyone in town, I am plain old Turia, or Pitty to my friends.

I remember standing in a reception line at the State Theatre in Sydney for the premiere of Angelina Jolie's film *Unbroken*. I had been invited to attend and meet Ange and Brad. I was pretty excited (more about Ange than Brad, to be honest). Michael was about as excited as Michael gets – half an hour before we were due at the theatre, he was online in our hotel room checking the next day's surf.

'The world needs more powerful women like you,' Angelina said as she shook my hand. For my part, I couldn't stop staring at her face. That complexion. Those eyes. And Brad. Kind of scruffy but oozing charisma, ridiculously handsome. I wasn't star-struck so much as bemused: a tiny voice in my head wondering how the hell I'd found myself here.

I was, however, star-struck when I met Kurt Fearnley – wheelchair racer, three-time Olympic gold medallist and all-round amazing human being. He's as close to a hero as I have. I read his book when I was training for Ironman – it's still one of my favourite books, and Kurt is one of my favourite people. To me, he epitomises strength of spirit.

He inspires me. The man has three Paralympic gold medals and has won thirty-five marathons in five different continents. He's achieved more in a wheelchair – and with his two remarkable arms – than most able-bodied people will achieve in their lifetime.

One of the things that really resonated in his book was a fear that he used to think only he felt, but has since realised is universal: a fear that when the test comes, you won't have enough. It's as if, no matter the training and preparation, you'll never completely eliminate that little glimmer of doubt about your capabilities. As I spent lonely days riding the backroads of Ulladulla training, to know that it wasn't only me who felt that way was an enormous comfort.

People tell me I am inspiring. I feel like a minnow next to Kurt Fearnley. So when I showed up for a gala dinner in Sydney and was seated next to him, I turned to jelly – I've never been as star-struck. I was so excited to meet him, I think I may have come on a bit strong. I can't be sure because I was in such a state of high excitement, but I vaguely recall him looking hopefully around the table for someone else to talk to as I babbled at him for two straight hours. I sent him an email the next day, apologising. I thought maybe I had overdone it! So unlike me ...

24

MICHAEL

At its heart, my story is a love story. As much as it is a tale of triumph over adversity – a story of the girl who was burned but not broken – it's a story of the boy and the girl whose love for each other couldn't be dimmed. A love that no fire could tear apart.

I reckon we all have different versions of ourselves. It depends on the day or the stage of life we're in. I can say without a shadow of doubt that the version of myself that I love the most is the version that I am when I'm with Michael.

He's my best friend. He knows me better than anyone. He not only lets me be me but he celebrates me – and indulges every single one of my crazy adventures.

Wherever I go and whomever I meet, I am asked about Michael. There's something about him that has captured the public's imagination. To my way of thinking, it's for one simple reason. It's because he has demonstrated what love is. He is a living example of the best, most dedicated partner a girl could ever hope to have.

I love him because I have a lot of respect for him as a man. He can talk to anyone and is nice to everyone, and I really look up to that.

I love him because he is gentle and caring. Even when we are out surfing together he will tell me where to sit while waiting for a wave. He's always encouraging me to push myself in the ocean. To be that little bit more brave, to try that little bit harder. Not because he wants me to be uncomfortable, but because he wants me to be the best possible version of myself. And that to me is the mark of a really beautiful person.

I love him because he's an ocean man. Not only does he teach me how to surf, fish and dive for lobsters, but he catches fish and hands them out to all of our neighbours.

I love that he is so utterly content with the person he is – so comfortable in his skin: a quality that is rare. It makes me more confident in myself. It makes me not try too hard. He reminds me all the time that there is no one else in the world who is like me.

I really love his family. They are such genuine, good people. They've given Michael a strong set of values that he never wavers from.

Michael doesn't need praise or affirmation. Everyone wants to be told they are good, but Michael doesn't need that. He is entirely contained. And his parents say he has always been like that. There's a kind of Zen calm about him. He is easily the most unflappable person I know.

He's also an excellent listener. When you talk to Michael he makes you feel like you are the most important person in the room. And he doesn't just do that with me, but with everyone. It's not forced, either. I don't think he realises what a special quality that is in a person.

For someone who is self-reliant and doesn't need affirmation: he has an enormous circle of friends. They're always dropping in to talk about fishing or surfing. But also they are dropping in because he listens to them when they talk. So he's shown me it's easy to be a good friend to someone. You call them, you send them a text message, you listen to them.

I almost feel like he's a higher being – like he is more evolved than the rest of us. Like a good-looking version of Yoda. Like an especially good-looking version. It's as if he figured out long ago what the secret to life is.

When people ask me, 'Did you ever think Michael would leave?' I tell them I never thought it for a moment. Why? Because he was there every day; he came back to me every morning without fail. And when someone is really committed like that, there's no room for doubt. Every now and then, out of pure frustration, I would try to push him away. I would lash out, tell him to go away, to leave me alone. But he never did. Never once did he complain. Which is just as well because deep down of course I knew I would have been lost without him.

I thought it was really cool how he bought the ring five years ago. I have asked him how he knew I wouldn't turn out to be useless, a shell of my former self. And he replies, 'I just knew who you were and who you would continue to be.'

He is wise like that, and patient and empathetic. I don't think I would have done this well in my life if Michael had not been a part of it.

He doesn't care about being famous or meeting famous people. He's all about 'just do what makes you happy, and if it doesn't make you happy, don't do it'. It's simple, but does life really need to be more complicated than that? He never makes up excuses, either. I sometimes still use the fire as an excuse.

For Michael, he's either not interested in doing something or he just gets on and does it. Simple. You make a decision and then you own it.

Nothing prepares a partner for the kind of thing that happened to us. And he's never had counselling, which I think is remarkable. He says he doesn't need it. Personally I think it couldn't hurt, but I'm not about to start pestering him about it; besides, he's got his own form of therapy – the ocean. Still, you can't go through what he's been through and not need to talk to someone about it. And certainly his parents Gary and Julie have been the most amazing support. They might not have sat around and talked about their feelings night after night, but Michael was never in any doubt about how solid was their backing, and it meant the world.

After the fire, I thought he would care that I looked so different. But whenever I felt self-conscious or ugly, when I would cry and get upset, he would hold me and tell me he had never loved me because of how I looked. 'They're going to help you get better,' Michael would say. 'You just have to be brave. We'll get through this together.'

That's the heart of our story. All of us on this planet want to find love. A lot of people are in relationships that may never be truly tested, so to have had our commitment to one another tested in the way it has been has actually been a blessing. There's no doubt our relationship is stronger now than it was before the fire. In a lot of respects, ours is a union that was forged in flames.

We are life partners. Before, there wasn't the deep connection we have now.

I always thought we would have kids. But now I know he is also my soul mate.

25

WEDDING BELLS

It was dusk and the sun had only just dipped below the horizon. The boat rocked gently. It was still as I stood at the aft with Michael, staring down at the water below. Three large manta rays were cruising lazily in the turquoise waters, dancing in and out of the light cast from the boat. It felt like they were performing an aquatic ballet, just for us. My hair was wet and still salt-encrusted from a day spent surfing and swimming. My bones were tired – but in a good way. It had been about as perfect a day as I could have hoped for. A light breeze blew in warm, gentle gusts. In the distance, I could just make out the flickering lights on one of the outlying islands of the Maldives.

From the other end of the boat, 20 metres away, came the murmur of happy banter – the sounds of our fellow sailors as they settled in for sundowners to cap another glorious day in paradise.

We were watching the rays, my mind was drifting contentedly when suddenly, without warning, Michael grabbed my hand. My heart started racing.

'Turia,' he said, looking up at me and taking my hand. 'Will you marry me?'

I've known for a long time that Michael and I would spend the rest of our lives together, but when the proposal came, it still managed to knock me for six. I'm not the girliest of girls, and emotion is not something I readily express, but having the man I love hold out a diamond ring and tell me he wants to spend the rest of his life with me – it was incredible.

It was day three of a six-night holiday in the Maldives. Exhausted from a year spent crisscrossing the country on speaking engagements, honouring an ever-growing roster of media commitments and flitting back and forth to Ulladulla, I had been looking forward to this break for months. The *Ocean Divine*, a stunning cruising yacht built by its owner, a Frenchman called David Mesnard, was to be our home for a week. Days would be spent surfing breaks on the chain of reefs off the Maldives, and nights would be spent lazing on deck. On the plane over there, I was practically bursting with excitement.

I remember grabbing Michael's arm at one point in the flight and saying, jokingly, 'Yay! You're going to propose to me on this holiday!' In typical Michael style, he just smiled back and said, 'Sure, Turia. Whatever.'

On the *Ocean Divine* were ten blokes and Michael and me. Not exactly conducive to romance. Our fellow guests were mostly Aussies – a bunch of guys from Byron Bay – there for the same reason as us: to chase far-flung surf breaks on a once-in-a-lifetime trip.

All the Aussies, and even the French owners – David and his wife, Gaelle – made a fuss when I stepped on board. They even had a copy of the *Women's Weekly* with me on the cover. Not awkward at all. But once we got past the introductions, I knew the whole trip was going to be wonderfully relaxed. With every hour that passed on the boat, I could just feel the tension and stress of the previous twelve months fall off my shoulders.

On day three, we woke to a picture-perfect Indian Ocean day. The sky was blue and cloudless, the sea was still and glassy. After a lazy breakfast, we headed off in search of a surf-able break. Our first surf of the day was pretty average, the second was better. I took my surfboard out and caught a couple of waves – enough to get my heart rate up and feel the exhilaration of surfing a break out in the middle of nowhere. Coming back to the boat later in the afternoon, I couldn't imagine how the day could be any more perfect.

When David invited me to take part in an exercise class he was holding up on deck, I jumped at it. My limbs ached already from a morning and afternoon spent surfing and paddling, but in this place, under that sky, I felt like I couldn't do enough to celebrate being alive.

After the class, I thought it would be a good idea to launch myself off the top deck of the boat and into the water below. I came down on my side and winded myself in the process. Michael stood on deck, looking down and laughing at me. As I clambered back on board, he made to move down the back of the boat.

'Turia,' he said. 'You have to come down the back and see these manta rays.'

So, here we were, four years after Michael had made his secret vow to his father that he would marry me if I stayed alive, with a diamond ring he had thoughtfully purchased from the mine I worked at before the fire. A ring he had secretly stashed in his daypack as we packed for this holiday – and then checked on every night and every morning since, waiting for the perfect moment to pull it out and pop the question.

If I had ever been in any doubt of how thoughtful Michael was, here was a proposal – a grand romantic gesture – to prove it once and for all.

'Will you marry me?' he asked as the mantas swam below. I looked down at the ring, I looked at the beautiful man holding it up and I felt a rush of happiness.

'Yes,' I heard myself reply. 'Yes. Of course I will marry you.'

We slid into the water, donned a set of snorkel and goggles, and swam with the manta rays. Just the two of us, in the ocean at dusk, in the company of these majestic sea creatures. A moment of pure bliss.

Back on deck, we joined our fellow sailors at dinner and shared our news. I called Mum and Dad, and Michael called his parents. They were none of them surprised: just delighted.

The following night, the boat's crew prepared a private dining area for us and scattered the tablecloth with flower petals. For someone who thought she wasn't the least bit interested in weddings and all their paraphernalia, I found myself unexpectedly excited about the ring Michael had given me – I couldn't stop staring at it. It wasn't so much the diamond itself – beautiful though it was – as the story that went with it. I blew me away that so much thought had gone into it. I felt truly humbled, and lucky.

Because of the damage to my hands, we decided we would buy a chain for the ring on our way back through Singapore, and that I would wear it around my neck.

Looking back now, the timing could not have been more perfect. And I don't mean the moment, the hour or the day that Michael chose to propose. I mean the stage we had finally reached as a couple. I had recovered sufficiently from my injuries to be finally independent. Michael had morphed back from being my primary carer to being my boyfriend. We had a much clearer perspective on life and were like a regular couple again. The proposal, the prospect of spending the rest of our lives together just seemed like the natural progression of things. And that was the best feeling.

In the grand scheme of things, it wouldn't matter all that much whether Michael and I were married or not. After all, how much more serious can you get than someone giving up their life for you for four years? A wedding kind of pales in comparison, to my mind. Not only that but, as far as I'm concerned, kids are a much more important test of a relationship, and a much more significant display of commitment, than any diamond ring or any wedding ceremony. To be honest, I thought Michael and I would end up having children before we got married. Maybe we still will. In Tahiti, that's the way they do it. People get married after they have raised a family together. The marriage is a celebration of a life as a couple. I guess the thinking is that you can't really celebrate something before you have done it.

Would we like a big family? I don't know. Three or four kids would be nice. But we'll just wait and see. One thing I know for certain: Michael would make the greatest dad.

But before I started off down the wedding planner route, I had one more challenge to complete. One more little mountain to climb.

26

IRONMAN – PART II

Ironman in Kona, on the Big Island of Hawaii, is often described as the greatest physical competition on the planet. The hardest race in the world. The kind of challenge that is undertaken only by the fittest people in the world. And the craziest.

It all unfurls in the volcanic west of this island at the north-ernmost end of the chain that makes up the fiftieth state of America. The race is renowned for its harsh conditions. A course that wends its way through barren lava fields; seasonal winds that have been known to knock cyclists off their bikes; and high temperatures. Any long-distance runner will tell you that the optimal outside temperature in which to run a marathon is 7°C. At Kona, the temperature in the middle of the day, in the month of October when the Ironman takes place – a race that involves a marathon on top of a 180-kilometre bike ride, which follows a 4-kilometre swim – often hovers around 35°C.

Throw into that mix a collection of the fittest, strongest, most dedicated humans on the planet and you have one heady, sweaty, terrifyingly intimidating combination.

The entire enterprise has been designed to push the human body not just to its limits, but far beyond them. And I reckon it was about two days after our plane touched down in Kona that I started to wonder what the hell I had been thinking in signing up to do it.

But first, a small recap.

After I'd crossed the finishing line of the Ironman in Port Macquarie, I'd felt an enormous sense of relief. The goal I had set in hospital five years before had been realised. I was finally comfortable in the knowledge that I had proved the naysayers wrong – and, more importantly, had made good on a promise I had made to myself in the darkest days of my recovery.

And then came the letter from the Ironman organisation inviting me to take part in the upcoming main event in Kona. I was ecstatic. Only the best of the best from all the Ironman events around the world are asked to Kona. The organisers take the top ten from every age group. The top ten female finishers from my age group in Australia had completed the course in Port Macquarie in under nine hours. My time was thirteen-and-a-half hours. But each year the organisers also hold a lottery in which anyone can win the chance to participate, as well as extending a handful of special invitations to competitors whose presence they think will be good for the race – either with respect to the media they will attract or the symbolism of having them compete.

I was one of the latter.

Michael and I flew into Hawaii two weeks before the race. I wanted to get to know the course, to acclimatise to the temperatures and use the time to taper off my training and try to get in the right headspace.

Stepping off the plane and onto the tarmac at Kona International Airport, I was hit by a wave of heat. The taxi that took us into town drove along the Queen Ka'ahumanu Highway – or the Queen K, as everyone there calls it. I recognised it immediately as the route on which the bike ride would take place. Outside, mile after mile of flat, barren lava field stretched to the horizon. The landscape was covered in a sort of low, scrubby, yellow spinifex-type grass. It looked lonely and desolate. I felt a knot in my stomach.

In town, the place was crawling with Ironmen and -women. There were six-packs everywhere you looked. Lithe, muscular, tanned and shredded bodies on every street corner. It was a scene of perpetual motion: people running, doing chin-ups, riding, knocking out crunches.

Then there was the gear. In Australia I had felt a bit smug about the quality of my stuff, but when I saw the incredible gizmos other competitors had, that feeling quickly faded. I began to feel a bit sick.

However, a year of training for Port Macquarie, and four months of intensive training between Kokoda and Kona, had taught me that races are run in the head: I just needed to keep my mind on my own race.

The first training session I did, I was exhausted after barely an hour. The heat was incredible. It knocked the stuffing out of you. In an attempt to replicate these conditions, I had already spent two weeks training in Thailand. The idea had been to go somewhere near home where the environment was at least as oppressive, but it had rained for pretty much the whole time I was there. My body just wasn't used to this heat, as well as the 90 per cent humidity. I began to worry I had bitten off more than I could chew.

Regulating my body temperature in Kona was, I knew, going to be a huge factor in determining whether I finished or not. I had chosen a cycling outfit with long white sleeves, specially designed to take in air and release heat, which I hoped was going to help, but as I headed out each afternoon along the Queen K for my training ride, with the sun beating down and radiating back up from the black lava fields, I began to have serious doubts.

On my first training run, my heart rate went through the roof. Still, it had done the same thing in Thailand. I was confident my body would adjust. In the meantime, my running training had to be altered. I would do a thirty-minute run and then have to come back to the hotel and hide in the air-conditioning.

There was also the wind. The western side of the island where Kona is located is flat and largely featureless. The other side of the island, where the volcano is, is lush tropical rainforest. In between, the climactic and geographic conditions conspire to whip up this powerful, hot headwind. Some days it felt like I was riding headlong into a blast furnace. I kept meeting people who had done the race before and been blown onto the rocks as they rode. On some of my training rides, my bike would get blown off the road. And I was thinking while riding, *Maybe I don't want to do this, after all*, knowing I couldn't back out.

The swimming training was at least comparatively pleasant. The water in the bay at Kona was clear and as I swam I would watch a multitude of colourful fish dart about the seabed below me.

The town kept getting more and more full of terrifyingly fit people. In some kind of sick mind game, it seemed to me that the universe was drip-feeding them into Kona – with each day that passed, a wave of even more shredded competitors than the day before would suddenly appear in our midst.

I'd meet people in town who would casually mention that they'd just done a 30-kilometre training run. 'Only a little run this morning, because I'm taking it easy today.' Or others who had knocked out a 90-kilometre bike ride before lunch.

'I don't think I can do this,' I said to Michael one afternoon, following an especially tough session on the bike.

In typical Michael form, he didn't miss a beat. 'So don't do it, darl.'

'But I have to!' I replied, incredulous that he could be so chill about the prospect of chucking in the towel.

'Okay, so do it, darl,' he said, barely looking up from his book.

No one handles me as well as Michael does.

In media interviews in the following days, American journalists who had been clued into my story asked me, 'Would you say Michael is your number one fan?'

I didn't have the heart to tell them that he couldn't have cared less if I won the race or went home tomorrow.

Thankfully, among the super-humans who made up the majority of my competition in the race, there were also a handful of mortals. Others who, like me, had been invited to take part. There was the first Iranian woman to compete (she undertook the course in a hijab), a female fighter pilot and a father and son duo – Jeff and Johnny Agar. Johnny, the son, had cerebral palsy. Together they had entered Ironman to prove that nothing in life was impossible, no matter the cards life dealt you. In the swim section of the race, Jeff was going to pull Johnny along in a little dinghy behind him. In the bike section, Johnny was going to sit in a specially made carriage and be towed along by his father. I felt humbled in their presence.

They were staying at the same hotel as us and we would cross paths regularly in the lead-up to the race. We'd always stop and chat, compare notes and laugh at how ridiculously intimidating the whole experience was.

'I'll be there at the finish line when you run across it,' I told Johnny one afternoon. And I meant it. These two were, after all, the living embodiment of the Ironman spirit. Their story was, in some ways, my story. Triumph over adversity. It gets you every time.

As race day approached and my support team started dribbling into town, I began to taper: pulling back on the intensity of my training sessions. Still worried about body temperature regulation, I would undertake a training cycle with my team along for the ride. They would wait by the roadside with an esky full of chilled water and douse me each time I rode past. It seemed to work. I figured that if, during the race, I could pour cold water over myself at each aid station along the course, I would be fine. I began to panic less. But only a bit less.

One thing that helped take the pressure off was the level of relative anonymity I enjoyed in Kona compared to Port Macquarie. Except for an NBC documentary crew who followed me for a bit and did a couple of interviews, there were no cameras recording my every training session, no interviewers asking me what time I thought I might finish in.

And I would love going down to Kailua Pier for a swim or heading off along Ali'i Drive for a training run and being surrounded by so many different languages. People from all over the world had descended – it was like the United Nations of fitness freaks. I felt like I was part of a special tribe – albeit the not-as-fast or not-as-fit member of that tribe. There was a parade of nations a day before the race. Looking at all the faces from every corner of the world, I felt a thrill. What an extraordinary honour to be here.

On the day of the race, I woke at 3.30 am and ate a bowl of Rice Bubbles and two bananas. My tummy felt unsettled, but I put it down to nerves. Michael and I set off to the course, where we pumped the tyres on my bike before heading to the marshalling area.

In the early morning light, the sight of two thousand people all nervously milling was something to behold. I put on my headphones, played my go-to song and did my best to get in the zone.

For the swim, in Port Macquarie we had all entered the water from the shore, pouring into the bay like lemmings off a cliff. Here in Kona the start line was out in the middle of the harbour, which meant swimming out and treading water for ten or so minutes waiting for the starter's gun to fire.

In my age category, there were about eight hundred women. There we all were, decked out in our speed suits, jostling for position in 5-metre-deep water; pushing, bumping – desperate to get going.

The cannon fired. A puff of smoke and the water around me began to churn. Eight hundred sets of limbs began moving. Momentarily, the turquoise waters of the harbour turned to whitewash, arms and legs going everywhere, everyone trying to swim over the top of everyone else, people actually grabbing you and pushing you backwards as they scrambled to get ahead. I tried to look to the harbour floor and concentrate on my breathing. Now was not the time to lose composure.

That time, as it happened, was about fifteen minutes into my swim. The queasy stomach I had put down to nerves began to grumble uncomfortably. I tried to ignore it and focus on my stroke, but suddenly, without warning, I felt the need to vomit, and before I knew what was happening I had thrown up. It had come on so quickly that I figured I must have swallowed too much sea water. I composed myself.

Then, as the race progressed and the field began to spread out, my head started to hurt from my goggles. The swim was one-and-a-half hours and I came out of the water with a bad headache. This had never happened before, and as I ran to find my bike I felt the beginnings of a rising panic. Was I sick? Was this going to stay around for the next twelve hours? How was I going to finish if I was vomiting and suffering from a splitting headache?

Bruce had told me that whenever a negative thought started to creep in, I had to replace it with a positive thought. So I pushed the fears back down. It wasn't a tummy bug, it was just sea water. It wasn't a headache, it was just a passing pain, most likely exacerbated by the goggles.

I was in the transition area for what seemed like ages, trying (and failing) to apply sunscreen and pull my white sleeves over my wet skin. For a brief moment, I thought about leaving them off, but I knew I would regret it if I did. Finally, I managed to pull them on, mount my bike and charge back onto the course.

It occurred to me as I left the transition area that there were a lot fewer bikes left waiting for their owners to emerge from the swim here in Kona than there had been in Port Macquarie. I tried not to focus on it as I put my head down and headed out into the heat.

I had 180 kilometres of cycling ahead of me – 90 kilometres out of town, into the black, barren moonscape of the lava fields, and back again. The temperature had already climbed into the thirties – from where it would only continue to rise as the day progressed. As usual I felt the heat radiating off the road, and as I rode out of town I could feel the waves of it emanating from the lava fields.

I knew that keeping up my energy levels and fluid intake was going to be vital, but each time I swallowed an energy gel or electrolyte drink, I vomited it straight back up again. My stomach had not settled and my head still ached. Whatever was going on in there was clearly more serious than a little bit of nerves or swallowed sea water. Of all the days to have a stomach bug, did it really have to be today? I pushed the negative thoughts away – determined to simply get on with it. Play with the cards you are dealt, I told myself. Don't psyche yourself out. You've come so far to be here, turn the negative thoughts into positive ones and just keep riding.

Indeed, for the first 90 kilometres – the occasional vomit notwithstanding – I actually felt fine. I had lots in the tank. I started to feel okay about the race for the first time. As if I might actually pull it off. So I wasn't about to break any records, and would most certainly come in with a slower time that I had recorded in Port Macquarie – but so what. This was Kona. The fact I was even here, competing, was a miracle in and of itself. Despite the heat, despite the vomiting, despite the feeling that – in all honesty – I would much rather have been anywhere else, the smallest of smiles crept across my lips.

At the 90-kilometre mark, I turned to go back. And that's when things started to fall apart.

The plan was, as I had drilled with my team in training, to stop at every aid station along the route and douse myself with water. The heat of the day and my inability to sweat made for a potentially lethal combination. Without the means to cool myself down, I could be in serious danger of overheating, with my heart working overtime to cope with the stress my body was under.

Aid stations were positioned at 15-kilometre intervals along the course, and as I approached the first station on the way back into town, I prepared to pull in, cool off with an impromptu shower and do a quick check of my heart rate.

'We're out of water, sorry!' came the cry from a volunteer as I cruised to a halt. I froze momentarily, hardly believing my ears. I was almost 90 kilometres from Kona – without water, and overheating as I stood there. There were other options for fluids at the station, but I couldn't use them because I needed to cool myself rather than rehydrate. Not wanting to make a fuss, I made an offhand comment about it being okay, put my hands in some ice buckets they did have, and got back on my bike.

It's okay, I told myself. Water is only 15 kilometres away at the next aid station. I put my head down and kept pedalling.

It was approaching mid-afternoon, the hottest part of the day. With every rotation of the pedals, I felt my body temperature rising. I watched my odometer nervously, counting down the kilometres until the next aid station.

After what seemed like an eternity, it came into view. Digging deep, I pushed towards it – finding a store of energy in the prospect of finally being able to cool myself down. As I coasted into the aid station, my heart sank. There was no water there either.

For the first time, I started to think: if there is no water at the next station I am in serious danger. The mercury had climbed to 35 degrees. The winds were starting to pick up, applying the blast furnace effect for which the island is renowned. It was all I could do not to cry.

My mind started to scramble. Suddenly it became hard to make sensible decisions. Also, I was running out of Gatorade, and any that I managed to drink I was throwing up anyway.

Still I pedalled. What else was I going to do? I had to ride to water. Then, somewhere in the funk that was my increasingly foggy mind, the survival instinct kicked in. I resolved that if I saw a car, I would pull it over and crawl into the back seat and ask them to take me back into town. I didn't need to finish this race. Who was I kidding? I hadn't come this far in my recovery only to be broken by something I didn't even have to be doing.

Almost at that moment, like some sort of mirage, a police car came into view on the horizon. At first, it was hard to make out – distorted by the waves of radiant heat rising off the bitumen. But as I drew closer, it came into focus. A police car, with a policeman. Ostensibly there to direct traffic, but in fact surely sent from someone up there to deliver me from this hell.

I rode straight for him and pulled up alongside.

'I need water,' I said.

He took one look at me and bolted to the back seat of his car, popping back up with three bottles of water. Without saying a word, he emptied the bottles all over me. It felt like the elixir of life itself was being poured over my head. I stood and waited for the water to take effect. Slowly, the fog began to lift. The road ahead seemed less fuzzy and my brain began to work again.

Each of the aid stations on the way back into town had water. Bit by bit, my race plan (such as it was) started to get back on track.

Then the wind picked up again. My average speed at this point of the race ought to have been 35 kilometres an hour – a fair clip that would have made relatively easy work of what was left of the cycle leg of this ordeal. But with the headwind, it was all I could do to maintain 12 kilometres an hour. Every stroke of the pedal felt like pushing through soft sand. I could feel the negative thoughts building: the desire to quit, to throw in the towel. I didn't have the energy to fight them; to push them down or turn them into positives. I started to cry.

There, in the middle of a sun-baked lava field, as twilight began to settle over the landscape, with my bike barely moving forward, the notion I had spent two weeks trying to quell, finally overwhelmed me. *I think I have bitten off more than I can chew.*

Somehow, and in a sort of delirium, I finally came riding back into town. I finished the bike ride in 7.5 hours: not a bad effort, considering. But I was shattered. And I still had a marathon to run.

For the first 20 or so kilometres, I ran like a machine – on track to do a sub-four-hour marathon. Drawing on reserves of energy from I don't know where, I pounded along Queen K highway, back out of town and into the inky blackness of an Hawaiian night. There were no street-lights illuminating the Queen K, no crowds lining the course: it was just me and the glo-stick around my neck – and up in the distance, the faint glow of fellow racers. And eventually my engine started to falter again. Dehydrated, starving and still unable to hold barely anything down, my body was starting to pack it in. Somewhere around the 22-kilometre mark, I started to walk.

Walking alone in the darkness, my own breathing and trainers on the bitumen the only sound, was an eerie experience. I tried to focus on the glo-sticks receding into the distance in front of me, but my brain was so addled, I began hallucinating.

About 8 kilometres from the finish line, I saw a white light coming towards me. It grew brighter with every step I took towards it, until soon I was able to make out that it was attached to a bike, being ridden by a man.

'Come on, Turia, you're almost there,' came a voice, in an accent so comfortingly familiar I almost cried.

His name was Craig. He had come all the way from Australia to watch the race. Beyond that, I learned nothing else about him – or if I did, I was too delirious to retain it other than that he was someone who, once more, had clearly been miraculously sent to get me across that finish line.

As Craig slow-pedalled beside me, offering up his water, I began to walk–run, slowly picking up my pace. On the horizon, the glow from the lights of Kona began to appear, and for the first time in hours my spirits weren't consumed with a sense of hopelessness – they actually began to lift.

The light from Craig's bike was heaven-sent – throwing a skinny shaft into the darkness ahead of us: just enough to make me think this darkness wasn't infinite; that, contrary to appearances, it did have an end point. He talked to me and I might have replied, I might have asked him questions, we might even have had a conversation, but I don't remember. All I recall is at one point asking if he would mind taking off my bike helmet.

'Turia, you're running,' he replied. 'You're not wearing a bike helmet.'

My mind was going off in all directions. As I reached the outskirts of town, the crowds began to build and the energy of the night changed completely. Picking up the pace, I passed parked cars with their doors open, music blaring, and I remember thinking, *No one will notice if I just go into one of those cars and lie down.* I began fantasising about lying in a bath then falling into a bed and not waking up for five days.

For the final 2 kilometres of the race I was well and truly back in Kona. And the crowd was going nuts. The clock had struck 9 pm. I had been racing since 7.15 am, and for reasons only an Ironman will understand, I was struck by a surge of energy. Suddenly, I felt like a boss – carried on the wave of cheers from the crowd. Before the race, I had spoken to a friend who admitted they had never done a race in which they'd finished knowing they had given it everything they had. I started sprinting.

I crossed the finish line in fourteen-and-a-half hours: an hour slower than my time in Port Macquarie. After Port Macquarie, I reflected on the race and thought I could probably have done more – swum a little quicker, run a little harder.

But here in Kona, I couldn't have gone any harder. I had thrown everything I had at it. And I felt really proud of myself.

Michael met me at the finish line. As cameras flashed and the crowd cheered, he folded me into his arms. I felt like crying: from euphoria, yes. But mostly relief that it was finally over.

For days after the race, I didn't feel like eating. I continued to vomit for most of the next day. Heat stress? Sunstroke? Or a poorly timed tummy bug? I didn't know nor much care. I had finished the Hawaiian Ironman. For all the pain, there was a deep sense of achievement.

Am I glad that I did it? Absolutely. Would I do it again? No way.

I showed what my body is capable of. Barely five years previously, doctors had stood by my hospital bed and told me I would be lucky to run again and most likely need to spend the rest of my life in an air-conditioned room. Yet I had just run the toughest race on the planet in the heat of Kona. The body is an amazing thing.

A couple of days later, Michael and I took ourselves off to a beach on the other side of the island. It was one of the most idyllic stretches of coastline either of us had ever seen. Dramatic cliffs falling into deep turquoise water, a sliver of palm-fringed sand, waves lapping gently onto the shore. We clambered over rocks and jumped into the sea from an over-hanging rock ten metres above the surface. We swam in caves, free-diving as we explored the underwater world. It was as perfect a day as either Michael or I could have imagined. Just the two of us, in the ocean: bliss.

As I paddled, I realised I felt light: as if an enormous weight had been lifted. It was over. The Ironman challenge I had set myself in that hospital bed all those years ago had been met. Now I could get on with the rest of my life. And I had a kind of epiphany. It felt like an end point: as if I had finally closed a massively formative chapter of my life. And the biggest revelation? When I stopped and thought about it, that chapter of my life had actually been closed for a long while. The chapter was still in the book, and always would be. But I had long since finished writing it.

I realised that the fire is part of me – and always will be. I am never going to get to a point when I am over the fire – when I have left it behind – because it is part of who I am. And I am okay with that.

27

CHASING THE 'BIG LIFE'

I've always said that to achieve any big goal, you need a strong emotional connection to it; you need a very good reason for it. Because when you're hating the grind and wondering why you're doing what you're doing, you need a foundation to fall back on.

Before the fire, I was an independent, vivacious go-getter. After it, I was apparently going to need a carer for the rest of my life – but, if I was lucky, there was always the possibility that one day I might drive again. I might even get married! And while I would never belittle those goals (I wanted and I want those things too), put together they didn't add up to what I would call a 'big life' – the kind of life I've always wanted to live for myself.

That was the reason I trained for and completed two Ironmans. That was the reason I kept grinding away with my training, waking up each morning in the dark and hitting the road. The reason I kept pushing myself, even when I wanted more than anything else to give up.

When I was training, in the middle of a six-hour bike ride, in the middle of a miserable downpour, I kept coming back to this reason: I want to be fitter than I was in the Kimberley. I hate being told what I can and can't do. I hate being limited. And the thing I hate the most is being underestimated.

What was the hardest thing about training for these huge events? The never-ending monotony of it. I struggled to fit in the training around my other commitments (much as I love my speaking engagements, or going to Peru to walk the Inca Trail, they take up a lot of time). There's no triathlon club in Ulladulla, so I tried to organise group sessions for the dates I was in Sydney, and consoled myself the rest of the time with the thought that training solo would only make me mentally tougher.

I faced it like I had faced everything else in my journey. Namely: how do you eat an elephant? One bite at a time.

In the same way, during my recovery from the fire I would congratulate myself for getting through yet another day in hospital (literally: every night before I went to sleep I'd say to myself, 'Well done, mate. You've made it through another day.') I would just focus on the day I had ahead of myself.

If it was a day in which I had to do a two-hour brick session (a full bike workout followed immediately by a full run workout), I'd get up in the morning, do it, and then not think about it for the rest of the day.

A lot of the strategies I used to train for Ironman were in fact similar to the strategies I'd used in hospital and throughout my recovery. For example, when I'd struggled through a particularly hard day of physio or a hard day of training,

I'd say to myself, 'Once you've done this, it'll be in the bank and you won't have to do it again.' Or let's say my physio sessions would go for an hour and they'd be really painful, I'd break them up into five-minute sections and reward myself with some Gatorade at these points.

When it came to Kona, I knew I was going to need some pretty specific, well-thought-out strategies. I knew it was going to be a tougher physical challenge than any I had ever taken on before. So, when things got tough:

- I thought about everything I had to be grateful for – Michael, Mum, being alive, having the opportunity to compete in this iconic race.
- I was careful not to let the enormity of the task ahead of me overwhelm me; to stay in the moment. I knew that if I thought about everything I had to do that day, it'd be too much. So I broke it down. In the swim, I just focused on getting to the next buoy, on the bike ride I just thought about the next 10 kilometres, and on the run I focused on the next 2 kilometres, aid station to aid station.
- I compared any physical pain to what I've experienced in the past few years – and it paled in comparison.
- If a negative thought entered my mind, I immediately squashed it. For example, on the bike ride when it was super-windy I got really cranky, but before that crankiness could poison the rest of me, I would replace that negative thought with a positive one. *Yes, it's really windy – but every other competitor has gone through the same thing today.*
- I used visualisation techniques. Often, I imagine that I'm a messenger for the Queen, and I have to get a message to her

otherwise a war is going to break out and I'm going to have the deaths of thousands of people on my hands. Sounds crazy, I know, but it works.

At the time, Port Macquarie was the toughest physical challenge I had ever undertaken. But Kona was for me another level altogether. And in life we need to empty the tank. We don't need to be the best, but we need to give our best.

For my training, I also had to be super-organised – I literally scheduled in each and every session for the months ahead. If I knew I was travelling a lot in a certain week, I'd let Bruce know and he'd tailor my sessions accordingly.

And I'd give myself a leave pass: no one is perfect. If I was travelling a lot for work, and couldn't fit in proper meals or training sessions, I'd just accept that that day wasn't going to be great. I set myself a ratio for my sessions, too: two per week had to be excellent, two could be sub-par and the rest I had to fully complete, even if I didn't excel in them.

One of the scariest things going into Kona was the pressure I felt. Sure, some of it was the pressure I'd put on myself, but I'd also told half of Australia that I was doing an Ironman in Hawaii, and there were moments when I worried what I'd done. Had I set myself up for failure? Again, I tried to reframe it: by telling the country that I was doing an Ironman, I knew that come hell or high water I'd finish it. Even if it meant crawling across the line. It made me accountable.

In fact, in Kona shit got even more real because I had financial backing from sponsors. It's tough when you know you have to go out there and perform *and* you're wearing a logo.

I also worried about how my body would hold up. I'd get overuse injuries (which most athletes get training for an

Ironman) and had to put in additional hours doing rehab or physio.

The thing about achieving a big goal is that it always gives back more than you put into it. I poured in hours and hours and hours and hours. I sweated, I cried, I wondered why I was doing it. I wondered what I was trying to prove. But in the end it was so empowering. It made me realise that the 'process' I'd used for recovering from hospital wasn't just a fluke. I wasn't just 'born this way'. I'd used the same strategies to complete Port Macquarie, where they'd worked; then I used them to go on and complete Kona, and they worked there, too.

Finally, doing Kona made me realise that anything I want to achieve in life *is* possible – if I'm willing to put in the work to get myself there.

Training for Ironman

Because I know that at least a handful of you out there share my love of a spreadsheet – and because there will also be enough of you curious to know exactly what sort of training is required to compete in an Ironman, I've laid it out below.

My training varied in intensity. Don't forget, by the time Kona came around, I'd been preparing for Ironman for two years. At the very start, my training was basic (see Table 1: basic training). Later on, when I was working towards Kona, it got way more intense, until it was kind of taking over my life (see Table 2: hectic training).

Having a strict regime worked, though – and the best thing about it was when I would start to doubt my fitness levels, I'd look back through the previous months and (maybe even years) and see how far I had come.

Table 1: basic training

	Training
Monday	**AM SWIM (1.3k)** 300m warm up 6 x 50m on 15s rest 200m easy 6 x 50m on 15s rest 200m cool down **PM RUN (20min)** 20min easy run
Tuesday	**AM BIKE (40min)** 10min warm up 8 x 2min intervals – 2min thinking about your pedal technique, 2min easy Cruisey spin to finish
Wednesday	**AM RUN (40min)** 40min run, counting your strides and aiming for 175-195 strides per minute.
Thursday	**AM SWIM (1.8k)** 300m warm up 200m kick with fins, 200m with pull buoy 5 x 200m 100m cool down
Friday	**AM BIKE (45min)** Spin on bike for 45min
Saturday	**AM RUN (1hr)** Easy jog. Run for 10min, walk for 1min.
Sunday	REST DAY

Table 2: hectic training

Monday	AM swim (3.5k)
	PM bike (1 hour)
Tuesday	AM run (40min)
Wednesday	Brick session (1hr ride + 30min run off bike)
Thursday	AM swim (4k)
	PM run (45min)
Friday	REST
Saturday	AM brick session (2hr ride + 30min run)
	PM 1hr open-water swim
Sunday	Seven-hour training ride

28

MINDSET

Nothing beats that feeling. The silence is total. It's almost like you're asleep, like you're in a different world. Like when you're in an aquarium, looking at fish. But instead you're the fish, and you're looking up through the water to the light playing on the surface above.

Part of the reason I love free diving is that there's no plan B. You have to commit. And once you've committed, you need to see it through.

It's quiet underneath the water. You feel disconnected from the world on the surface, and part of another whole new world. It's quiet because there are no bubbles. You have no tank, no oxygen and the pressure compresses your lungs to the size of an orange – every cell in your body is electrified. Your body is in survival mode, pushed to its extremes. Your every instinct is telling you to surface, to head for the light – away from the darkness – and yet, with self-control, you push ever downwards.

The feeling of coming up to the surface – having spent maybe more than two minutes underwater without breathing –

is indescribable. And how you feel – panicked and gagging for air, or totally blissed out – comes down to your mindset. I've been for short dives and been out of breath after twenty seconds. Other times, I've hit the bottom and almost fallen asleep I feel so zen.

While I was pushing myself to my physical limits in the Ironman in Hawaii, Michael decided to take a free-diving course. The aim was to reach a depth of 20 metres comfortably (at 20 metres your lungs decompress to one-third of their original size) and then push through to 40 metres.

He would begin each dive by breathing up on the surface: three-second inhales followed by ten-second exhales. This allows the heart to slow, therefore using less oxygen in the bloodstream.

After a day of practice, he got down to 20 metres. He gradually increased the depth with every dive. To get to 40 metres was something else, though. More important than mastering the physical was conquering the mental. At 20 metres, every synapse in your brain is telling you to surface. To quell the anxiety and push on, you need to find your happy place. We all have a happy place, somewhere we can visualise in our mind and our body in which we instantly become relaxed.

And so down he went. Counting his kicks, equalising all the way, releasing his mask as it squeezed to his face. Arm over head to create a streamline, accepting the water pressure surrounding his body, forgetting about his breathing, relaxing. Finding his happy place.

For the next two days he kept reaching 30 metres and turning around. He just wasn't comfortable: his mind was thinking about too many things. On the last day he kept it simple. Rather than kicking down, he took hold of the weight that takes the guideline to the bottom. He let go of all the tension in his body and went into his own little world. It felt like only a matter of seconds and the line went tight, he was at 40 metres. He would tell me later that he felt total euphoria – no urge to breathe at all. He surfaced with a total dive time of just over two minutes.

Deep under the ocean, the water pressing in on all sides, in a profound meditation; totally at the mercy of the sea, with only your own self-control keeping disaster at bay. It's an incredible feeling. You feel so alive.

Everything in this world is in our heads. And when we get our mindset right, when we get our mindset working for us and not against us, it's amazing what we can achieve. It's almost magic.

It will come as no surprise that I enjoy challenging myself. Why? Because if we always do what we know we can do, we never grow. We like our comfort zone because it's warm and safe. But staying in your comfort zone is a sure way to stagnate.

Even in the early days of wearing my mask, I had to constantly push my own boundaries. At first, that meant getting used to not wearing my mask around Mum and Michael, and then my close friends; then I'd go out for a walk around the block. I built from there. It's not like one day I wore my mask, and the next day I took it off. I consistently stretched myself and pushed myself that little bit further.

It was the same with the rest of my body. I used to wear long-sleeved pants and long-sleeved tops. Then I moved to wearing three-quarter-length tops and three-quarter-length pants. Now I can wear a singlet and shorts and feel completely at ease. But if I hadn't done the legwork – the slow process of gradually getting used to my skin – I'd still be in long shirts and pants. We have to get comfortable being uncomfortable.

I remember the first time I went into the Ulladulla Coles after my accident. It was a mission. I told Michael to stay in the car. My heart was pounding as I went through the doors. I felt like everyone's eyes were on me and my mask (they probably weren't – people are more worried about what they're doing to bother focusing on you). I grabbed a packet of biscuits, paid, and went back to the car. A pretty ordinary thing for anyone else, but at the time it felt as much of an achievement as running a marathon.

Even in France, when Michael dropped me off at the rehab centre and was kind of hanging around, I realised that having my security blanket wasn't going to help my recovery. It was time I started stepping up and doing stuff by myself. If we have a plan B or a back-up plan, sometimes it can do us a disservice. Like on Kokoda – if there had been a helicopter waiting every night to take people who had had enough, I guarantee that a lot of people would have left (me being one of them!).

I still challenge myself, but it's on a grander scale than going into Coles to buy biscuits. That's why I do stuff like free diving and rock running underwater (when you pick up a boulder and run across the seabed). That's why I undertook two Ironmans. Because it's only when you challenge yourself that you see what you're made of.

So, how do we get our mindset working for us and not against us? You get comfortable being uncomfortable (hate standing up at work giving presentations? Give more presentations). You challenge yourself to step outside your comfort zone.

You back yourself. You accept and acknowledge the grind. You set stretch goals.

A lot of people tell me that they've got ten goals for next year: 'Finish the bathroom'; 'Pay down the mortgage by ten per cent'; 'Enrol my child in high school'. But to me these aren't goals: these are things you put on a to-do list. If it doesn't stretch you, if it doesn't intimidate you, if it doesn't scare you a little … Is it really a goal? I don't subscribe to the 'SMART' goal methodology, either (SMART: specific, measurable, attainable, relevant, time-bound). Again, if a goal is achievable or attainable – is it really a goal?

People also ask me how I got so much confidence, and how I've managed to rebuild my life. I think a huge part of it has been my goal-setting. By setting a stretch goal, by working towards it and eventually achieving it, you gain confidence, self-esteem and greater resilience. It's important here to say that you can't compare yourself to anyone else. Your goals and your stretch goals are going to be totally different to everyone else's. If you run 5 kilometres regularly, a 10-kilometre run probably won't give you more confidence in your abilities. Training for a marathon, on the other hand, will. If you've never run a day in your life, however, a 5-kilometre fun run will be a stretch for you.

I also think that we often sell ourselves short. We *don't* take on goals that will really push us outside our comfort zones, that terrify us a little bit. Because when we take on goals that seem impossible, be that a 10-kilometre run or starting a new business, and we do the work to achieve them – that's when the magic happens. That's when we get more confidence, more resilience and a greater sense of self-belief. We get all that in spades and we can use it to take on new goals.

I hear it all the time when people are telling me about their goals. 'I'll do the marathon once I'm a bit fitter!' No! You do it the other way around. You sign up for the marathon first. Then you tell everyone. And then you start training like a mad person because you've literally told the whole world you're doing it.

Because I was constantly being asked by people how I managed to not only pull myself back from the brink of death but also to rebuild for myself a life that exceeded all expectations, I created Turia's School of Champions: a seven-week online course designed to help people remove the mental obstacles that stand between them and their goals.

I've been running the School of Champions for more than a year now and have had thousands of people through. It's been such a privilege for me to work with these people, who have entrusted their most profound desires and ambitions to me. And to be able to teach them to believe in themselves. On top of that, it's great to hear about the changes these people have made in their lives. Like I've said before, I love it when people tell me what it is that I've inspired them to do. I think anything is possible when we understand our mindset and know how to best use it.

I've been luckier than most in that I've had a second chance at life. I've been written off for dead, and had an opportunity to claw myself back into existence. And when that happens, you learn not to take a single moment of a single day for granted. Because we only get one turn at this thing called life: why wouldn't you make the most of it?

EPILOGUE:
FIRE WALKER

The music is thumping. It's a crazed, dance music beat. It feels like it's in time with my heart. As the volume ebbs and the lights stop their frenetic flashing, I take a moment to compose myself.

Up on stage, Tony Robbins is weaving the magic that has made him millions. It's like how I imagine revivalist tents of the old days used to be, just as I suppose some of those charismatic Christian church groups are today. No one is talking in tongues (yet) but it wouldn't surprise me if someone suddenly did.

As the afternoon stretches out into evening, I've managed to quell the rising sense of panic. Every now and then, when Tony feels like the crowd is losing interest, the air-conditioning is cranked, the temperature drops and we're all made to get up and dance.

I can't help but admire him. He has a stadium full of people eating out of the palm of his hand; hanging off his every word, obediently standing, sitting, dancing whenever he says so.

Then, just to keep the tension in the room, sometimes on the large screen behind him, up flashes footage from outside: a long, thin bed of hot coals glowing red against the fast fading light.

For the first time in a long while, I am overcome with fear.

'Screw this,' I think to myself. 'I don't need this in my life.' I pick up my handbag and make for the nearest exit. One of Tony's people is guarding the door. He stops me and says, 'Tony knows who you are. Tony wants you to fire-walk.'

I look the man square in the eye and reply, 'Oh, yeah? Well, mate, you can tell Tony to get stuffed.' I am not here to dance to anyone's tune but my own. I am no performing seal. I will walk across the coals only if I choose to. And I will make that decision in my own time. Yet I find myself sitting back down in my seat.

For the next four hours, as Tony variously prowls the stage and the auditorium floor – pontificating about self-belief or picking people out of the crowd to share their story – I'm a bundle of mixed emotions. I've spent years distancing myself from the fire: trying to outrun it, why would I go back?

'Because we need to be honest about what's holding us back,' booms Tony. 'We need to face our fears and confront them head-on.'

But haven't I been doing just that ever since I regained consciousness in hospital? Hasn't my every waking moment been dedicated to rebuilding my life? What more do I need to prove? And who am I proving it to? And why – more importantly – should I be taking my cues from this borderline crazy man?

'Look at the list you wrote this morning of the things you know are holding you back!' implores Tony. 'What are the excuses you reach for when you don't think you can achieve something or if things aren't going your way?'

I look down at my notepad, and two words stare back at me.

The fire.

For the most part, I honestly think I am good. I rarely use the fire as an excuse for all the things I cannot achieve. But if I am in a bad mood, or if I'm worn down or tired, it can't help but come bubbling to the surface. I focus on all the things I cannot do because of that fire. And it makes me angry. Sometimes when I can't do what I want to, I won't care, I'll shrug my shoulders. But on other days it doesn't seem fair, any limitations make me want to scream in frustration, make me feel like the world is against me.

The crowd is swaying now, as if in a trance. There are people crying, there are people wailing. I'm both caught up in the spectacle, and still thinking it's all a bit silly.

And yet. And yet.

I look at the time. It's almost ten at night. We've been in here, listening to Tony, watching him minister his flock for almost twelve hours. We've had lunch and a few snacks, but nothing else to eat. I'm tired and wired all at the same time. If I surrender myself to the moment, if I think about the reasons I came here in the first place, I can see why I have no choice but to walk over the hot coals outside. This is just another test, like the many hundreds I have had to face since the fire. If anything, it pales in comparison to most of the other challenges I have stared down.

There's a sort of electricity in the air as the human tooth-paste commercial up on stage brings the day's proceedings to close. More music, more fist-pumping, more ululating from the crowd who by now – starved and delirious – have been whipped into a frenzy.

'Are you ready, Sydneyyyyy!' Tony is screaming. I feel a hand on my elbow. It's Tony's people, they're back.

'It's time,' one of them says, leaning in.

I am led backstage. Through a tangle of wires and TV monitors and sound desks, we come upon Tony. Six foot seven, black shirt, black shorts. He towers over everyone around him: big teeth, big hands, big everything. He definitely has an aura about him.

'I've heard your story, I've heard all about you,' he tells me, fixing me with a stare. 'You are amazing. So inspiring.' He pauses to let the compliment breathe. 'So, you ready to do this?'

I take, from the fact that he is already making for the door, that this is a rhetorical question. Before I know it, I am walking in his wake, heading back through the crowd and stepping through the doors of the stadium into the night air.

It has started to rain and the temperature has dropped. There's a chill on the air. I'm barefoot and trembling a little from the cold. We round a corner and I see a sight that makes me pull up in horror. A space about the size of a small oval to my left is covered in burning coals, glowering menacingly. I feel the radiant heat and my heart instinctively starts to beat faster. 'There's no way I'm walking across that,' I think to myself. 'He must be fucking kidding!'

But then to my right I see ten neat laneways of hot coals, each about two metres in length. And by comparison they seem not so daunting. A little disappointing, even.

'You can do this,' I am saying over and over to myself. 'You can do this.'

Before I know what has happened, Tony is off. He's removed his shoes, given a primal scream, whacked himself on the chest and charged barefoot across a lane of coals.

He turns at the other end and looks around at me expectantly.

Here goes.

I push down the fear, I shut out the shouting in my head. With a guttural scream, I lurch forward – eyes straight ahead, too scared to look down. I feel heat under foot, but there's no pain. It's over before I know what has happened. As I step off the coals, I am grabbed under either arm by two fire-walking assistants. They are shouting at me to wipe my feet on the mat – to remove any embers that may have attached themselves to my soles – but while they are right next to me, their voices seem miles away.

For a moment I am lost in a reverie. I feel exhilarated, unstoppable. I sit on the ground and watch as thousands pour out of the auditorium and charge across the coals. Each step for each person is the end of one journey or the start of a new one. The rain is falling like a soft mist and I feel unbreakable.

POSTSCRIPTS
SKIN

Hold out your hand in front of you and consider it for a moment. How many times a day do you see it, even if only in your peripheral vision, and take it for granted? Now consider for an extra moment the skin that covers it – and stop and think about how incredible skin is. It is, in my humble opinion, the most underrated, underappreciated organ in the human body. It protects us; it insulates us; it forms a simultaneously delicate and oh-so-strong barrier between us and all the nasties of the outside world. It protects the veins and arteries that carry the life-giving blood coursing through our bodies. It helps regulate our body temperature.

Now imagine if you had an accident after which you lost or permanently damaged your skin. Thanks to the miracle of modern medicine, we can now transplant a heart or lungs or a liver or a kidney if one of those fails in our body – and happily there are increasing numbers of generous souls who are donating their organs for just that purpose (though still nowhere near enough). Skin, on the other hand, is very hard to come by. The donation rates for skin remain stubbornly low – both here in Australia and overseas. Which is why I almost died on the operating table back in the dark days after the fire.

It is thanks to an eleventh-hour emergency delivery of skin from the Musculoskeletal Transplant Foundation (MTF) in the US that I am here today. Michael tells me that within hours of donor skin being given to me, my vital signs started improving and within a few days I was stable. Of course, I didn't know any of this at the time – I only found out about it when I woke up in hospital a month later. It was mind-blowing to me, then, because I had never even realised that tissue donation was a thing, or thought about its importance and uses.

So when I was well enough, I wrote to the people at the MTF to thank them for the vital part they played in saving my life. Not long after, they replied to tell me that the skin that saved me had come from sixteen donors. From that moment, I resolved to live my life the best I could. I wanted the families of my donors, wherever they are, to be proud of everything I've done since the fire. And I felt I owed it to each person who had essentially saved me to not take for granted a single day of the life I had been gifted.

Then the MTF invited me to America to visit their facilities, meet their staff and see the work they do. I jumped at the chance.

Michael and I set off from Sydney one warm December day and touched down twenty-four hours later in an icy-cold New York. I had never been to mainland America before. So many people had told me about the hustle and bustle of the city that never sleeps, and I wasn't sure if I was going to like it – I'm a South Coast chick at heart. But the place was buzzing with energy and dynamism – I was smitten straightaway.

And Americans have such a wonderful, can-do approach to life: nothing was too much trouble, everything was possible. A celebration of those who have a go seems to be hardwired into them all. I loved it.

Meeting some of the people who were directly involved in preparing and sending over the skin tissue that saved my life was humbling. You know those moments when you are in the presence of people – really good people – who do amazing, life-saving work on a day-to-day basis and it puts things into perspective and makes you feel like what you do is a bit silly and flippant in comparison? It was one of those moments.

I learned that one donor can help to save and heal the lives of up to 100 others. A pretty incredible number. But as a donor recipient, I know the impact of the gift reaches so many more – the ripple effect on friends and families cannot even be quantified. The other thing I learned was that every donor and donor recipient has a story. Mine is just one of them.

I didn't get to meet the families of those donors whose skin saved my life, but I did meet many other donor families. One woman's story especially touched me.

Her name was Pam. She was a beautiful, open-faced woman in her mid-thirties. She and her husband were volunteer fire-fighters in their local community – because, she told me, they both wanted to give something back. One day they decided together to fill out the form to become organ donors. For a couple so committed to helping others, it was a no-brainer. Two weeks later Pam's husband was killed in a car accident. When I met her it had been two years since his death but you could still see the pain of it etched on her face. Pam told me that because of the way her husband died, it wasn't possible to harvest any of his organs for donation, but his skin and tissue were viable and went on to be used in life-saving surgeries for no fewer than fifty-seven people. Imagine that. One tiny act of posthumous generosity – the passing on of tissue and organs for which you no longer have any practical use – made the ultimate positive impact on the lives of all those other people. She told me she missed her husband every day but got an enormous sense of solace knowing that those people had lived because of his selflessness.

Part of the invitation from the MTF was to take part in the famous Rose Parade in Pasadena, atop the DonateLife float. The Rose Parade is a big event on the American cultural calendar. Held each year on New Year's Day, the parade is renowned for its elaborate, floral-themed floats and marching bands.

The 2017 parade featured forty-four floats, nineteen equestrian units with approximately four hundred horses, and twenty-two marching bands. It was big, exuberant and wonderfully, unapologetically American.

The DonateLife float had been crafted to resemble an outrigger canoe. On its two sails were the faces of sixty organ donors – fashioned entirely out of flowers. I was among twenty-four organ recipients in the canoe, 'rowing' our way along the parade course. Walking alongside the float were donor families.

It was a sunny winter's day in California, the crowd lining the parade route was ten-deep. The soundtrack provided by the marching bands – some of which had travelled from overseas to take part – was relentlessly upbeat, and the mood on our float was one of celebration. But every now and then I would catch a donor family member walking alongside me lost in private thought – waving to the crowd, a smile pasted to their face, but caught for a moment by the calamity that had brought them here in the first place. I felt lucky and humbled in their presence.

I might never meet a single one of the sixteen families whose loved ones bestowed the ultimate gift, but nevertheless I wrote them a letter and asked the MTF to send it on to them:

> My name is Turia Pitt. I am a humanitarian, athlete, motivationalist and burns survivor.
>
> In 2011, I was running in a 100-kilometre ultramarathon in outback Australia. During the race, I was trapped by a grassfire, and received burns to 65 per cent of my body.
>
> I was evacuated and eventually sent to Concord Hospital in Sydney.
>
> My surgeons desperately needed skin to cover me, but there was none in Australia. So they turned to America, where a life-saving shipment of skin was quickly sent.
>
> This brings me to the purpose of this letter.
>
> Your loved one's skin was the tissue that was used on me. It was the skin that saved my life.
>
> Because of your loved one's gift, I have been able to live my life to the max. I have raised over one million dollars for Interplast, a burns charity that works in developing countries. I work as a motivational speaker, bestselling author and mindset coach – inspiring thousands of people in Australia to make positive changes in their life and achieve their biggest goals.
>
> This year, I achieved a goal held since the early days of my recovery, when walking and running again

seemed impossible, by competing in the Ironman World Championship in Kona, Hawaii.

I have also become engaged to Michael, my beautiful partner, and we are planning on starting a family next year.

I am eternally grateful to your family.

Yours,

Turia

Nothing would make me prouder than if, as a result of reading this book, more people signed up to become tissue and organ donors. It takes only a few minutes to do, and it could save a life. It's important before you register for organ or tissue donation to have a discussion with your loved ones, so they are aware of your desire to give life after you have gone.

For more information, or to register as a donor, visit:

Australian Organ Donor Registration
www2.medicareaustralia.gov.au/pext/registerAodr/Pages/
DonorRegistration.jsp

Donate Life (USA)
www.donatelife.net/

EVEREST ... INTERRUPTED

A shiver of excitement passes through the plane's passengers. A series of snow-capped mountain peaks are poking out of the bank of clouds to our right. The Himalaya. No other mountain chain in the world is as steeped in legend. Craning our necks, we all look for a glimpse of the most famous peak. The one that reaches higher into the sky than any other. The mighty Everest.

As the plane prepares its descent to Kathmandu Airport, I fasten my seatbelt and say a silent prayer. I'm nervous about the next couple of days, about the secret I am carrying.

It's May 2017 and once again I am on a charity fundraiser challenge. The charity: my favourite cause, Interplast. The challenge: to climb through the mountains of Nepal to Everest Base Camp. My company for the trip: no fewer than twenty-seven very excited, soon-to-be Everest climbers.

For the first few days in Kathmandu we wander about the ancient city, marvelling at its beautiful decrepitude. It's only been a couple of years since the country was devastated by the worst earthquake in a century, and everywhere you look there are signs of the destruction it wrought. The place is bustling, in that slightly manic way Asian cities do, but there are still people living in temporary shelters; temples without roofs, and piles of debris scattered about the place.

We spend the first few days acclimatising, taking in our surroundings, getting to know one another and visiting some of Kathmandu's remarkable sights. We marvel at the staggering workmanship of the temple complexes. The whole city is a kind of living museum, with people living among ancient buildings. Ornate wooden doors and windows with the most intricate carvings date back hundreds of years. It's inspiring to be here.

One of our Kathmandu days is spent with Interplast representatives, visiting a local hospital to understand the work done there. It's important that the group about to tackle base camp see how the money they're raising can help – it gives the whole effort context.

The night before the team is due to fly out to Lukla, from where they will set off to base camp, we gather for a pre-trip briefing. Time I came clean.

'I'm really excited, and also really nervous about what I'm about to tell you,' I hear myself saying. Puzzled looks are exchanged between the trekkers. 'The thing is, I won't be joining you tomorrow when you set out for base camp.'

There's a rumble of confusion. One woman begins to protest.

'It's because . . . I'm eleven weeks pregnant.'

A beat passes while the news sinks in, and then a cheer erupts and I am mobbed.

So. How did we get here? Well, as I went on to explain to countless well-wishers in the ensuing weeks and months, if

I need to explain that, clearly your parents didn't do their birds-and-bees duty well enough.

Michael and I had been thinking about starting a family for some time. Having climbed the Ironman mountain (twice), and become engaged, it felt to us like the natural next step. Perhaps some might say that marriage is the natural next step, but we felt well and truly married already. So, while I wouldn't say we started trying for a baby, we stopped trying not to have a baby. And frankly, much as I love you all, that's as much detail as I'm prepared to give.

About four weeks before leaving for Everest, I began to feel lacklustre. I was training for base camp, throwing myself into the physical preparations with my usual gusto, loving having something to work towards again, but noticing I was not my usual energetic self. I felt tired all the time. So on a whim I went out and bought a pregnancy test kit.

As I weed on the stick I had a little shiver of expectation, but I never really expected a positive result. Michael and I had been not-not trying to avoid conception for only a month or so, and by all accounts falling pregnant isn't always easy. But as I stood in the bathroom, two fateful grey lines came slowly into focus.

'Hmmm. That's odd,' I thought.

After breaking out another stick, and the appearance of another two lines, I felt a tingle of excitement.

'Hang on,' I heard myself say to my reflection in the bathroom mirror. 'I'm supposed to be going to Everest, and then we have Namibia planned, and a surfing trip to the Maldives.'

Back to the toilet I went, and back came another set of grey lines.

How did I feel? Confused, I guess. Unless the three white plastic paddles on the edge of the basin were faulty – and I had no reason to think they were – I was pregnant. Carrying another human. There was a baby on-board.

I waited for what seemed like an eternity for Michael to come home. Later, when he was in the bathroom brushing his teeth, I leant against the door jamb, the pregnancy test in my hand. 'Check this out.'

His eyes widened when he registered what I was showing him. With a mouthful of toothpaste he spun around, picked me up and started jumping up and down.

'We're having a baby!' he yelled to the empty house. 'We're having a baby!'

The next few days were a mix of emotions. Excitement at the new life we had apparently created, but anxiousness, too. Would it all be okay? Would this little embryo go the distance? We knew that many pregnancies miscarry in the first three months. We resolved to try to keep a lid on the excitement, didn't want to get ahead of ourselves.

But there was the small problem of Everest, and the twenty-seven people who had booked their flights and paid for a ten-day trek to base camp. And the charity for whom we were doing the walk in the first place. Suddenly, I felt like there was more than just Michael, me and the little human we had created in this equation, and it began to concern me. Should I forge ahead and do the trek? I would only be twelve weeks' pregnant – physically it shouldn't make a difference, right? Yes, I was feeling more tired than normal, but I had done two Ironmans. How hard could an Everest Base Camp trek be, carrying a few hundred extra grams?

Not so much hard as unnecessarily risky, according to my doctor. The flight to Nepal was nothing to worry about. Being in Kathmandu – provided I ate and drank well and avoided contracting any nasty bugs – was going to be fine. But climbing to an altitude of 5380 metres in the middle of a remote mountain range, far from medical assistance, in a developing country? My doctor recommended that I cancel the trip. Michael didn't want me to do it either, and I realised that the risk just wasn't worth it.

So I decided to forgo Everest, but I wanted to tell the trekkers in person. I knew a lot of them had signed up for the challenge to spend time with me, and I felt I owed it to them to accompany them at least to Kathmandu. As it happened, my angst about how they would receive the news was unnecessary. As we sat around dinner in a Kathmandu restaurant, this band of relative strangers could not have been happier for me.

In the weeks before leaving for Nepal, Michael and I had also told our families. It was early days in the pregnancy but Everest was forcing our hand. There was no way we could share the news with the trekkers before telling our own parents.

It will come as no surprise to you to learn that Mum almost hit the ceiling she was so happy. Overjoyed is the word that springs to mind. She's over-enthusiastic at the best of times; the prospect of me and Michael producing a grandchild for her was almost more than she could cope with. There were tears, there were screams of joy, there was singing of Tahitian songs.

She had dropped by one morning and I had purposely left the pregnancy test on my bedside table in our bedroom – in full view. 'Mum, can you please grab me a hair elastic?' I asked. 'There should be one in there on my bedside table.'

She trotted into my room. I started counting the seconds, waiting for the scream. Nothing.

'Darling,' came her voice. 'I can't find the elastic.'

'It's on the table!' I said, a note of irritation creeping into my voice.

'Nope. I can't see it.'

I marched into the bedroom, swept up the pregnancy stick and waved it in front of her face.

Cue the tears of joy.

Dad was a little more subdued. They're nothing if not pre-dictable, my parents.

'Hey, Dad,' I said, during one of our regular phone chats. 'Guess what?'

There was a slight pause. In my mind's eye, a wry smile was working its way across his face.

'Let's see,' he replied. 'You're either pregnant or you're getting married.'

'Nailed it in one, Dad. We're up the duff!'

'That's great news, darling. I'm so happy for you.'

Michael's parents? We had them around for dinner and announced the happy news as we sat down to eat.

'Guess what, guys?' I asked.

'Oh no,' Julie replied. 'What crazy adventure are you dream-ing up now?'

'Parenthood,' I replied, barely containing my excitement.

I might have imagined it, but I could have sworn I spied a tear in the corner of Gary's eye.

Throughout my recovery my doctors had always assured me that there was no medical reason I couldn't bear children.

I couldn't help worry that with all the operations I'd had maybe my fertility had been affected; however, though the fire had scarred me on the outside, none of my internal organs were damaged. And the burns I had sustained, while extensive, were not as deep on my abdomen as they had been on other parts of my body. I had been assured on multiple occasions that the skin is a remarkable, and a remarkably elastic, organ. Of course, my doctors would monitor the progress of the pregnancy closely, but they reiterated now that there was no reason it would be any more complicated than most.

As the weeks ticked by and I began to read up on all things pregnancy, I came to realise that the accident I'd had six years before was the least of the potential impediments to my successfully carrying this baby to term. The more I read and the more I spoke to people, the more I realised how precarious all pregnancies are, no matter who is carrying the child. A low-level anxiety, it seemed, is just part and parcel of having a baby.

Now that my family knew, and now that the group halfway up Everest knew, the next step was to consider how to announce the news to the Australian public, who had become so invested in my life. I was inclined to let the news trickle out of its own accord but Mum was adamant. 'People have invested in you, Turia!' she said. 'This love story of yours – a part of it belongs to Australia. You have to share it with the country.'

I thought she was being a little overblown (so not like her . . .), but after discussing it with Michael we decided the best way to make the announcement was via the same public platform on which our story had begun all those years ago.

It didn't take much to convince Ali Smith, our friend from *60 Minutes*, to scramble with a camera crew and reporter Ally

Langdon to make the trip south from Sydney to Mollymook. After a morning spent surfing for the cameras, we sat down in our living room and shared our exciting announcement with the country. A *Women's Weekly* cover story followed a couple of weeks later to complete the circle.

The outpouring of love and support following my *60 Minutes* and *Women's Weekly* outings was overwhelming. I knew that my story had resonated with people, and I knew that Michael's and my plight over the last six years had been carefully followed, but I still couldn't have anticipated the wave of love that washed over us.

Grateful. It's a word that's used a lot (not least by me), but it sums up perfectly how I felt in those weeks. Contented, happy and so very grateful.

After the all-important three-month mark, we underwent all the usual scans: the ultrasound to test the thickness of the nuchal fold, the blood test to check the baby's DNA. During that process, Michael had learned the baby's sex; I was comfortable not knowing. There was talk of a gender reveal party, but I had seen them on YouTube and thought they were a bit naff. Neither Michael nor I was sure that the melodrama of a special event at which an oversized black helium balloon containing blue or pink confetti was popped was really the way to go.

However, finally, I came around to the idea of inviting over a few of our nearest and dearest and popping that balloon to find out if I was having a boy or a girl. Blame it on the hormones.

If you've seen the video I posted on Instagram, you'll know what I mean when I say that for someone who already knew the sex of the baby, Michael behaved like *the* single most excited expectant dad on the planet. When I punctured the balloon, sending blue confetti all over our living room, he jumped around like a kid on Christmas morning. Hopping up and down on the spot with undisguised glee.

A boy! We're having a boy!

DANCE OF THE WATER

Michael and I went sailing together in Tahiti some years after my accident, and we found ourselves in the Marquesas Islands. The Marquesas are a chain of volcanic peaks rising out of the blue waters of the Pacific – easily some of the most beautiful places I have ever visited.

The setting was spectacular, but it was a special holiday for another reason: it was the first proper trip Michael and I had taken since I had regained much of my independence. We skippered the boat ourselves – hoisting sails and navigating reefs. It was a marker of sorts that life was not only returning to normal but held out the promise of being so much better than either of us had dared to hope.

During the trip we found ourselves on a tiny island, hanging with the locals. There was a mum in the group nursing a baby. Quite possibly the coolest little kid I had ever met. You know how they say that some kids have a wisdom about them? A sort of calm that apparently makes people think they have been here before? That was this kid. He sat in my arms contentedly for ages – big brown eyes, blond hair, skin the colour of mocha. His name was Hakavai – which in Polynesian roughly translates to 'dance of the water'.

I took a photo of Michael holding Hakavai and it became the screensaver on my phone for the next few years.

Why? Hope, I guess. I'm not much into visualisation, but I always hoped that one day Michael and I would have a family. If we were lucky enough for it to happen, I knew it was something that would make us really happy. And Hakavai Hoskin has such a good ring to it. A nod to my Polynesian heritage, a meaning that spoke to Michael and my shared love of the ocean and a reminder of a beautiful kid we had met on one of the most special holidays we had taken together.

So that photo of Michael looking so relaxed on holidays, so happy holding little Hakavai, became a constant reminder of the life we were hopefully working towards building. I say hopefully, because you just never know. It's not until you start trying for a family that you properly realise it's a gift not everyone receives. There wasn't a day of my pregnancy when I didn't stop to take a moment and be grateful. So many women don't get to experience it – and for many that can be painful. I was aware of that and I didn't take a second of it for granted.

But, honestly, if it hadn't happened for me that would have been fine. Life is so full of other adventures. Michael and I would have figured it out. Dealing with the curveballs that life throws at you is kind of what we do. Maybe we would have adopted, or moved to Africa, or become free divers – whatever. Having kids is not the be all and end all.

It's funny. Since I fell pregnant, I've had so many people say it must have been the reason to live. The prospect of one day holding my own child must have got me through. But it's simply not true. Waking every morning with the possibility of a day swimming in the ocean, snuggling up next to Michael on the couch, a good meal, a laugh with friends, the simple joy of being alive – these are the things that kept me going. Being pregnant and having a baby is the cherry on top of the icing on the cake.

I reckon if you get one healthy, happy kid, you are really blessed. If you get two, you are doubly blessed. The plan is to have more than one. I'd love a brood of mini-Hoskins running around the living room – their hair tousled from a morning in the surf. But I also know – perhaps more than most – that life doesn't always go to plan. So we'll gratefully accept whatever life has in store for us and make the best of it.

Michael and I had been planning a trip to Namibia for more than a year. A former German colony tucked away in the south-western corner of Africa, wedged between South Africa and Angola, it's a remote, sparsely populated country pretty low on the list of must-sees for most Aussies.

Our French friends from the Maldives, David and Gaelle, had raved to us about Namibia. To them it was the closest place to heaven outside of their beautiful charter boat, the *Ocean Divine*. Plans had been hatched long before I fell pregnant to take a trip there together.

After checking with my doctors, who were finally convinced that Namibia's relatively modern medical facilities were fit-for-purpose in the event of any unforeseen emergencies, in the middle of my second trimester Michael and I jetted off for Africa. Little Hakavai had started to kick, which gave me a thrill every time it happened. I was feeling more energetic than

I had for months. This was probably going to be the last proper holiday Michael and I would have together as a twosome.

Namibia is an awe-inspiring place. As with many eastern and southern African countries, the place is teeming with wildlife. There were days we would sit out in the savannah, the only humans for miles and miles, set up camp for the night and watch a herd of giraffe loping slowly along the near horizon, perfectly silhouetted against the setting sun.

Our accommodation for the trip was the tent on the roof of our four-wheel drive. Each evening we would find a glorious stretch of desert – maybe at the bottom of a rocky mountain or smack-bang in the middle of a plain – pull up, unfurl the tents and lower the ladders that allowed us to access them. We'd eat by a campfire, marvelling at the stars, then climb the ladder and crawl into our rooftop bed. Often we would fall asleep to the sound of lions roaring in the distance. One night, I awoke to hear elephants shuffling about our campsite, sniffing around our vehicle. I was terrified. Michael was in his element.

One day we were driving in convoy in an area not far from the Angolan border when we came upon a collection of mud huts with thatched roofs and – to David, at least, who had been in this area a couple of years before – a few vaguely familiar faces. We had found a small community of the Himba tribe – a people who, like the Maasai in Kenya and the Pygmies in Congo, make regular appearances in the pages of *National Geographic*. The Himba are known for the ochre paste their women cover themselves with, giving them a red hue. They live as they have for centuries – herding goats and cattle. It's a harsh, simple life. And as we pulled up to this settlement, with smoke wisping from a small campfire, a couple of emaciated dogs moving listlessly about the camp, it looked like the last place on Earth you would want to live.

One by one the tribe emerged from their huts and began to form in a group around us. They were timid, and without any language in common we mostly stood around gesturing at one another. I spied a girl – she couldn't have been more than seventeen – standing back among the women. She was clearly pregnant, so I walked over to her and pointed at myself. I lifted up my shirt and showed her my belly. A ripple of laughter passed through the tribe. For the next few minutes we stood and admired one another's bumps. Neither understood a word the other was saying, but it didn't matter. The universality of pregnancy was enough. Both our bodies were hard at work gestating a new life. And as I stood there in the afternoon sun, it struck me how completely different the lives of our two babies would be. More than that, as I looked around the village it struck me that this girl probably wouldn't be seeing a doctor during the course of her pregnancy, and when it came time to deliver she'd likely be doing it in one of those huts.

As we got back in our cars and waved goodbye, I felt an overwhelming sense of gratitude, knowing I would be returning home to an excellent medical system, to give birth in a well-equipped hospital. And as I write this, it occurs to me that the young woman would have given birth by now. Maybe one day we'll take Hakavai back there. Maybe when he hits those difficult teenage years. Just for a bit of perspective.

I think I had it pretty good during my first pregnancy. I was tired in the first trimester, but at least I wasn't struck down by morning sickness. I didn't exercise as much as I was used to.

Though admittedly that's coming off a pretty high base. The most energetic I managed was the odd class of yoga here and there, a spot of Pilates and a lot of soft-sand walking (wearing a weigh vest – just to make it that little bit more challenging . . .).

I continued to surf throughout most of my first trimester, but eventually lying on my belly got too uncomfortable. So I switched to a body board, and finally to a surf mat. My last surf was at the seven-and-a-half month mark. The wetsuit was too tight by then, and when I was out past the break my arm rope got ripped off as I tried to duck dive under a wave. I watched as my board got carried onto the beach, and started swimming back to shore. I was so exhausted by the time I got in I figured maybe it was a sign that it was time to hang up the board for a bit.

All my friends who have kids tell me I'm in for the shock of my life. And people are always asking if we have prepared the nursery. But surely the little fella is just going to sleep in a basket for the first few months. How much stuff does one baby need? And birth plans. If he's anything like his mum, Hakavai will do exactly as he pleases on the day. So my only preparation is a mental one. I'm going to tackle the challenge not unlike I tackled Ironman: I know it's going to be a long day and there will be periods when I'll want it all to end, and periods when I will be just so grateful to be experiencing it. Because, really, it's one of the great privileges of being a woman.

It's funny the sorts of questions I get from people about my pregnancy. I've lost count of the number of women who ask me if I am worried about getting back my pre-baby body. It seems like such a strange question. I will never be the same after being pregnant and having a baby: everything will be different.

Why should my body be any exception? Someone actually asked me if I was worried about getting stretch marks. Seriously.

And that's another weird thing. When you are pregnant you become public property. Random strangers on the street come up and touch your belly. Most of the time that's fine, but it's still a bit weird. Then there are those who insist on calling it a miracle. When it's not really. It's just biology. I mean, I get it: maybe it's hard for people to imagine that a human body could go through everything mine has and still be capable of performing one of its basic functions. I know it comes from a good place, but I am not frail, I am not sick, I am not weak. I have done two Ironmans. People ask if it's hurt as my belly's stretched. Not especially. I've never been pregnant when I wasn't burned, so I don't have anything to compare it to, but I'd hazard a guess that it's no more or less uncomfortable than it is for any other woman.

At about the six-month mark, I decided to enrol in a calm birth course. Dragging Michael by the scruff of his neck, we rocked up and sat in a circle with a bunch of other expectant mums and dads. We went around the circle, introducing ourselves. When it was Michael's turn to speak, I nearly died.

'To be honest, I don't really want to be here at all,' he said as I looked on in horror. Honesty is always commendable in my book. But even so . . .

'I'm basically here because my partner made me come,' he continued. 'No offence, but this is the last place I wanted to spend my weekend.'

All the other guys in the room laughed out loud. I was mortified! But afterwards I got to thinking. So often childbirth is framed as being a scary medical procedure, and as a woman you are always told how hard it is. To me, as with so many other things in life, it's all about mindset. I determined from that day to reframe the experience. Instead of thinking of it as vaguely scary and painful, I would frame it as Hakavai's birthday. The day a little 'dance of the water' came into our world.

A LETTER TO HAKAVAI:
The Day You Were Born

My darling Hakavai,

It's been just over a week since you were born and I am still floating. I've just put you to sleep and I spent five minutes hovering over the crib, staring down at you, drinking you in, marvelling at how, only a week ago, we'd never met. Yet now I can't imagine my life without you.

I figured one day you would grow up and might want to know the story of your birth. So here it is.

Patience, it has to be said, has never been on of my virtues. Just ask your dad. I have an active personality; I'm more of a 'take action and make things happen' sort of person than a 'sit around and wait for things to happen' kind of girl. So you can imagine how good I was at waiting for you to decide you were ready to come out and meet the world. By the time the forty-week mark came around, I was done. I felt fat and tired, I couldn't get comfortable and you were kicking me in organs

I didn't know I had. Carrying you for the last nine months and watching my body transform in that way women's bodies have since the start of time was amazing. But the party was over now. I was ready for you to come out.

So, at forty weeks and one day, I looked down at my enormous belly and heard myself say aloud, 'Okay, mate, it's time for you to come and meet the world.'

I hoiked myself into my swimming cossie and, together with your dad, waddled down to the beach. A kilometre of ocean swimming ought to do it, I figured.

Thirty minutes later, I heaved myself up onto the sand and lay on my back, panting. Nothing.

'You even think about making a beached whale joke and I will actually kill you,' I said to your dad, who just smirked and looked out to sea.

I made an appointment with my chiropractor and went along to get my pelvis aligned. Surely that would do the trick, I thought. Get everything down there in order – smooth the path, as it were. But still, nada.

An acupuncturist was the next on the list. Girlfriends who'd had babies had raved about the effectiveness of a few needles, strategically placed, as a sure-fire labour-starter. Forty-odd needles and a couple of hundred bucks later, there was still no movement at the station.

Clearly nothing I did to the outside of my body was going to get you moving. It was time to try the food trick. Back here in 2017, if you searched the internet for 'best labour-inducing foods' you got all sorts of crazy stuff. Pineapple, spicy foods, licorice. A pineapple licorice curry. You name it, there was a half-baked (pun intended) theory on how certain foodstuffs would absolutely, definitely kick-start the birth process. The one that jumped out at me was a recipe for eggplant parmigiana from an Italian restaurant in the US.

The walls of Scalini's restaurant in Atlanta are apparently lined with more than 300 photos of babies whose mothers reckon they went into labour almost immediately after eating the chef's signature eggplant parmigiana. So I cooked it – following the recipe to a tee. It was yummy. But it didn't budge you, my little buddy.

Later, your grandma and I were mucking around on the couch. Your dad was rolling his eyes at our shenanigans. Suddenly, out of nowhere, I broke wind – in quite a spectacular way. I blamed it on the baby, because, as you should hopefully know by now, I am normally far too ladylike to do that in company. Anyway, the shock of the noise sent me and your grandmother into a fit of hysterical laughter. And it was at that point that my waters finally broke.

I know, right? Glamorous.

But then, as I was about to find out, there ain't nothing glamorous about childbirth. It's about as primal as it gets.

Panicked, excited and confused all at the same time, I looked at your dad and said, 'Um, I think my waters just broke.'

Your grandmother – who's frankly never met a bit of melodrama she wasn't attracted to – flew immediately into panic mode.

'Call the hospital! Get an ambulance! Go now!'

Your dad, on the other hand, calmly suggested I check I hadn't just wet myself from laughing too much. Ever the pragmatist.

I hadn't wet myself. My waters had broken. And so began my first tentative steps into the crazy miracle of birth.

Taking my cues from your Zen-like father – and ignoring your grandma's mounting hysteria – I took myself to the shower while your dad called the hospital. We were told to start making our way there.

The drive up the coast to the hospital was going to take two hours. I played calm birth meditation tracks in the car on the drive – worried that at any point you might decide to make your entrance into the world. Your dad drove calmly and sensibly beside me. It was going to be all right. I felt calm and positive.

By the time we arrived at the hospital, I'd had a few minor contractions, but nothing serious. I had been able to breathe through them. Once inside, I was admitted and sent off to a birthing room, where nurses spent a whole lot of time looking for a vein underneath my scars to put in a cannula. My obstetrician, Dr Walton, popped his head in.

'This could take a while,' he said. 'If you don't have the baby tonight, I'll see you in the morning.' And with that he was gone, leaving us in the capable hands of our midwife – a total legend who was happy to leave your dad and me alone to do our thing.

We waited. And waited. And waited.

We put some music on. I stared out the window a lot. We prepped my fitball. But it remained all quiet on the southern front. The occasional contraction would ripple through my body – stopping me in my tracks. But it would subside as fast as it came on.

It wasn't until ten o'clock that night that things started to really heat up. Which was just as well, because there was nothing on TV, and your dad and I had run out of conversation – and patience.

The intensity of the labour pains started to build, which is when things really started to hurt. But just as I thought there was no way I'd get through the contraction, the wave would pass and I'd feel normal. They never tell you this about labour but you actually get a bit of 'downtime' when you're not in pain and you can talk normally between contractions.

I laboured all through the night, and called the midwife in a few times, each time insisting, 'Okay, this is it, I need to push now!' She would always give me a kindly look and reply, 'Sorry, love, you're not quite ready.'

The pain eventually became overwhelming. I remember looking at the clock and scarcely believing the time. It was four in the morning. Why hadn't this happened yet? Five am came and went. Soon it was six o'clock. And all this time the contractions were becoming more and more intense.

At seven am Dr Walton came in. By this stage I'd been labouring for nine hours. I was tired but feeling pretty pleased with the progress I must surely have made in that time. The doctor inspected me and told me I'd done well, but that the whole night had essentially been for nothing. Nine hours of what he called 'ineffective labour'.

It was a bit soul-destroying.

'You've dilated three centimetres,' Dr Walton informed me. 'So, you can keep doing what you've been doing, at which rate Hakavai will probably be here tomorrow morning, but there's a real risk that we may have to opt for a Caesarian section if you get too exhausted.

'Or we can give you an epidural now, you can have a bit of a sleep, and the baby will most likely be here in a few hours.'

I opted for the epidural, and from the moment it went in I never looked back. It took about thirty minutes to kick in, at which point I promptly fell into a deep sleep. I slept for almost three hours. The next thing I remember is Dr Walton shaking me gently on my shoulder, 'Turia, it's time to wake up. You're ten centimetres dilated. It's time for you to start doing some work.' Then he laughed and said, 'It's called labour for a reason!'

I started to push.

Another forty minutes passed. The contractions were getting closer together. Still I kept pushing – being careful to follow the instructions of my midwife and doctor. Only afterwards did I look back and think about what had happened. I was surrounded by technology, doctors and midwives, in a state-of-the-art hospital, yet when it came down to it, it was just going to be you and me, working our way together through a chain reaction of physiological marvels that constitute the miracle of birth.

And then I looked down and saw a shock of black hair. It was your head! After a few tense moments you were with us. The sound of your cry filled the room and my heart filled with joy. My son!

I felt elated. I felt exhausted. I felt dazed and confused. But as they handed you to me – all covered in blood and vernix, your eyes puffy and your head misshapen – I hugged you to my chest. You were just perfect.

Your dad cut the umbilical cord, tears welling. His look was one of pride and of the deepest love. The doctor placed a big wet kiss on my cheek.

'Congratulations, Turia,' he said. 'You're a mum.'

And there it was. Whatever else I had been, whatever else I would go on to be or do: this one was going to be a constant. I was a mum.

Everyone left the room and it was just you and me.

Mother and son.

This Is My Message to You

It's been just over a month since Hakavai was born. And whenever I've had a few minutes to myself (which hasn't been all that often), I've been jotting down some thoughts about my experience as his mum so far. I don't want to forget this period, and writing has felt good – I want to record something of this most extraordinary first few weeks of him being here on planet Earth, document the beginning of what I know will easily be one of the most important relationships in my life, and hopefully in his too.

Dear Hakavai,

Yesterday you were screaming uncontrollably. Your little face was screwed up and red, and when you cried all I could see were your gums.

I'd checked your nappy. I'd checked to see if you were too hot or too cold. I tried to feed you. I even tried a dummy on you.

My poor darling. What's bothering you?

I took you out onto the balcony and held you and we both looked at the black cockatoos and listened to the ocean.

I started to sing (badly) the Bob Marley 'Don't worry' song.

You looked right at me and you smiled, then laughed, as if to say, 'Mum, don't worry. Everything's going to be just fine.'

So now, whenever I'm stressed, overwhelmed, anxious or just plain flustered, I pick you up, sing that song, breathe in your intoxicating scent and remind myself not to get too far ahead of right here, right now.

To stay in the moment, and enjoy each and every one of them.

Turia xx

It's a lesson I'm determined to carry with me from this day on. When I'm working towards the things I want to achieve this year, I'm determined to try not to get too far ahead of myself. When it all feels too overwhelming, or when life gets stressy and messy, I'm going to stop and take a deep breath.

Because all you can really do, and *need* to do, is focus on this moment, and the small step forward you can take today.

The rest will follow.

It's true – everything is going to be just fine.

FAQs

What gets you out of bed and keeps you motivated?

I always have a goal in mind, something I'm working towards. But it's just as important to have a clear reason for wanting to achieve that goal. The main thing I try to remember is that you'll never regret the sacrifice that goes into working towards a goal. I never finish a hard swim session and think, *Man, I should've stayed in bed!* I never work on my School of Champions and think, *I should've watched TV instead.* So that thought of *You won't regret it* also keeps me motivated.

Who's your inspiration?

There are a lot of people who inspire me! In fact, I think if you're relying on only one person to inspire you, you're limiting yourself. I find new sources of inspiration almost on a daily basis. It's important that we keep topping up our tanks.

Different people inspire me for different reasons at different times. When I was in hospital, I loved Sam Bailey's book, *Head Over Heels*. Sam Bailey is a farmer who had a car accident and as a result became a quadriplegic. He's still a farmer, as well as a motivational speaker and helicopter pilot. He really showed me that it is possible to rebuild your life after tragedy.

I love watching TED talks as they're usually short and are a great pick-me-up when you're feeling flat in the middle of the work day.

What should you say to a friend going through adversity or illness?

This one's a hard one – everyone's unique and everyone responds to situations differently. But the number one rule is to say something. Don't think, *Oh, I don't know what to say so I'm not going to give her a call.* Call up your mate and just say, *I don't know what to say. But I'm here for you anyway.*

What's your idea or understanding of success?

Success for everyone comes down to the same broad stuff we all need. We crave great connections. We want to challenge ourselves, and we want to feel confident and happy. And ultimately we want to feel we're achieving the goals we set for ourselves. If we can do all of those things, that paints a pretty good picture of success.

You're really determined. Do you reckon you were just born like that?

I think for sure my mental fortitude started to develop when I was younger because of the way I was brought up.

The thing is, though, I don't believe I have any more determination than the next person. My strength has just been tested in ways most people won't experience. I think we all have an infinite amount of strength and potential, and it's our excuses that keep us from tapping into it.

It's like when people say, 'I don't have enough time,' when time is the only thing distributed evenly between every single person on this planet! We can get into the habit of using excuses to justify our behaviour, too: 'It's all right for her, she's got an awesome partner,' or 'Well, he makes heaps of money.' Saying, 'Oh, you're really strong – obviously you were born that way' is just another excuse.

I think I've got some of the best excuses around! I was catastrophically injured during a fire; I've lost fingers; I look different; and I can't regulate my body temperature. If I wanted to, I could very easily use the fire as an excuse for not living my life the way I want to.

Anyone can develop a strong and positive mindset with the right tools and the right strategies. That's why I'm passionate about helping people to tap into their potential, drop their excuses and nail their mindset.

Tell us a little more about Interplast. How can we get involved?

There are a couple of ways you can get involved with this incredible organisation. You can come on one of my annual adventures (the best way to find out about these would be to sign up to my newsletter: bit.ly/TuriaNews). Or you can volunteer to work with Interplast, or donate directly to them, by going to their website: www.interplast.org.au.

What are the words (or quotes or statements) that you live by?

I try hard to start each day with gratitude. The coolest thing about practising gratitude is that when you're truly grateful, that's the only experience you'll have. You know, you can't be grateful and angry at the same time, or grateful and bitter, or grateful and sad. Every morning (and, in fact, all throughout the day), I make a conscious choice: am I going to make today a bad day, or am I going to make it a great day? We may not be able to control what happens in our day, but we definitely have control over how we respond. In fact, our reaction and our feelings are the only things we do have control over.

I'm going through a tough time ... How do I pull through?

First up, it's important to remember that every single person on the planet has tough times. It's normal. Even if what you're going through feels unique, remember that someone else on the planet has very likely gone through it. I'm not trying to diminish your experiences, I'm simply trying to normalise them.

Here are my pointers for getting through those tough times:

1. Nourish your mind with something that inspires you, motivates you, or gives you perspective (see my resources bank for some good movie and book ideas).
2. Move your body – I don't care if it's weights, sprints or a walk. When you move, you get endorphins, which make you feel better.

3. Find a role model – maybe someone in a similar position who has turned their life around (Sam Bailey was mine). What did they do? What did they do that you can do?

4. Find someone worse off and help them. We can get into the habit of being so introspective. Helping others gives us much needed perspective.

5. Practise gratitude. Focus on everything you do have going for you.

6. If necessary, see a professional. Organisations such as Beyond Blue, the Black Dog Institute and SANE can help you to find the support you need. Their details are all online.

I'm interested in your School of Champions. Can you tell me more about it, and how do I sign up?

My School of Champions provides anyone with the tools and resources they need to set and reach any goal they want to achieve, whether it's to lose weight, change careers, quit smoking or even run a marathon. *Anything* is possible once you understand the psychology behind the goal-getting process.

School of Champions unpacks my own goal-getting framework. Over the course of seven weeks, you'll discover what motivates you (it isn't what you think!), and be given strategies to overcome your challenges, ditch your excuses, boost your confidence and self-belief, and form life-changing habits.

This is the framework that I used to rebuild my life after being trapped by the fire, and to get across the Ironman finish line (twice!). It's what makes me strong. Confident. Resilient.

Visit turiaschampions.com to join the team and get direct access to me and a whole bunch of legends who are kicking big goals inside the private community. Together, we'll say goodbye to whatever is holding you back and move forwards – towards the life you really want.

RESOURCES BANK

Cool movies

The Blind Side, *Million Dollar Baby*, *My Left Foot*, *Good Will Hunting*, *The Shawshank Redemption*, *Forrest Gump*, *Erin Brockovich*, *A Beautiful Mind*, *The Diving Bell and the Butterfly*, *The Intouchables* (French film), *Cool Runnings*, *500 Days of Summer*

Yes, I watched all of these when I was recovering. These days I watch a lot of series when I'm recovering from an operation – I love *Game of Thrones* and *House of Cards*.

Cool books

Man's Search for Meaning by Viktor Frankl
Head Over Heels by Sam Bailey
Never Tell Me Never by Janine Shepherd
Don't Die with the Music in You by Wayne Bennett
The Happiness Trap by Dr Russ Harris
The Power of Vulnerability by Brene Brown